My Father's Eyes

a memoir

Mary Bonina

Červená Barva Press
Somerville, Massachusetts

Červená Barva Press
P.O. Box 440357
W. Somerville, MA 02144-3222

www.cervenabarvapress.com

Bookstore: www.thelostbookshelf.com

Cover Design: Andrai Pawlak Whitted (front)
             William J. Kelle

Inside and front cover photos courtesy of the author
Author Photo: Lynn Wayne

ISBN: 978-0-9883713-8-5

Library of Congress: 2013945744

These are my memories. Others of my family no doubt have theirs. I have done my best to be true and to render the historical moment in which this story is set.

My Father's Eyes includes chapters previously published in somewhat different form. "Inheritance" appeared in the *Zingology* anthology on power. "Sidekick" was featured in *Hanging Loose*. "The Wanderer, 1962" was published in *Gulf Stream*.

My Father's Eyes

Also by Mary Bonina

Living Proof

Clear Eye Tea

Dad

Biagio John Bonina
November 5, 1922 - June 3, 1993

Close both eyes/ to see with the other eye.
—Rumi

Greater than scene, I came to see, is situation. Greater than situation is implication. Greater than all of these is a single, entire human being, who will never be confined to any frame.
— Eudora Welty *One Writer's Beginnings*

… and for Mark and Gianni,
Peg, Kate, and Jack

One

KEYS (1956)

As my father turned out of the driveway and headed up Norwood Street that last day he ever drove a car, he was singing a song I sometimes heard him whistling. The words were about making the darkness light. Earlier, when I had returned home from Church, I'd found him out in the driveway, waxing and polishing the Packard. He was using Turtle Wax and I wondered if it was made from turtles. My father had laughed and told me that if I wanted to help him— and to go for a ride after— I should go into the house to change my clothes. I had on a fancy organdy dress—light pink, the color of cotton candy—and a white straw hat with a ribbon streamer the same pink color and decorated all down its length with a ladder of daisies. My two sisters and I had a closet full of Sunday dresses and hats. I was the oldest, "five going on six," that day.

I went running inside to our second floor apartment, taking the front hall stairs two at a time, and singing as I went, "On the Good Ship Lollipop." I loved to hear my voice and tapping steps echoing in the big, cool, empty hall. A feeling of lightness would come over me on a warm spring day: the weather, the flimsy fabric of my dress, my straw hat and shiny black patent leather shoes, would make me feel like singing and dancing. That was what Shirley Temple would do when she was happy. I had seen some of her movies, so I knew when a song and dance should happen.

But on that Sunday, the only day in the week when my father was home from work, I cut short the dance I usually did when I reached the wide open landing. I was in a hurry to help.

After I'd changed my clothes, I breezed through the kitchen on my way out the back door. My mother was

3

moving about the room, setting dishes on the table, sliding the rack out of the oven to check on dinner, stabbing at the baking potatoes with a long fork to see how near they were to being ready. This Sunday would seem at the start to be like all the rest, and it was for a while anyway. However, as it turned out, it would not be like any other, although the afternoon began innocently enough with the day's simple routines.

My father's 1941 Packard 180 touring sedan was a sleek animal. I rubbed the chamois cloth, buffing the headlights clean, just the way he showed me. I thought of the lights as the animal's eyes. My father took care of what looked like a nose, then the grillwork—what I called the teeth. I was short, so I did the bumper, the fat lower lip. I worked really hard at removing the soapy film until the chrome shined and I could see myself in it, my features all distorted.

While he did the finishing touches and fooled around under the hood, my father let me sit behind the wheel. I loved sitting inside. There was fabric on the seats—and even the ceiling—a soft grey pin striped cloth that reminded me of the Sunday suits my dad wore to church. I wondered if he'd bought them so they would match his car, he liked it so much.

Every once in a while I hollered out, "This is New York City! I'm driving through New York City!" I hit the horn twice, three times.

My mother looked out whenever she heard any commotion in the driveway. The car was parked right under the dining room window, and looking up from behind the steering wheel and out the front windshield, I could see her well.

"John!" she yelled, sounding mad at my father while trying to take the old wooden screen out of the second-story window. She had to push hard with each hand, so it folded up like a fan. She had trouble with it, like always. It was stiff and would stick. "Damn thing!" she cursed. "What good is it anyway?"

4

Once she'd removed the screen, she put her head out. "What's the matter?" she demanded. She sounded angry that the beep of the car horn had taken her away from whatever she'd been doing.

"Nothing," my father answered, pointing to me sitting behind the wheel, that I was the one who'd tooted the horn.

"You be careful!" she yelled.

"Just don't touch the brake," my father said.

I thought my father knew that I wouldn't, but he said it anyway, I guess to let my mother know that he was watching me, taking good care of me. She was afraid, always expecting that I was going to get hurt. "You'll get hurt," she said to me more than anything.

My mother pulled back from the window, slamming it down, not bothering to put the screen back in.

When my father felt satisfied that the car shined like new, he opened the driver's side door and said, "Slide over there now," and that meant that we were going for a ride somewhere.

I liked going for rides with my father and I was especially excited on this particular Sunday afternoon, because he had not recently been behind the wheel. I didn't know why. Until later in the day I would have had no reason to suspect that he was having any trouble with his eyes. Maybe I was too young to have noticed and still incapable of imagining that my father was not perfect.

He turned the key and the car started right up. He put his head out the window and listened. "Quiet a minute," he said when I wanted to know where we were headed.

"What are you listening for?" I asked.

"Birdies, honey."

I stuck my head out the window to listen, too. "Pigeons?" They were lined up on the roof edge of the house, cooing loudly. "Jays! That's it, right? Jays!" They fought all the time with the cat next door. I watched it prowl along the granite wall below where they nested in the viney branches of our backyard willow. I had a collection of their beautiful blue and black feathers that fell to the ground whenever they swooped down to tease the cat, and I intended to make an Indian princess headdress when I had enough of them.

"No, no, not jays. Or sparrows. Or pigeons. Birdies in the engine, hon." He laughed.

What birds would live in an engine? I had looked under the hood. That was no place for birds. My father got black grease on his hands and arms when he fixed things under the hood. Maybe the birds were crows, their wings already oily black.

He stepped on the gas pedal and the engine got loud. Then he took his foot off and listened again as it quieted down. Was this the way he checked for those black birds? Was he trying to scare them out? He did this a few times, then seemed to be satisfied that there were no birds and the car was running just fine.

"Purrs like a cat. Let's go for a spin."

"Why don't we have a saint in our car?" I asked my dad as we began our journey.

"We're in a different boat," he said.

I was remembering my recent trip in my Aunt Margaret's new car. She had a plastic statue of St. Christopher, the patron saint of travelers, decorating the dashboard of her snazzy turquoise blue Oldsmobile with brilliant white-wall tires. That saint stayed glued to the dashboard, as if it were watching out the front window for us while she drove, looking out for any trouble that might lie ahead.

My father looked very comfortable in the driver's seat, slouching a little, relaxing. Seeing him as he was, anyone would have been able to tell that he loved driving that car. He rolled his window down on nice days. He kept his left hand on the wheel, and rested that forearm on the door's window track, his elbow hanging out in the breeze. He stretched his right arm over the back of the passenger's seat, and the fingers of that hand drummed out the rhythm of whatever song was in his head; then he started humming or whistling.

He was a great whistler and his singing voice was pretty good, too. He liked to sing opera, especially when he was in front of the bathroom mirror, shaving. He always sang along whenever he watched *The Hit Parade* on television, and when he was driving, he'd sing mostly songs he'd heard on the radio.

By the time he turned the corner onto Woodland Street, the bright afternoon was beginning to fade. Clouds were starting to take over. Every once in a while the sun still peaked through the full-leafed trees that lined the streets of our neighborhood. The ride went along as usual until suddenly there was something bothering me. I felt that I was not quite safe. I had butterflies in my stomach. It was a feeling that would come over me sometimes, but I had never before experienced it when I was with my father. He had stopped singing, and I was watching him, trying to figure out why.

When I think of the way he looked that day, I see him suddenly sitting up so straight that he reminded me of the lifeguards at Holbrook, the way they watched swarms of kids in the water on a hot day, never taking their eyes off them. As he drove along he looked too much from side to side, giving the shade trees a lot of attention. This was the way we went, the same route we took out of the neighborhood whenever we went anywhere. What new thing could he be looking for? I wondered. He had both hands on the wheel like he was holding on tight for some reason. He looked hard at things, as if he were trying to protect us both from some terrible danger, something he knew was out there just around the corner from home, waiting to get us.

Driving down Woodland Street he slowed up whenever he got to a side street, and I thought: *Here is the problem. At Oberlin Street.* Then when we got to Claremont and the same thing happened, I thought: *Might be at Claremont where the trouble is.* As we went along I began to realize that I was worried that whatever the danger was, it seemed to be everywhere. The way my father was acting made me feel that it was riding along with us, a passenger in our car.

Just seconds after I began to feel that my father looked like he knew something was about to ambush us, something did. Yet even as the events and revelations of that afternoon played out, I was not able to fully appreciate their meaning. We reached the end of May Street where it intersected with Main, and then I was absolutely sure that something was not right with my dad. The buildings near the corner were a deep rusty red and not the faded pink color the brick façade took on when it was bright and sunny. I thought that maybe it was going to rain, and I was disappointed in the sudden change of weather.

It happened so fast.

My father panicked when he drove into the intersection. "Ree," he yelled. He needed my help. I knew there was something wrong. But *what*, I did not understand.

"What color is the light? Hurry! Quick!"

"It's red! It's red!" I shouted, but my words could not make the light change to green, nor could I change the fact that he'd kept on driving although the signal was red. What was worse, my father didn't turn the wheel so the car stayed frozen in time for a few seconds in the middle of Main Street.

I looked to the left and realized that we were in danger. The Number 19 Cherry Valley bus was coming into the intersection, too. My father looked left and saw it. He woke up from whatever spell had come over him.

"Damn!"

He turned the wheel sharply to the right and stepped on the gas. There was the sound of squealing as our car took off.

My father let out his breath in a loud sigh as we narrowly missed being hit by the bus. The driver leaned on the horn, blasting us as we got away.

"We have the green light now," my father announced.

Did he want to let me know that whatever was wrong with him back at that corner had passed like a sudden thunderstorm, the danger gone away down the road to

Leicester or Spencer or some other town, where it would find another girl and her daddy to scare?

"Yes, Dad. Nothing coming."

"Nothing coming," he repeated. "Coast clear."

But he didn't continue up Main Street. Instead, he pulled over to the curb and parked. He was taking me to *Alexander's Ice Cream Creations*, even though we hadn't had dinner yet. We got out of the car, walked back to where the place was at the corner, went inside and took seats at the soda fountain. He ordered a chocolate ice cream cone served upside down in a sundae dish for me. "To catch the drips," he told the waitress.

I got some on my jersey anyway, so he dipped a napkin in a Coke glass filled with water and dabbed at the chocolate drips. "Dinner must be ready by now. We have to hurry. Don't mention this to your mother."

"Hope it doesn't stain," I said. "Mummy will be mad."

Did my father stop for ice cream with me that day in order to gain his composure? I don't think so. We were by then so close to home, just a few streets away. I would think that he would have wanted the drive over with as quickly as possible after what had happened. Did he stop simply for my sake, to soften the blow of the experience, to help me forget it? If so, ironically, it may be that going for ice cream with him is what made this memory from my childhood indelible.

As he drove up the hill to our house, I could see my mother out in the driveway, pacing. She was shaking her fists angrily at the car when she saw us. I thought only: we must be late for dinner. Although I didn't understand what it was that was making my mother so angry that day, it was clear to me that there was something wrong, and I quickly realized that it was nothing as simple as being late for dinner. I heard my mother's fear loud and clear.

"What right have you?" she screamed at my father.

She stopped for a moment as if she didn't know the right words to say what was wrong. She called on God to help her,

"Dear Blessed God in heaven!" she prayed, looking up at the sky. "God, give me strength! Did you think that doctor was kidding? Is that it? Didn't he tell you not to drive? And didn't you promise you wouldn't?"

This was the first time that I had heard of any doctor telling my father not to drive. I wondered what was wrong, but my mother and my father, too, seemed that day to have forgotten that I was right there with them.

She stooped down to look at my father in the car window, "And what do you mean by taking her with you on a joyride? What were you thinking, doing such a thing?"

I don't remember my father answering her. But I do recall that he looked as if he'd expected an argument, and perhaps that is why he didn't reply.

"You gave me your word!" she kept yelling.

My father parked the car then and took the keys out of the ignition, holding them out to me and finally speaking. "Give the keys to your mother."

I opened the car door to get out.

"Give me those keys! You just give me the keys to that car!"

I dangled them from my extended hand for her to take and she yanked them from me, as if she had expected that I would be holding tightly to them.

My father got out and went over to where my mother was standing and kissed her on the cheek. I could tell that he felt relieved, just as I did, to be home safely—even though, now that he was, my mother was hollering at him.

After he kissed her she just got more worked up. She kept asking him what business he had taking me on a joyride.

"One last spin," was all he could say to her.

"You bet it is your last. You bet it is."

She turned on me then, "And you! You! Going with him like that, not telling me where you were going!"

I started to cry then, not because she'd grabbed me roughly and shook me, but because I didn't understand why she was angry with me.

My mother turned on my father again. "You have your nerve! Where did you go with her?"

He didn't answer, only stood there looking at her blankly, as if taking the medicine he deserved.

I stopped crying, suddenly remembering the afternoon's pleasure. "Ice cream. We had ice cream," I said, knowing immediately that I'd broken my promise not to mention it.

"Don't you ever—ever—drive that car again!"

Because it was a warm evening the windows in our upstairs apartment were open. With all the noise coming from our house, the neighbors could not possibly have eaten dinner in peace. My father didn't defend himself, but it made no difference: my mother didn't stop yelling until she began to cry, which seemed to take forever. My sister Peg, who was four, had been crying all along and hollering, chastising them the way Mum reprimanded us when we fought with each other. "Stop it you two. Stop it!" Peg yelled at them. Katie, who was only a toddler, hid under her bed. I stood off to the side in a corner of whatever room my mother and father happened to be in, watching and listening to their argument unfold.

I remember my confusion that day. I didn't understand why my mother thought that I should have asked her permission to go with my father for a ride. During the week, when he was at work I didn't ask *his* permission to go places with *her*.

My mother's anger at my father that afternoon for putting us both in danger must have gained its power from the fact that she was being forced quite suddenly to begin to face the potential consequences of his going blind. I wonder now, had she told me about the problem with my father's eyes before that afternoon, to try to warn me, and had I not understood her meaning or what the implications were for me? Is that why she was so angry that I hadn't told her I was going for a ride with him—that she thought I'd understood why the car had stayed idle all those weeks? Was it perhaps a failure on her part not to recognize my age, and given that, that I had limited knowledge of what might go wrong in life? It seems more likely though, that mother had not told me that something was wrong with my father's eyes. Was she hoping to let me hold on to the illusion of a carefree childhood for a while longer? Or was it just that in those days there were things parents did not think children needed to know?

The truth is though, that there was no turning back for me that afternoon. From then on I became totally preoccupied, trying to figure out what was wrong. If my father's sight had been lost all at once, so that it was quite evident what his problem was, I would have had no mystery to solve. But in fact, his vision would diminish gradually over time. The car ride was the spark, too, that set in motion something else that made my childhood distinctive: *I began to watch out for my father.* His last ride in the Packard was my initiation in the role of being his guide. It would take time for me to fully appreciate that fact, to come to realize that as my father's vision worsened, I would be expected to watch out for him more and more. Accompanying him as guide, I would in essence be needed to describe the world for him. Is this what gave me a love of words and the inclination to tell stories?

Memorial Days

The last day I saw my father alive was Sunday of Memorial Day Weekend, 1993. It was our backyard picnic to celebrate my husband's birthday and a way of ushering in the summer season with a gathering of friends and family who look forward to the occasion every year.

Our son Gianni was going to be two in July. He climbed his slide and hollered out to my father from the top step, just as he was ready to go down. "Gampy, see me! See me go down, Gampy!"

My father turned his head toward him then, his eyes stopping right where Gianni's voice originated. To watch him do this anyone would think that he could see Gianni. He waited until he heard, "Taddah!" Then he clapped enthusiastically for him.

Gianni ran to him. "I did it!"

"Very good. How did you learn that?" my father asked him, nestling his face in the crook of Gianni's neck, smothering him with ticklish kisses, just as he used to with my sisters and brother and me when we were that young.

"I don't know," my boy answered. "Watch me again, Gampy!"

"Ah, the love of repetition." I laughed.

Being bothered by a bee and not having much luck trying to whack it away, my mother got up from her lawn chair and dragged it over to the other side of the yard.

Our picnic must have seemed ordinary to any of the neighbors sitting out on their decks and porches overlooking our small yard. In addition to family, Mark and I had extended the invitation to several of our closest friends as well, finding that doing so kept everyone in the family on their best behavior. The party gave me an excuse to do a lot

13

of cooking, something I have enjoyed ever since the college summer break when I worked as a cook at a hotel on the coast of Maine.

Watching Gianni and eating was the main entertainment for the afternoon. Everyone except my father ate a good amount. He declined the grilled chicken, fish, and beef. He passed up roasted potato salad, black bean salad, salad made of early lettuce from Mark's garden, basmati rice salad, and cold Thai noodles. He even rejected his favorite—the Italian sausage.

"I couldn't, Ree," he said every time I passed a different dish. He made a face that made me think he didn't feel well. "Too heavy," he said.

"What would you like?" I asked.

"How about fruit? What kind of fruit do you have?"

I told him I'd have a look and headed upstairs into the house, to the refrigerator where I found a grapefruit I didn't know we had.

"Great!" he said, beaming as if I'd offered lobster or filet mignon.

He peeled the grapefruit and ate every section. The other guests, seated all around in a circle, had a little of everything, most of them refilling their plates several times over. My father ate only the grapefruit and a slice of Mark's birthday cake, a chocolate Grand Marnier torte with apricot filling between the layers, a cake I made for the first time that day.

"Very good," my father said about the cake. "I like the combination of chocolate and fruit. It's good."

The day was warm. Plants all around were coming into bloom, and the roses on the garden wall were thick with buds.

"You'll have a lot of roses this year," my father said, adding to his prediction: "It's going to be a very hot summer."

Somehow, with all the talk of roses budding, my father was reminded of the crab apple tree that used to be in the side yard of our family home while I was growing up in

Worcester. "That would be full of blossoms every spring," he said. "Wasn't it beautiful?"

I remembered the tree well, loved its simple white flowers. It was in the yard below the south-facing window of the bedroom I shared with my sisters Peg and Kate. One late fall afternoon of my childhood, my father took the crab apple tree down to its roots, so I was surprised to hear him remark about its beauty. I thought I'd take the opportunity, since he'd brought it up, to ask why he'd cut it down then. "Why? Why did you do that?" I had cried the day it had happened, but I'd received no response. The forsythia, too, which bordered the front of the house was nothing but a short stub of sticks when I saw it as I was coming up the hill that day, approaching the granite front steps of the house on Norwood Street.

I had my father's full attention, and so I asked him the question that had haunted me, "Why, Dad? I never understood it. Why did you cut down that tree and hedge?"

"Jack," he said.

"What do mean?"

My father clamped his lips shut and raised his eyebrows, the way he would when he intended to keep quiet about something.

My brother, who is six years younger than I am, was the only one of my siblings not present. He'd stayed home to be with his wife, whose own father was very ill.

"Was he helping you with yard work, Dad?" I asked. I had been by then, a teenager, and most likely out with my friends and therefore not the one helping him.

My father still would not elaborate.

"Did he misunderstand what you wanted him to do?" I persisted, thinking that perhaps my brother hadn't realized that my father only meant for him to help prune and shape the tree and the forsythia.

But once again, I got nothing in the way of explanation from him that afternoon. It wasn't until a few years after, when I'd asked my mother if she knew what had happened that day, that she'd confirmed that Jack had indeed been helping my father with the yard work and had misunderstood what my father wanted him to do, resulting in the loss of the plantings.

The crab apple tree was one of the loveliest things about our yard. Growing up I looked forward to its display of flowers every spring, had watched the tree grow fuller and more lush with blooms. When I was small, after it had rained, I'd collect the creamy white flower petals that were dotted with pale yellow shadings. As I gathered them up from the grass after they'd been shaken loose from the branches, I used to cup them in the palm of my hand, like treasure—and I would examine them the way I'd look at a little bug, or one of the holy relics the nuns so often passed around my classroom. I loved the silky feel of the petals, when I rolled a few between thumb and index finger.

Once when I was very young I wanted to save some of the blossoms, to keep them for winter. "They won't keep," my mother said. "Flowers fade and dry up." But after giving me fair warning she found an old envelope I could put them in. First though, she used her fountain pen to scratch out the return address inscribed in the upper left hand corner. "I don't want everyone knowing my business," she said, as her determined strokes obliterated the name of Massachusetts Eye and Ear Infirmary in Boston, eliminating the evidence, she thought, of my father's impending blindness. I guess she could not have imagined that day, the very public life my father would later lead, in spite of losing his sight.

In full flower, the crab apple and forsythia brought me a private happiness, a glimpse of possibility at a time when all of us in the family were living with a profound sense of life's limitations. The blooms brought with them a lightness of heart, an attitude that for me routinely accompanied the first soft, warm days of spring so characteristic of Central Massachusetts. With the apple blossoms as evidence I felt the definite arrival of spring. Inevitably though, the sultry days of summer set in; then, some days I would be rendered helpless, trying to push against the heavy home atmosphere in the face of the new season's humidity.

I would like to believe that my mother and father planted the tree and hedge together on a better afternoon, one bright with the promise of their marriage—perhaps the first spring they lived on Norwood Street—as a way of celebrating their new home and the family they would raise there.

Shadows gradually took over the yard. Without the sun shining on our picnic, the late spring air was chilly, so we got out of our aluminum chairs, folded them up, and leaned them against the porch wall. We said goodbye to our friends and went into the house.

I heated up some soup for Gianni. He sat in his high chair, calling out to my father, "Gampy, see me eat soup!"

When he was finished and let loose, he ran to my father with a new picture book in hand. The book was called, *Building a House.*

"Read this," he said.

My father took it from Gianni and lifted him up gently and settled him on his lap. He opened the book, looked up at me and asked, "Do I have it right side up, Ree?"

His question broke my heart.

My father proceeded to "read" to Gianni. He knew how to build a house. Gianni would guide him through it.

He opened the book to the first page and asked, "What's that?"

"Blocks. Wagon," Gianni said, pointing first to one, then the other.

My father said, "To build a house first you make the foundation. Show me those bricks again," he said, and Gianni pointed to the load of bricks.

They went through the whole book this way, my father saying, "What's that?" to get clues about which aspect of the house building process was shown in the illustration and covered in the text of each page. Gianni guided him, giving him the names for objects that tapped my father's memory, and in that way he was able to identify each step in the construction process. Gianni pointed and answered him, "Wood." My father told him about framing rooms. They made the journey together all the way to the end of the book, and they were both happy.

Two

EYES (1947 – 1956)

I picture my father, Biagio John Bonina, as a young man still in his twenties, before the diagnosis of retinitis pigmentosa—a gradual degeneration of the retina, leading to blindness. He is driving through small towns in Massachusetts. Most of these towns are even smaller than his own of Milford, near the Rhode Island border. To get to Worcester he follows Route 140 for thirty miles or so through Hopedale, Mendon, Upton, and on into Grafton, where the road meanders around Lake Ripple. He is not married yet, although that is the point of his traveling; he is looking for a wife.

It is 1947. Route 140 north is a country road with only an occasional streetlight. He drives it often, so he knows it well. Most Friday and Saturday nights he and his friend, Nove Marcone, head for the big city to go dancing. Now that the war is over, they are hoping to meet the women of their dreams.

I know the fancy gowns and dresses my mother wore when she went out dancing. They were still in the closet in the back bedroom at my grandparents' house while I was growing up. I loved getting dressed in them and playing dance queen with my sister, Peg, the two of us pretending that we were in one of the musical numbers in the old movies we watched on Sunday afternoons. My mother's dresses were made of satin and tulle. The gowns were black, white, emerald and Nile green or deep red—a whole array of colors and styles. I found that wearing them was magical. I suppose I must have put on the same dress my mother wore the night she met my father, but she never did tell me which one it was. In recounting their meeting she told me that he wouldn't take no for an answer when he asked her to dance.

Dressed in a tailored suit cut from fine woolen fabric that hung just so on his slender frame, she thought he had panache, and that made him irresistible. She didn't know any Italians, not really. Yet he seemed familiar. Frank Sinatra came to mind. Something about him reminded her of Frank Sinatra. He could have put his shoes under her bed any day. The eyes of her new admirer were dark brown—not blue—but that didn't matter. When he looked at her those dark eyes made her feel that he could see right through her. She calculated that he stood at about the same height as Sinatra, and he moved in that same suave way—except sometimes—and that troubled her.

At a club or dancehall he wouldn't always take her by the arm as they wove in and out around the tables on their way to and from the dance floor. He fell behind, following her instead of leading the way. It was as if she were a guide blazing a trail for them. She wasn't used to being with a man who acted like that, not after going dancing with others who proudly took her arm. Why couldn't he show her common courtesy? If he didn't have that, she considered, then what good was it to be so handsome? She asked herself—*What kind of people are these Italians, anyway?*

She demanded an explanation: *Why was he always waiting for her to cut a path through the crowd?* She had no intention of letting him go on that way, always lurking in the background whenever they were out in public. It was as if he were afraid of his own shadow. She put it to him finally, "Don't you know how to act when you're out in public with a woman?"

"It's my eyes," he told her. A doctor had given him glasses for the problem and he wore them, although they didn't seem to help much. "That's all it is, Mary," he told her. And don't you know there isn't another woman I know as beautiful as you are?"

He explained to her that his eyes gave him the most trouble when he walked inside from a dark parking lot to a bright foyer, or when he walked out into the blackness of night when they were heading home. That is he reason he said he had her take the lead. And when the lights in the dancehall were dim—and they usually were—he knew he might stumble if he did not have his hand on her elbow, nudging her ahead of him.

She thought about his problem only briefly. So what? Lots of people wore glasses, she thought. His explanation put to rest the uneasiness she had been feeling about what she'd perceived as inconsideration. She was not thinking clearly, she would tell you now. She must have already fallen for him. She thought that there would be a simple solution to the problem—a new doctor and new glasses. She couldn't have understood the serious implications for him, for her, and for their future children. He had no idea himself.

We never know what lies ahead for us, but I think that my mother knew less than many of us do about life. When I was growing up, she freely admitted time and again, that she was a bit naïve, telling one story or another from her youth to illustrate how innocent she was. Always, whenever she repeated this one about how she had met my father, she would say, "Boy, was I green!"

"She was a blue baby," my grandmother so often proclaimed when talking about my mother, referring to the oxygen deprivation she'd experienced during birth. She might have died, which is the reason everyone was especially good to her. Because of all the attention she received, her younger sister—my aunt Margaret—used to call her "Queenie." As a child myself, not knowing what my grandmother meant when she talked like that, not understanding that her baby—my mother—was born with the umbilical chord wrapped around her neck and nearly suffocated, I would try to picture what my mother must have looked like at birth. I sometimes stared at her baby picture displayed atop the piano at Gram's house, and I tried to visualize her face in turquoise, azure, and sometimes, dark blue.

Did her troubled arrival in this world make my mother the darling of her grandmother's proper residence on Jacques

Avenue, a three-story brick house dating from Victorian times, like the family living in it? Her mother's two sisters, her aunts Mary McCarthy who was a schoolteacher, and Margaret O'Brien, a nurse—as well as their brother, her Uncle Tom and his family—all lived at Jacques Avenue. My mother was such a frequent visitor, that it was a second home to her. Doctor Tom, as he was called, was one of the city's most prominent obstetricians and he took a great interest in my mother's well-being.

My grandmother would tell the story of my mother being blue at birth, whenever she was melancholy, routinely remembering my mother's birth right after telling of how she had lost her only son, David, just a day or so after a man had come to the house begging for food. It was just before the Great Depression, and this man came often. She would generally help him. As the story went, that day in question she had not exactly refused him. She would have fed him, except that she was busy with baby David. When she told that man that she couldn't help him right away, he got angry and he cursed her, cursed her baby, too, and then her baby died.

When I was old enough, my grandmother asked me to memorize a poem that must have reminded her of her dead son. The poem described a child's toys, dusty and rusting on a shelf, never seeing use, still waiting for the boy who was meant to play with them. I memorized the poem because she wanted me to do so, and I recited it for her whenever she asked for it. "Do it to please me," she would say. It was a poem in a collection by Eugene Field. I became accomplished at reciting the lines on command, for company and sometimes for her alone, even though I could tell that it made her sad, "The little toy dog is covered with dust but sturdy and staunch he stands / the little toy soldier is red with rust, and his musket molds in his hands." Again and again over the years, she'd say, "Recite it now, will ye?"

The Irish have a way of never forgetting tragedy. It is their history no doubt that has ingrained this aspect of personality in them. So when misfortune hits them dead center the way it did my grandmother—and my mother, too—they live for it, for the telling of it, and the loss lives in them for the rest of their days. I suppose, since I am descended from them on my mother's side, I have a trace of that characteristic myself. Why else would I tell this story?

My father couldn't stay away from her, my mother says. He kept showing up at all the dancehalls. No matter which one she went to, he was there. At Norumbega Park, the Indian Ranch, and Club Cosmo. And then he began asking if he could visit her at home. She said no to that, too. A lot of difference it made. Her assessment: *He was so damn stubborn.* He always was that, but it served him well when he went blind. Once she let him in the door, he began driving to the city to visit her two and three times a week. Finally she thought, *Oh, might as well let nature take its course.*

That is the closest my mother ever came to admitting to me that she loved my father, but she must have. She stayed with him, pushed him to face his denial and to get the help he needed.

*

My father owned the Packard at the time he began courting my mother, having traded in his 1938 Dodge, which had been famous in his hometown. Once, when someone had given him a calf, he put it in the back seat of the old car and drove it home. When my father was not allowed to keep the animal, he showed the kind of resourcefulness that would later help keep the wolf from the door of our family's house: he held a raffle to find a home for the baby cow, releasing it to a farm in Blackstone.

When he was growing up, my father's family had chickens, a large vegetable garden, and a simple white house that was bursting at the seams with family. Anna was born ahead of him, as well two boys who died as infants of influenza; and born after him were Marguerite, Evelyn, Jean, and Tom —

who looked enough like him to have been his twin. In addition to the eight children born to Bellonia and his father Biagio for whom he was named, the house also sheltered his grandparents—his mother's mother and father, Gitano and Marguerite. On the street level of the house was "Testa's," the family market.

My father was the only one of the six children in the family to leave Milford permanently and establish his home in another place. It was a bold move for the oldest son born into an Italian immigrant family to move to the city and leave that small town in which even unrelated families became an extension of your own. What must have required a greater courage though, was marrying a woman who was not like anyone else he knew—not Italian, but Irish—and from educated people.

"We were refined. Don't you forget that," my mother would always say, referring to her own upbringing. She reminded us of this fact whenever the issue of etiquette or acceptable behavior surfaced in our family. She chastised us this way, too, if we complained of being slighted or scorned by other children in our parochial world, once my father's eyes changed not for the better, and as a consequence, our financial circumstances did as well. Through it all, my mother refused to accept that marrying my father and living as we did changed anything about her. After all, she had an uncle who was a well known doctor, unmarried aunts who were teachers, nuns, and nurses, and one off her uncles wrote poetry and another was a Catholic missionary priest of the Passionist order who'd made their union official, marrying my parents in a formal ceremony in Worcester at St. Paul's Cathedral, then heading to his post in Jamaica, West Indies, where he later built a school.

My father had learned the trade of machine tool-making after leaving high school without finishing up, frustrated by a problem with his eyes. During the war, unable to serve—because of his bad eyes—he worked as a toolmaker at the

Charlestown Navy Yard. He saved his money and he bought a Packard to get him where he wanted to go.

Years before he met my mother, my father had begun to experience night blindness. Somehow that did not keep him from pursuing her, which meant driving the thirty miles or so from Milford to Worcester and back again in the dark, negotiating the curves and bends in the road that followed Lake Ripple, just to take my mother dancing. I have always thought that there was something magical about my father's ability to navigate in the dark. Knowing that he did this, that he drove a car to Worcester as often as he did to see my mother, and knowing that he travelled mostly at night when his eyes were least reliable, I cannot help but wonder how he could have found his way, except for love.

My parents married a year after they'd met. I have a photograph of my mother dressed in her "going away suit" and she is wearing sensible shoes, all ready for their honeymoon road trip to Canada in the Packard, my mother descending the front steps of her family home, being showered with confetti by her sisters Margaret and Sally.

Almost two and half years after that June wedding day I was born, in November of nineteen-fifty.

*

Over the years I have created in my mind a scenario of the two of them with me—still a babe-in-arms—being shown the house they would buy, inspecting and considering whether it would satisfy as both an investment and a good place in which to raise the family they hoped to have. They were excited about it after months of looking. They didn't want to spend another winter in that dark Victorian house with my mother's aging and crotchety aunt, Margaret O'Brien.

It was spring and my mother was wearing a straw hat and a colorful dress when the Realtor took them inside the twenty-one-room house offered for sale by a doctor. It was Victorian, too, but brighter—with shiny oak and gumwood—

some of it stained a dark mahogany color, but most of it cherry and honey-colored. There were thirteen-foot ceilings on the two bottom floors. The pitch of the high roof made the ceilings slope on the top floor and light poured in. As they walked through the many rooms of the house they were aware of how much space there actually was, and a feeling of freedom overwhelmed them after living too many months with a baby in an old woman's house full of heavy furnishings. This house had three fireplaces on both the first and second floors, each of which had seven rooms. There was even a second pantry, a butler's pantry as it was called, with a dumbwaiter from one kitchen to another.

"We wouldn't want all this space," I heard my father say in my imagination.

Who was it made the decision? Who saw the possibility of income if they were to remodel, make separate apartments that would house three different families. Doctor Wegan and his family had lived in the whole house before them, but they couldn't afford that. They'd need the income from tenants. Did the Realtor suggest it, the owner seeking a buyer, or my mother with genes for owning rental property handed down by her grandmother who came over from Ireland with gold bars and bought property on Bradley Street, a three-decker tenement house to rent out to other immigrants? Or my father maybe thought of it. Maybe he'd been interested in buying property suitable for tenants, worried even before the diagnosis, that one day he would be blind and out of a job with a wife and children to support, and they would need something to fall back on. Perhaps it had been a mutual decision, to buy something that was a sound investment. The spirited colorful dress my mother might have worn the day she and my father signed the purchase papers would have been an indication of her high hopes as well as her innocence.

On the day they celebrated their decision by planting the crab apple tree and the forsythia hedge, as I imagine it, my mother could not have known for the life of her, that the lovely wrap-around porch on the house would have to be torn down, because keeping it in good repair was not something they could afford to do. She and my father hadn't given a thought to the fact that the house would be drafty and that it would be expensive and inefficient to run a furnace with so many fireplaces and high ceilings. I am sure that when my mother saw the fireplaces she could not picture them walled up, especially the one in the front room that would become their bedroom. The sunroom, too—with its yellow stained glass windows, where she planned to put her babies—would disappear off the side of the house. My mother didn't know any of this then, because on the afternoon they'd put the tree and hedge in the ground, it was long before my father was given the prognosis of gradual blindness with no known cure, when I was an infant, and before Peg, Kate, and Jack were born.

By the time summer came around the year I was entering first grade, my father had been given the diagnosis that he suffered from the hereditary retina condition that would, over a period of years, gradually lead to blindness. In the years that followed my mother, although reserved in showing affection, would however, begin to freely express anger, becoming easily flustered when a routine was even slightly upset, or when our behavior fell short of her expectations. My grandmother would explain, "She's high strung." And Auntie Margaret often said, "She goes off at the drop of a hat." And through it all, my father would plead, "Mame, simmer down, will you?"

The adults around me talked like this always, leaving me to visualize simmering pots on the stove, hats on the floor, and taut violin strings. And when they spoke of my grandfather, saying that he was "as deaf as a haddock," fish went flipping and flopping in my mind. My mother would call me in for supper, and when I finally heard her, she stood at the door chastising me, "What do you mean you didn't hear me?" she would ask in disbelief. "I can be heard from here to Halifax?" My memory went then to the map of the Atlantic Ocean I had studied on one trip to Maine, and I found myself sailing in my mind to Nova Scotia. I got so caught up in the vivid images of their speech that it was very hard for me to understand even a little of the more important things that were mentioned by the adults all around me.

Only rarely and much later, after I had deciphered a good deal of information on my own, did anyone speak sensitively about my father's encroaching blindness. I did not generally ask either for explanations, preferring instead—since no one was forthcoming—to learn things on my own. And so it was that I devoted a good amount of time to thinking and imagining what was happening to my father—what it meant to him, to my mother, to me, my sisters and brother, the rest of the family, and to our community—that he was going blind. My private investigations and subsequent interpretations of goings on bred in me an anxiety about our future as a family, assigning my child's heart a weighty responsibility. Hiding in nearby rooms, I listened unseen to telephone conversations and to hellos and goodbyes whispered to visitors in the front hall. And late at night, I sat on my bedroom floor behind the chintz-covered chair next to the door—which I insisted be left open "just a crack"—so that I could look out into the living room, and eavesdrop on adult conversation. And what I heard bewildered me for years. And worried me, too. It took a long time to make sense of any of it, and perhaps I have not yet.

Memorial Days

The evening of the Memorial Day barbecue was pleasant. The following day was the actual holiday, offering another day's respite, making it a long weekend; no one had to rush home to prepare and rest up for the start of the coming work week. Worcester was only a one-hour drive from Cambridge, so the family extended their visit, lingering past dark, telling stories, playing with Gianni, and drinking iced tea and soda. As usual my father dished out advice good-naturedly. The mood of our gathering gave me the feeling that we were as a family, entering into an easier time of being with each other. Gianni was out of infancy, making it possible to relate to him more as a little person. We had a house now, thanks to my father's help—a house with a yard for picnics.

I wanted nothing as much as to be able to see my father relax in a lawn chair in our back yard for many summers to come. He had so few of the basic comforts people expect when they work as hard as he did. Since we had moved into our first house, the season had changed, bringing better weather with it. During the week when my father telephoned me in the evening, if he thought the phone had been ringing too long before I picked up he said, "Were you sitting out in the yard?" I could hear in that question *his* longing to relax. He was imagining me being able to do what he could not on those weekday evenings. For years he had been staying during the week in a furnished room he rented in Cambridge and going home only on weekends, so that he wouldn't have to commute to his food service business—from Worcester to Boston and back again each work day, as he once did. I knew that he sat outside on the stoop of the YMCA where he spent weekday nights, not wanting to miss the arrival of better weather or to take in a necessary breeze on a hot and humid night in the city. Asking me if I had been sitting out in the yard, he was letting me know that that was what he would have been doing, had he been in my situation. These thoughts came to me, as I looked at him and saw how washed out, tired, and much thinner he seemed than he had been just a few weeks before, when he'd taken the family out for dinner at Tiano's, a good Italian restaurant in Worcester, to celebrate my mother's birthday. That night he'd thoroughly enjoyed his meal, raving about how good it was.

We were all seated around in the living room. I was taking in the scene from the wing chair opposite the couch where my mother, Peg, and Kate, were sitting in a line, facing me My father sat in the black Morris chair to my right, on the edge of the leather seat, because he was enjoying listening to Gianni who was on the floor at his feet, chatting away as he played with Duplo blocks. Mark and my sister Kate's husband, Bob, were sitting in Windsor chairs they'd brought in from the dining room. In our small apartment it felt like we were a crowd.

I was worried about my father. He was ill, I thought, considering how he looked not just thinner, but old all of a sudden—ten years older since the last time I'd seen him. Whenever my father was around I watched and anticipated his needs out of habit. In truth, I worried about his welfare whether he was present or not. But I thought, looking at him, that I had real cause for concern. I was certain that there was something wrong with his health. Did anyone else notice? It seemed not. He'd made a valiant effort all afternoon, entertaining our friends with stories of his childhood, even though he rarely spoke of that time in his life.

After everyone went home and when Gianni was asleep in his crib, Mark and I lay down next to each other in the dark, talking about whether it would be possible for my father to come live with us. Mark knew that I was pained thinking of him staying all week in a room at the YMCA, while I was living comfortably with my family in a house that he had helped us finance.

"You know we can't, that we don't have room," Mark said gently.

"If only we had the money to fix up the attic," I said, not wanting to hear obstacles to my plan. "If we did, we could move our study up there and give my father that little room off the front hall. It would be perfect. That room is too small for both of us to use as a study anyway."

I knew that we didn't have the money for such a home renovation, and I knew, too, that there was no one we could ask for help. Meanwhile I could see that my father was getting old and sick while living alone most nights of the week in a furnished room. It felt wrong. But in spite of the fact that Mark and I had always lived simply and worked hard in our professions, buying a house in Cambridge had depleted our resources, even taken our small retirement fund. Without a modest gift from my father with the understanding that Mark's parents would match it, we would never even have had the required "safety net" bank account to secure our thirty-year mortgage.

Following the gathering on Sunday of Memorial Day weekend, my father had gone home to spend what would be his last night there. On Monday evening when he got back to his room in Cambridge he called me, as he always did, when he got in. There was a message on the answering machine when we came home after having dinner with friends. He sounded as if he were in distress.

"Where are you? Pick up the phone, will you, Ree? Are you there, Ree?"

I was worried. When I'd seen him the day before I had told him that when he came back to Cambridge the next day, we would be out to dinner at the time he regularly called. He wasn't generally forgetful. From his tone, I thought I heard a rising panic more than the impatience that was sometimes reflected in his voice. The message seemed to be further confirmation of my worry that he was ill. I wanted to call him, but he had no phone, only the use of the public pay phone in the lobby. I thought of calling the desk, but I had done that once during a major snowstorm. With true bravado he had gone out walking in a raging nor'easter. He'd led a couple of other blind but permanent residents of the YMCA, who were afraid to go out on their own, on an expedition to find a place where they could have dinner. Hadn't he been angry with me then for calling to check up on him? I felt that he would be upset once again, if I called and asked the desk clerk to knock on the door of his room to see if he was all right. I suppose I was only trying to rationalize my fear. I knew my father. I should have remembered, too, that he'd been known to display a bit of machismo from time to time. I knew how he hated to admit that he was not feeling well. Hadn't he had a heart attack preceding a more major one and kept even that secret?

But it was late, and if my father were asleep I knew that I didn't want to wake him, knowing that he got up to get ready for work at four a.m.; the day before he had looked so tired. I suppose I had fooled myself into thinking that he was all right because I received no further messages: no news is good news, I pretended. But he never left my thoughts and I was often distracted, thinking of him as I went through my evening routine with Gianni.

After listening to the phone message and hearing what I thought was controlled panic in his voice, I went over the next day's commitments, hoping I might find time to track down my father. A writer friend of mine would be in Boston on the following day. We had kept our friendship alive for twenty years since our days as undergraduates, communicating entirely by telephone and letter in the intervening years; we had not seen each other in all that time. I was anxious already about seeing my friend again, and more so, because to do so required managing Gianni's childcare so that I would be able to spend a good chunk of the day in Boston, attending a reunion lunch with group of college friends, all of us pleased that one of our own would be receiving a prestigious literary award that evening. I could not imagine missing any of it, but I was torn by a sense of responsibility that I ought to take care of my father, to see to it that he was okay. I had always tried to be a good daughter. Yet I did not even try to call him. I was caught up in my own life in a way that was rare for me in those early years of motherhood, when my own needs often went unmet.

Two days after I'd received that worrisome phone call, my father called me again when he got in from work on Wednesday. He sounded better. His voice was stronger and without even a hint of panic. And he seemed happier as we got talking. I was relieved. He did not let on that there had been anything at all wrong on Monday evening when he'd called and left me that message. He said simply, "I forgot that you were going out."

I had a lot to tell him, to explain where I had been since we'd last talked. He remembered my old college friend who was now the acclaimed writer, honored by the likes of Jacqueline Kennedy Onassis and George Plimpton. I told him that I'd met the former first lady. "Isn't it an amazing irony," I said, "that it was Jackie honoring him, hosting a reception for *him*?" He had grown up in D.C., his family poor and struggling, at the very time when the Kennedys were in the White House, and there he was, sitting next to Jackie herself, so many years later, being honored by *her*.

"Life is funny," my father said. "Did you speak to her besides to say 'hello'?" he asked.

I laughed, "Are you kidding? What could I have possibly said to her?"

I was worried as always when I met someone of that stature, of sounding inane or fawning.

"Well," my father said, "you could have told her that you thought it was important for a minority writer to be honored in this way. That would have been something to talk about, wouldn't it?"

He was right. I could always count on my father to be direct about his opinions. It was exactly what I'd been thinking, having learned something about justice, being his daughter. It was what I should have said. He would have said it, and it wouldn't have mattered a bit to whom he was talking; nothing stopped him from diplomatically saying whatever was on his mind. But I'd been tongue-tied.

I ran down the day's whirlwind of activities for my father, knowing how much he lived vicariously through me. I told him about my stint as a tailor after lunch that afternoon. Forgetting that he was going to be in Boston and not Washington, D.C. where he lived, my friend had assumed that he would be able to find a tailor on the spur of the moment to hem the pants he was going to wear that evening for the award ceremony and reading. None of us at lunch had a clue about where he might have the alterations done, so I boldly offered to do the work.

I remember standing with another of my college friends in the foyer of the St. Botolph Club—in the foyer, because we women were not allowed in, since it was for males only at the time. It was a bastion of Brahmin splendor on Commonwealth Avenue, where our writer friend was being put up by the organization sponsoring the awards event. We were on the outside looking in. On tiptoes, we peered through the glass window of the front door at the entryway. We saw what was either a dining or sitting room. We were both struck by the irony of our friend staying at such a luxurious place. We knew him as a humble man, and he had seemed uncomfortable taking us to see that he was staying in such elegant, formal surroundings.

We waited for him to go upstairs to his room to retrieve the slacks that needed hemming. When he returned, I did a cursory measurement of the proper length—the three of us standing in the foyer; then my old college friend and I flew like the wind, back to Cambridge to get the pants ready for the evening festivities.

I was not a seamstress, not by any stretch of the imagination, but as an antidote to boredom one afternoon of my childhood, my grandmother Feeherry had taught me how to baste a temporary hem. I could improvise, too, and that was fortunate, since I found that I did not have a spool of black thread anywhere in the house. I knew that my toddler would be home from childcare soon, and that there was not time to go out to the store to buy one; so I salvaged some. I took down the hem on a pair of black slacks I no longer wore, and completed the necessary alterations using that thread, humming in my mind all the while, the feminist anthem "I'm a Woman," about the ridiculous amount of multi-tasking required of a woman with a family.

My father laughed at the story. "You did that?" Hemmed the pants he wore that night? I didn't know you could sew, Ree."

He sounded at once amused, surprised, and proud.

Then he saw himself in the story of my experience. It was some thirty years before. He remembered hemming my brother's dress pants in a hurry, for his First Communion. It was a particularly poignant story he told. My mother had been in the hospital for one of her many operations or bouts of pneumonia. She was too sick to take needle and thread in hand and apparently it was too late to involve my grandmother, who had been a dressmaker when she was young, and was therefore often pressed into service to sew hems and even the angel costumes my sisters and I had to wear for school holiday pageants. So my father took it upon himself to alter the suit Jack had to wear the next morning. He sat there in a chair in my mother's hospital room, sewing. It must have been after he had been through the rehabilitation program, because I remember him telling me that he had learned to sew as part of a curriculum designed to cultivate independence in the school's students who were all newly blinded adults.

My father laughed at the memory of sewing my brother's pants, and of me sewing the pants my friend wore to the awards ceremony.

"I didn't know you could sew, Ree," he repeated.

"Only in a pinch," I said, laughing along with him.

"Gianni asleep?" he wanted to know.

"Yup, he's asleep." I lied. Gianni had already had his bath and Mark was reading to him, the last step before a lullaby in his hour-long bedtime ritual. I knew that it would be upsetting if I disturbed the routine, after the pains Mark had taken to create a smooth transition to sleep.

I did think for a moment: perhaps I ought to let Gianni talk to my father. They took such delight in each other. I had a strange feeling that I would regret not doing so, but I didn't call Gianni to the phone.

"Well," my father said, "I think I'll go upstairs now and listen to the Red Sox game on the radio."

I think of my father listening in the dark to his radio until he fell asleep. Did the radio comfort him as my transistor radio had comforted me during difficult times in my teenage years? I hope so. I didn't know it then, but that would be the last conversation I would have with him. He had fooled me into thinking that he was feeling better, so the events of the next day seemed to come out of the blue.

Three

BARRICADE (1956)

After our Sunday joyride in the Packard, when my mother had ordered my father never to go near the car again and then saw to it that it was put up for sale, there were no longer family Sunday outings after washing and waxing the Packard. What it meant to my father was that he had to walk to and from his job at the pressed metal company, where he worked the three to eleven P.M. shift, often six days a week. It was nearly a two mile walk each way, requiring him to leave the house earlier in the day and it meant that he'd get home later at night than he had before, when he'd been able to drive the distance. My mother did not know how to drive at the time my father had to turn in his license, so the car stayed idle in the yard until it was finally sold. Everyone—except me—ignored it. I watched it as if I had been given the responsibility of guarding it for my father.

One morning when I got out of bed and went into the yard to check on it, as I did at various times of the day, I found that the car had disappeared. I had been not been told that a sale was imminent. I remember only the fantasy I created about the loss.

I had a fantastic imagination. I settled on the idea that the car not only looked like a wild animal, but that it really was one after all, and that it had gone back to its real life as a big cat. I remembered my father always said that the car purred whenever he started it up. I knew from my Aunt Margaret telling me, that bears and big cats still roamed the woods of Maine, and I imagined that maybe the car had taken off in that direction. Like most children, I was interested in wild animals and curious about places where men and women rode horses and were free as the breeze. I read books that took place in wide-open spaces and mystery stories, too. With my idea of the car transformed into a cat, just like one of the Transformer toys my own son played with when he was younger, and drawing on the plots of adventure shows I watched on television on Saturdays back then, I imagined the car—the cat, in its new life—sneaking up on Penny and that Sky King would have to rescue her, although it would be dangerous and difficult for him to land his small plane in the mountains. I pretended, too, that the car-turned-cat was waiting at some mountain pass to pounce on the Lone Ranger and Tonto.

I guess I felt sometimes, like galloping away myself, so I did so in my imagination.

"You kids will be the death of me yet," Mum was always saying.

We didn't know what she meant. We just wanted to run sometimes.

"You'll crack your skulls open and have to get stitches at the hospital emergency room. Can't you find something else to do?"

Peg and I skated in our stocking feet on the newly polished wood floors.

"You'll get slivers, I'm telling you."

We begged her to let us go to Coes Pond where we knew other kids went swimming.

"No, and I don't want to hear any more about it. Do you want to get polio? Every Tom, Dick, and Harry swims at Coes Pond. You never know what disease you might get!"

I was bored and so I sometimes retreated to my hideout, the bedroom I shared with my sister Peg. I closed the door and sang, "Home on the Range," passionately—the lyrics about being in a place where there hardly was a discouraging word spoken and where there were no cloudy days. Or else I went quietly down the back stairs and out to the yard. When it got to be winter I wouldn't go out of the house; instead, I sat inside the hall on the bottom step, as far away as I could get from the upstairs door to our apartment.

But when I went out in summer, I used the front entrance and enjoyed the coolness of that big hall. With its oak staircase, vanilla colored toile wallpaper decorated with scenes of country ladies in long dresses strolling or sitting under sprawling willow trees near ponds, the front hall was a great place to dream. On the second floor landing there were three long windows in a bay and built into the wall in front of them, an oak window seat that opened up when you lifted a small brass ring. Inside I found that there were books, some probably there, my mother said, going back to the time when the house was first occupied. I knew that there was a book called *Ben Hur* stored somewhere in the window seat. Driven to search for it, I used to take it out sometimes, just to look at it and touch it. The pages of *Ben Hur* had gold edging. I would turn the book on its side and feel its smooth golden thickness; I was in awe of what I thought—from the looks of it—must have been an important book. I would find it under large, heavy books with titles like, *Drafting* and *Crafting Machine Tools*. "Leave those there," my mother said when I wanted to know about them. "Those belong to your father."

When I stood on tiptoes near the bottom stairs of the lower landing, I could create a new world by looking in first one, then another, of each stained glass windowpane. I loved making our unchanging neighborhood change. Looking through one pane of glass I saw that it was yellow, in another it turned blue. I looked in all the other squares of colored glass and I could make it red, green, or purple. I liked seeing Mr. Sadowsky in his yard next door. He looked best yellow. He was a scary looking old man in the first place, and in yellow he looked more so. I told my sister Peg to try it, to see how creepy he looked when he was yellow and she said, "Stop scaring me."

Sometimes I visited Bill Roche who lived across the street from us in the funny eight-sided house. "A real octagon," he told me. I'd find him sitting in a rocker reading the newspaper on the front porch or else he would be out puttering in the big old barn behind his house. He had a lot of junk in there, lots to do. The place smelled of oil from fixing things and sawdust from his other projects. He was always doing something. He put up a swing just for me, made from a tire's inner tube that hung on a thick rope attached to a hook in the rafters. The swing was right at the front entrance to the barn and the doors were always wide open.

"Hold on, now," Bill advised me as he pulled back the rope that held the old Goodyear tire. When he let go I flew out the barn door, my feet aimed right at my family's house. I closed my eyes and let gravity pull me back into the barn, and Bill pushed me out again.

Swinging was relaxing, and so was sitting in one of the rockers on the porch. I liked my conversations with Bill, wherever they happened. Bill had a wife named Mary—like me, like my mother—and I often wondered how many Marys there were in the world anyway. Sometimes he told me to go into the house and say "Hello" to his wife, that he knew that someone had just given her a box of Schraft's chocolates and that she might be willing to share them. If I couldn't decide which one to take from the assortment I was offered, Mary told me that pinching one until it bled its strawberry or orange cream was allowed. When I was at home and tried her technique of deciding which chocolate to choose, it gave my mother yet another reason to yell. "Where did you learn that?" she wanted to know, and when I told her she said, "Hasn't Mary Roche ever heard of germs? Don't let me ever see you do that again."

I knew the streets my father had to walk late at night, after he didn't drive anymore. I had heard my mother say that he ought to ask someone to give him a ride home from work. If he didn't want to do that, she thought that at the very least, he shouldn't take the Beacon Street route.

"Forget Beacon. Walk up to Main. At least it's got more street lighting. And cars go by even at that hour."

Although parallel to Main Street, Beacon was much darker. A large part of the street—the stretch my father walked near midnight—was lined with brick factory buildings, creating a tunnel effect. Did the industrialists with their particular brand of nineteenth century optimism give the street such a bright and promising name?

Perhaps my father was afraid that his eyes might play tricks on him, and that is the reason he did not walk the other way. What I know now about the progress of his shrinking vision is that all the different varieties of lighting on the Main Street route would have been jarring to him. He would have had trouble adjusting his eyes to competing neon signs and the headlights of passing cars, while also accommodating the regular pattern of streetlights broken by intervals of darkness on the outer reaches of the business district.

I am spending a lot of time sorting out fact from fiction. That is the hardest part of what I am trying to do. I have found that once I get people and events straight in terms of time, the pieces almost write themselves. For example, I spent one day thinking, trying to sort out the truth of my memory of the night when I found that, coming in from work near midnight, my father had barricaded the kitchen door to the back hallway.

My memory was sketchy. My mother wasn't present in it for some reason, and that perplexed me. I knew that I was very young and I also believed that this event had happened soon after the last ride I'd had with my father in the Packard, which I am fairly certain took place in the late spring of 1956. Not only did I remember that my mother was not involved that night I want to describe, but I also remembered that she was in hospital for some reason. She was hospitalized often when I was growing up, as it seemed so many women were in those years for surgeries. Or she'd get pneumonia or let some minor infection get out of hand. I realized though, that those health problems came later than 1956. That led me to these questions: Who then was taking care of us, if my mother was not there; and if she was in hospital, what was the reason?

I was the oldest. I celebrated my sixth birthday on November 2, 1956. Peg was a year and nine months younger, and Kate, that much younger than Peg. Someone had to dress us, take us to school, give us breakfast, lunch, and supper, and bathe us before putting us to bed at night. Who? Once I could answer that question, I was then able to determine that yes—my mother was in hospital in fact— and more importantly, I knew why.

Was it Auntie Margaret watching over us? My mother's sister was, I thought, the one most likely to have been taking care of us at night in my mother's absence. In my childhood memories she is always there.

My meditation led me to a series of associations by which I was then able to determine that it was not my aunt Margaret taking care of us, but rather, my Aunt Jean, my father's youngest sister who was just a teenager then. She would not have seen what my father did, barricaded the door when he came home, because she was tired out from taking care of us and went to bed early, when we children did. Because she lived out of town she was staying with us, not just babysitting for the evening.

"I sleep like the dead," she said to me when I asked her all these years later if she could remember anything about that night. She knew something had happened but her memory was vague. Still, I knew it was Aunt Jean staying with us, once I recalled having had a conversation with her on Ripley Street, just outside the building where my first-grade class was located. We were walking home. She'd come to meet me at school. I was in the first grade in 1956. The first graders were the youngest children at St. Peter's, and the lower grades were at that time, set apart from the others in an old wood frame farmhouse just up the street from the main building. Aunt Jean was walking me home from school. We were on the sidewalk there.

To my amazement, in my memory of us talking I could even visualize the direction we were facing on the street. I remembered snippets of our conversation. The subject was memorable because I had asked my aunt if there really was a Santa Claus, and that question is surely a milestone in a child's life. I was brought to the topic because I was no doubt thinking that Halloween was coming soon. I suppose that I may have associated then that my birthday was right after it in November, which meant that Christmas was not far away. It was that time of year when there was one childhood occasion after another for me. Aunt Jean, being so young, was more like an older friend rather than an adult, and I thought she might tell me the truth about Santa, and she did.

That is how I dated this event. My mother had gone to the hospital to deliver my brother Jack, who was born on October 27th the year I turned six.

That night I'd discovered the barricade I was startled awake and wondering about the unfamiliar noise keeping me from dozing off again. It was not one of the sounds I generally heard in the house late at night, when it was extremely quiet—the whirring of the refrigerator, the muffled footsteps of the upstairs tenants, or the pipes knocking when someone in the downstairs apartment ran the water. This was different, and I didn't know what it was. Not having a clock in my bedroom, I didn't know the time, only that it was still dark when I decided to get out of bed to investigate.

According to the clock on the wall in the dining room, it was midnight. Perhaps what I had heard was only my father coming in late from work. Because he walked home—the factory not being on any bus route and buses in our city not running that late at night anyway—he didn't usually get in until midnight. I knew that my father never asked anyone to give him a ride home. I had heard my mother telling him over and over again that he should.

I could see a light on in the bathroom and a shadow in the frosted glass window of the door. Water was running in the sink.

I went into the kitchen and that is when I found out what the noise was all about. I saw the barricade. The table—Formica-topped, and with curved metal legs like the chairs that went with it—had been moved—dragged across the linoleum floor from the middle of the room and put in front of the door to the back hall. The chairs, too, were there, standing— not on the floor—but on top of the table, the way my father stacked them in pairs when he was going to wash the kitchen floor. They were stacked seat-to-seat, one placed upside down in the lap of the other. But it was after midnight, too late to be washing the floor. The three sets of chairs on top of the table looked like they were waiting to have guards seated in them.

On the stovetop counter there was a pack of Lucky Strikes, and I knew that meant my father was home, so I went to the bathroom door and called to him.

"Dad?"

"Dad," he answered.

When he came to the door he was drying his chin with a towel. He must have just come home. He was still wearing the army green colored shirt and pants, his work clothes.

"What are you doing out of bed?" he asked.

"I have to pee," I pretended.

He came out of the bathroom and I went in, closing the door behind me. I did not really have to pee, so I waited a minute, then flushed the toilet and ran water in the sink, while counting to sixty before coming out.

In the kitchen I saw my father standing, staring at the back door. He seemed to be looking past the table and chairs, past the door even, and into the hallway outside. He didn't look like he was seeing anything, but he was listening hard I could tell—for someone—something? He held his head still, as if tuning into some very small sound, little as the click of a key in a lock.

"A noise woke me up. I didn't know what it was," I said, hoping for an explanation.

"Just me probably," he confirmed. "Don't worry."

He said no more, so I had to ask.

"Why did you move the table and why are the chairs on top of it?"

"The lock on the door is broken," he answered. "Someone will come fix it in the morning. The chairs and table are there just to be safe."

"I missed you, Dad."

My father looked the way I suppose I do when I'm scared and pretending not to be. Although he told me that night that everything was all right, I worried. I wondered if he was frightened because he thought that someone had followed him home, tracking him along the midnight streets. I had heard him saying to my mother not long before, that when he was walking home he thought sometimes that he could hear footsteps behind him. My mother said that he was imagining things, that he was afraid of his own shadow. What if there really had been some person—someone who wanted to rob him, some burglar who would try to get into our house in the night while we were sleeping? Or what if there was someone who wanted to hurt my father? Would his barricade help keep out such trouble? These were thoughts I had that night when I saw what my father had done and how he was acting.

Before leaving the kitchen to go back to bed, I stopped at the window above the yard. I looked out, but I didn't see anything moving outside, just the branches of the trees swaying in a gentle wind and something rolling around in the gutter, maybe a paper Dixie cup or the cardboard roll left from a Rocket push-up ice cream treat. The floodlights were always on at the furniture store on the corner and one could see clear to Main Street.

"I don't see anyone outside, Dad. Not a person, a car, or anything out there."

I remember that when I looked back at him he was still standing, listening near the door.

"We're safe," I said.

He smiled. "Now you really should get back to bed."

"I'm going, " I said.

We all had our fingers crossed that when my mother came home from the hospital she would bring back a baby boy. Did my father send me to bed that night, telling me to say my prayers before I went to sleep, "Pray hard and maybe we'll get a boy this time?"

I said "Goodnight" to my father and went to my station behind the slightly open bedroom door. There I sat in my usual snooping spot where I would often fall asleep while eavesdropping and would be discovered there and have to be carried into bed. On this night though, I stayed awake, waiting in the dark until the house was quiet. When I was sure that my father had gone to bed, almost certain that he would be asleep, I got up and went silently to the front bedroom. I stood there like a statue—not even breathing—at the foot of the bed to check on him. Once I was sure that he was asleep, I went back out into the kitchen knowing that sleep would not come for me until I had checked the lock on the back door. I didn't believe what my father had said, that the lock was broken and that was the reason for his barricade. I knew my Aunt Jean had locked the door earlier. I'd watched her lock it after Peg and Kate and I came in for supper after playing out in the yard all afternoon. I remembered I'd asked her why she was locking the door. I told her that our mother never locked the door when we were at home, only when we were going out. Aunt Jean wouldn't unlock it though. "This is the city," she said. "People need to lock their doors in the city." Aunt Jean lived in Milford. It was a small town. It was like the country where she lived.

The room was full of moonlight, enough for me to see, so I crawled under the table to get to the lock. I reached up and slid the bolt over, then turned the knob to see if the door was locked.

It was—just as I had thought.

I wondered then why my father hadn't told me the truth about his reason for barricading the door. I wondered if someone really had been following him or if he had just been imagining things like my mother said I did, whenever I was scared of the dark and thought I heard someone in my room. Even with the barricade, I did not feel safe. I went to bed, but

I was frightened, and I wanted to know what secret my father was keeping from me.

Next to the bed I slept in with my sister, Peg, who had not stirred, there was a chest of drawers. I kept a photograph in there of my mother and father. It was one that I had secretly slipped out of a family album at Grammy's house. I had hidden it for those times when I was scared and confused.

There was not enough light over at the window. The moon had moved and I could see that it was shining brightly on the aluminum roof of the garage next door. I knew that I might wake Peg, but it was the chance I took, putting on the light just long enough to take a look, knowing that seeing the photograph would help me get back to sleep. I gave Mum and Dad in the picture a kiss goodnight.

The year 1947 is stamped on the back of the scallop-edged snapshot that I still have, taken before they were married, before they became my mother and father. They are standing outside the house that I recognize as my aunt Margaret's summer cottage in Maine, standing in front of the porch in the patchy dry grass. The Packard is there in the background. I had had my own picture taken in that same spot. Whoever the photographer was, he didn't pay any attention to the sun. In the picture my father squints, looking pale and not like the dark-skinned man I knew. My mother smiles just like she is in some advertisement for toothpaste in one of the ladies' magazines she used to read. She does not look even a little camera shy. Her blonde hair is very light, lighter than it really was when she was young, almost white—the way it is now in her tenth decade.

I can tell from this picture that they were in love, just by looking at the way they were holding on to each other. My father has his right arm around her shoulder and his hand on her upper arm as if he is protecting her. Her arm is looped around behind him at the waist, and I can see one of my mother's small hands on my father's hip. They are a good-looking couple.

That night my father barricaded the door and I had discovered his fear—and mine, too—I shut off the light after looking at the photograph. I crawled into bed and closed my eyes. I could still see the picture in my mind of my mother and father together, and soon I fell asleep.

Memorial Days

The phone rang in the early afternoon, and it was my brother Jack telling me that his wife had received a call from Massachusetts General Hospital with the information that my father had been taken there. The caller asked that my brother contact a certain doctor. Jack was telephoning, asking me if I would. I thought that Jack was asking me to make the call because I was in town, and I could go there if need be, to see what was up. Worcester to Boston was a long-distance charge, and I knew that whoever called would probably be kept on hold while the doctor was paged. I understood, therefore, that it was efficient on more than one count, if I did the calling.

When I reached the doctor, I told him that I was calling to find out why my father had been brought in, and what his condition was.

"He was brought in from the JFK Federal Building by ambulance," the doctor said, sounding as if he were reading the information off a report.

"Yes, he works there," I said. "His business is there. And what is his condition?" I was impatient and anxious.

"Our efforts to revive him were unsuccessful. I'm sorry," the doctor said.

I was stunned, completely unprepared for the words the doctor had spoken so flatly and routinely, devoid of emotion or even the slightest bit of empathy. I could not speak for a moment, yet the doctor rambled on about an autopsy.

"What?" I said finally, interrupting him, disbelieving. "What happened?"

"Sudden death," he said. "That's why we would do an autopsy."

"That won't be necessary. I can tell you what was wrong."

I reviewed my father's medical history for him then. In a couple of sentences I demonstrated for the doctor that it was not surprising really that my father had died suddenly, given his ailments and his resistance to accepting treatment for them. I described the stress of his lifestyle. I explained to the doctor that my father had suffered a massive coronary at the age of fifty-two, that his doctor had advised him that he would live perhaps another ten years—at most. As I spoke, I pictured my father almost *twenty* years before, sitting on the couch in the living room of the house in which I was raised, looking—not frightened—but disgusted, telling me, "Ten years. Ten years, that's all I've got."

"He lived almost ten years longer than he was told he would after his last heart attack," I said to the doctor. "He was a diabetic, too. He was told not long ago that he ought to be taking insulin shots, but he wouldn't."

My father took pills before eating and attempted in vain to control his diabetes by paying attention to his diet. He knew all sorts of people; he talked to everyone. I don't doubt that he thought that at his residence during the week there were addicts renting rooms; that kind of thing is often the downside of living in a rooming house in the city—even one like the Y. I can't help but wonder if he'd been afraid of being a target for someone who could put his syringes to another use, had he relented and consented to taking insulin intravenously. He was too smart, too streetwise, not to have considered that. The alternative would have been for him to solicit help from someone on the staff at the residence, or from the nurse at the JFK Federal Building at Government Center where his snack bar/newsstand was at the time. But he valued his independence too much to admit to any kind of vulnerability, even an illness that was life threatening, but which might have responded to treatment. He was too self-reliant and stubborn about it, too private, and used to deflecting attention away from himself and giving it to others instead—even when he was in need.

In that phone conversation I didn't tell the doctor that my father ate on the run—sweets and food that did not meet his dietary restrictions. I did not say how hard he worked or that he hadn't taken a vacation since I'd been a teenager more than twenty years before. I didn't tell the doctor that in the car on the way back to Cambridge the night of the party my sisters and brother and I had given for our parents in celebration of their fortieth wedding anniversary, that my father had talked hopefully to my husband and me, about retiring eventually and then taking my mother on a cruise on the QE2. I don't think I even told the doctor that my father was blind.

I didn't need to say anything more. He had heard enough.

"Well, in that case," the doctor said, "we can avoid doing an autopsy."

It was four days after our backyard picnic that my father disappeared from my life as suddenly as the crab apple tree and forsythia hedge had. Sudden death. Stricken at work.

I was alone in the house. I called my friends Joan and Paul, and Paul answered. When I told him what had happened, he asked, "Are you alone?"

I had never felt so alone.

"We'll be right over," he said.

It was only after I hung up that I could hear Mark and Gianni out in the yard, returning from their walk. It sounded like they were coming in the back entrance.

I looked out and could see them from the bedroom window.

"My father's gone," I told Mark quietly as they entered the kitchen. I didn't want Gianni to hear.

"What?" Mark said, not understanding my meaning, his puzzlement showing in his expression. "Gone where?"

"He died," I answered.

"No. Oh, no," Mark said.

I felt at first defeated, more than sad. But I began to make dinner in spite of the news. Roast chicken. I brushed it with honey and covered it with crushed walnuts. I'd invited Joan and Paul to come to eat with us.

When I brought the platter to the table, Joan said, "Oh, look at this. We should be cooking for you instead of you doing this."

"Well, it's done now. It gave me something to do. I didn't know what else to do."

I had always taken care of myself, always taken care of others. I knew how to do it. Why should this evening have been any different?

We put Gianni to bed without letting on that his grandfather had died and was gone out of his life forever. I tucked him in and when I leaned down to kiss him goodnight, he had a question for me.

"Mom?"

"Yes, Gianni, what is it?" I asked wearily.

"Mom, where did Gampy go?"

Four

ELVIS (1956)

One wintery Saturday afternoon when snow was on the way and taking its own good time arriving, I was sitting in the living room watching *The Lone Ranger* or some other show I regularly watched, when my father came home carrying a small suitcase of red vinyl with tiny white polka dots all over it. It did not look like a man's suitcase, so I thought that maybe my father had bought it for me. I had caught the travelling bug, going to Maine in the summer with my mother's sister, my aunt Margaret.

My father put the suitcase down on the living room floor and crouched next to it.

"Look what I have for you," he said, opening it up.

I stared into it, seeing that it was more than a suitcase, that it had things already inside it—dials and knobs and at the center was a round, think chunk—of *rubber* was it? Yes, it was a circle of grooved rubber about the size of a sandwich plate.

"Ever see anything like this?" my father asked.

I had not.

"*This* is a portable record player," he said.

The only record player that I had ever seen was the one at the Crowley-Phillips house, next to my aunt's cottage in Maine. I loved being invited there after dinner in the evenings, as we sometimes were. We ate salty white pistachios while the record player droned on. It was a Victrola, nothing like this one that was a hot new item in the 1950s. The Victrola was the opposite of portable. Coming out of its case was a large bloom, like an Easter lily—only huge and made of metal—and it played heavy records, that except for their thickness, felt like the pieces of slate that I sometimes found in the back yard, fallen off the roof of our house. The records smashed the same way as slate did, too, I found, dropping one of them by accident during a visit. The Victrola had a sound that was both distant and yet too near, making all music strange, as if from another world. We listened to songs like "Swanee River" about the sad and dreary and lonely world we live in. And I remember thinking when I heard the song, "All Through the Night" played on the Victrola and sung by a woman whose voice wavered so, that it made me think that it was the singing voice a ghost might have. I barely recognized the music as that of a familiar lullaby that my grandmother played for me on the rare occasion when she sat down at the piano. "Sleep my child and peace attend thee / All through the night."

"But where's the horn?" I asked about the suitcase record player.

My father laughed a little, but not the way he usually laughed when I said something silly. This time he laughed like he had a magic trick—the disappearing quarter trick or something else—to show me.

"This," he said, "doesn't need a horn. It's got speakers built right into the case. And wires, so you don't have to crank it up. You just plug it in; turn it on—put the record right here—this is the turntable," he said. "Then... Music!"

He had not put the record on yet, so there was no music really.

I picked up the two records he had brought home. They were thin and light and fit inside a small box with handles, a box like a pocketbook.

"You should always keep the records in their case, so that they don't get scratched and you know where they are. It's very important. Scratches ruin records. If that happens you won't have music anymore."

My mother, who had been out in the kitchen must have all of a sudden realized that my father was home, because she came bursting into the living room.

"What's this?" she asked.

My father pointed to the records, then to the suitcase player. He was smiling at her.

"I don't know what you were thinking, bringing something like this home. She doesn't need that. She's not old enough for that."

"It's for all of us," he said.

"What do we need that around here for? I don't need it. I don't have time for anything like that."

"Well, I'll listen to it," he said.

"And when are you ever here to listen to anything? This isn't something you give a kid. She's not old enough to appreciate something like that."

She did not realize that my father had taken care to bring home as well, a recorded story meant just for me. My mother didn't regularly read to us, though my aunt sometimes did, if she was around at bedtime.

"Sure she's old enough," my father said. "She'll get lots of pleasure out of it."

"Until the novelty wears off," she replied.

But I would put on the record of "Peter the Church Mouse" whenever I wanted to hear a story. I played it so much that I wore it out. I still remember the point at which the record would get stuck, and if I were not right next to it, to gently rest my index finger on the arm to move the needle along, it played the same fragment of a sentence over and over until I did—"...that Peter the Church Mouse put on it...that Peter the Church Mouse put on it." In addition to receiving the recorded story as a present, the record player itself may have been a late birthday gift for me. When my birthday had rolled around that year—on November second—it was the week after Jack had been born, when we'd all been caught up in the excitement of having a new baby in the house. In addition to the record he bought for me, my father had also purchased a copy of Elvis Presley's "Love Me Tender," which was the number one hit record in the country on November 3, 1956.

It was a waste of good money my mother thought about the record player. I didn't know what she meant, why she would think that about something so wonderful. I knew she liked music—or rather, that she used to. She was always talking about St. Gabriel's School of Music where she had learned to sing when she was young. "I was on stage all the time," she told me. "After St. Gabriel's your aunt Margaret and I both were. We sang in the Light Opera and in the Worcester Chorus for the Music Festival." I was sure that it wasn't music that made my mother mad at my father for bringing home this present.

"How does it work?" Show *me*, Daddy," I said, turning my back on my mother.

Of the two records he'd bought, I knew which one was for me. But that was not the record he took out of the paper envelope and put onto the turntable, pressing its center with the fingertips of both hands until it snapped on.

"So it won't slide off as it goes around, " he explained.

He pointed to the letters RPM and a set of numbers: 16, 33 1/3, 78, and 45.

"Now this is where you set the speed."

I wanted to ask *why*, but I couldn't. He was talking so fast. I had to keep listening or else I would miss something.

"And over here you have the volume. Soft. Loud."

"Now don't have that thing turned up so loud. Do you hear me?" my mother yelled, storming back in from the kitchen three rooms away, when the sound got very loud for just a second. "You'll wake the baby."

"I'm just demonstrating, Mame," he said, barely loud enough for her to hear him, not yelling as she was.

He didn't like it that she always interrupted him when he was talking. I could tell by the way he twisted his mouth when he answered her that it made him angry that she would think that he'd keep playing the music so loudly. All he was trying to do was to explain to me how the machine worked.

"Oh, demonstrating are you? Aren't you swell?"

I suppose that my mother had her reasons for not liking machines. They broke down, like the Mercury my father bought for her once she decided she'd learn to drive. *I had to sit around in that damn garage all day.* Or the washing machine—

I've been waiting an eternity for that repairman to come. And the furnace—*We have to have heat. I've got four kids and tenants upstairs and down.* And it was the machine shop that took my father away from us for long days of work. *He's never home,* she complained constantly; yet when he was, she didn't seem to like him being there, arguing with him day and night. It was no wonder that she thought that learning to use the new record player would be a waste of time. She saw it, I suppose, as just another machine to disrupt her life.

"Play it," I said.

"That's Elvis Presley singing," my father said, as the song began.

"Never heard of him," my mother said.

My father reminded her that this was the singer that everyone was crazy about. They had seen him on the *Ed Sullivan Show.*

"Oh, that one. Well, I don't think he'd be able to fulfill my dreams. He looked like he had St. Vitus Dance, the way he squirmed all over the place on stage."

This made my father laugh and made me wonder about St. Vitus—who he was and why anyone would name a dance after a saint.

When I heard the Elvis Presley song I thought of kissing. The song was what my mother would call "mushy," what she said my father was, whenever he tried to kiss her, telling him after he did, that he needed a shave, or stopping him from kissing her, saying he shouldn't bother her, that she was busy doing something.

"Listen," he said to her. "Shhh."

My mother, though, didn't seem to care that the reason my father had bought this record was so they could listen to it together. I remember thinking that the words were like a Valentine.

"Am I going to have to listen to that mushy stuff all day now?"

Why didn't my mother care that my father was trying to tell her he loved her that day—and that he had bought this record for her? Was it that she no longer believed that he could fulfill her dreams?

My mother's dashed dreams surfaced now and again throughout my childhood, coming into play always when she was in the middle of some argument, under real or perceived verbal attack, or when she was being teased. When she remembered her dreams, out came angry words directed at my father and all of us. I remember when she had no words once, only the Melmac dinnerware, that "unbreakable" stuff, which she managed to crack into pieces, hurling it so hard across the kitchen floor during one of their arguments.

She'd laugh and make a comedy of struggling to get into clothes that no longer fit her, but when we joked along with her, or when she was trying a new diet drink called Metrical, she hit back with a dream that had escaped her. "I had to leave nursing training because I only weighed eighty-five pounds." She was petite, barely five feet. When she said this, I would wonder if she'd grown heavy because her thinness was responsible for her losing her dream of working in a hospital, alongside doctors like her Uncle Tom, a place where she might have found a husband who'd have given her a life that wouldn't have involved the kind of struggles—financial as well as emotional —that she had to deal with, marrying my father. She had expected a whole other kind of life, like one in the movies she loved watching, free of the kind of difficulties she had in her life.

I thought my father had bought the record player for me, and suddenly I felt left out. He was singing to my mother about wanting her to love him and forgetting about me.

I didn't understand how putting the record on the machine produced music we could hear. All that mattered to me then was that it gave me an intense feeling of happiness to listen to music or a story and know that I could play those records whenever I wanted. I accepted its magic and embraced the mystery of it, just as I did when I saw a movie being broadcast on the television or the screen at the Loew's Poli. But my father would not stop explaining. He wanted me to understand how things worked.

"RPM means revolutions per minute," he said. "The number of times the record spins around every minute is its speed."

"Is that right now? You don't say," my mother said, interrupting again.

She may have wanted him to tell *her* this, not *me*. She turned on him though, rather than admit it.

"Now where did *you* come into all this information?"

This was the same thing my mother said to me sometimes, when I wanted to tell her something new I had learned, or when I thought that she was wrong not to believe something that I knew to be true.

I understood my father's explanation this way. The letter R in RPM means revolutions, like when my mother would blame my father for "starting a revolution over nothing," when they began to argue.

He tried to explain about the speed using the example of the revolving doors at the Denholm & McKay Company downtown, the place that my grandmother referred to as "The Boston Store."

"It's a revolution," my father said, "each time the door goes completely around. Each time it makes the circle."

But the doors made my mother think of something else— like the record player, like the song must have.

"Well," she said, changing the subject, "those were the kind of doors they had the Cocoanut Grove."

The Cocoanut Grove was the premiere Boston nightclub after Prohibition ended. My mother and my grandmother, too, sometimes talked about the horrible fire there.

"Those revolving doors are dangerous," she said remembering that, "in the big fire people got trampled or stuck when trying to get out of those revolving doors. Burnt alive, when they'd just been out for a good time."

Her story about the people in that nightclub fire being trapped in the revolving doors reminded my father that records too, could get stuck.

"But you can get them moving," he said.

He showed me how.

"If you just put your finger very lightly on the arm, right at the tip where the needle is—very gently—that will move the needle over the spot that is scratched. The scratch makes the record play the same bit over and over again." He flipped the arm up and rubbed his finger once over the needle, so that I would know where it was. It coughed, making a sound like the one the microphone made when the priest went to the pulpit to give his Sunday sermon.

I didn't care that my mother hated the record player and what it brought to mind for her. I admired the little machine in a suitcase. It was small like I was. And watching my father use it, watching him point out for me all the little things that made it go, I saw that I could learn to use it, too. When I think back on that day, I love my father for having that belief in what I could do, and I love him also for trying to tell my mother he loved her with the Elvis Presley record.

Memorial Days

My brother came to Cambridge the day after my father's death. When my father was taken to the hospital he had on the white uniform he wore at work, and he carried no wallet or other identification on his person. A family member would have to identify the body.

I intended to go to the morgue in spite of being advised not to by friends.

"You don't want to remember him that way," a librarian I knew told me. She said she had been the one to identify her brother when he died and had regretted it ever since.

But I wouldn't hear of staying home when Mark and my brother were going to the morgue. I insisted on being with them, and they agreed to allow it, but Mark made it clear that he and Jack would make the identification of the body and that I would stay out of the room.

At the time, the morgue for city of Boston looked like a fortress—a huge rundown brick warehouse on the fringes of a highway. When we got out of the car to enter, we saw that there was a bell at the door, a feeble-looking device and a sign that said something like "Ring then Enter."

"Hmmm," Jack said, almost to himself, when he saw the sign and the bell.

I thought: great, a do-it-yourself morgue, right out of a horror-movie set. Without a guide, someone from within, it seemed so frightening a place. I feared my own vulnerability, and there was something more important I did not want to face—the indignity of my father being within those walls. The morgue was, I knew, primarily a place for indigents and criminals, a place that seemed to have been created without any consideration for those left behind. I thought of my father living in that furnished room on weekdays, so that he could work in Boston, living among those who may have been without family and were a short step away from being homeless. Having him end up here at the city morgue, it suddenly seemed that my father might as well have been homeless. This place denied that he had a family and more particularly that I had always cared so much about him and done everything in my power to help him.

I remember his savoir faire, dressed in a tuxedo at my sister's wedding, greeting guests; I see him in a pinstriped suit at Gianni's christening at the Slover's mansion in Brookline, raising his champagne glass in a toast to his grandson, hoping that above all Gianni would have courage in his life. My father met ever day with courage and dignity, and a place like the Boston city morgue erased that history. It corrupted the kindness, intelligence, and humility he radiated, and it defined as failure, the simplicity with which he had lived his daily life. How could he possibly have ended up in this place? I had tried hard I thought, to help him have a different kind of life, one that would have a different ending.

Once we went inside I felt only worse. Directly opposite the entrance was an amphitheater with a garish gold and black ornate door—inconsistently ornate within the context. We didn't dare open it, but instead began wandering through the building, looking for someone to help us. It was the strangest place I have ever entered. For the first few minutes I felt as if I had been sucked down to another level, as if I were experiencing a different plane of reality.

I think all of us had in mind that we were going to an official building, a place, if not entirely like City Hall, at least one with a staff and a sense of officiousness. But that was not the case at all. This building seemed to have been abandoned on the outskirts of the city. We couldn't find anyone in the building; it appeared empty—except, we imagined, for the corpses that lay on slabs beyond the walls of the rooms we could access.

We wandered throughout the building, up flights of staircases reminiscent of those in late nineteenth century schools, mill buildings, and factories, of the kind that I was familiar with from having grown up in Worcester—although the ones I knew were better preserved and certainly cleaner. It was a place that even without the knowledge of its purpose would make your skin crawl. I don't remember how many floors we stopped on, but they were all the same: empty long corridors that brought us to large areas of open office space as a central point of each floor. These offices looked like those of the abandoned bureaucracy of a defunct government. There were old dark green metal desks covered with files of papers and folders and the same army green color-coordinated file cabinets all around. "But where were the office workers? And who was in charge?" we wondered. Had the morgue taken over a building that had once had another purpose and had everything been left, as it had been, no need to remove the vestiges of the past? I wondered—but only for a moment—if this could be some kind of cruel joke the employees played on unsuspecting visitors in order to liven up their work place. I imagined the employees hiding, crushed behind a door, trying to contain their laughter as they scared us out of our wits. But no, this was no television sitcom; I knew that. My father was dead and his body was somewhere in this building.

We called out—quietly at first. Were we afraid to yell, afraid to wake the dead?

"Hello," Jack called feebly. "Anyone here?"

"Let's split up, see if we can find someone," Mark suggested, sounding like a character in a young adult mystery.

"No, don't. Don't leave me."

"I'll look," Jack offered, and he set off bravely down the corridor by himself, so that Mark could stay with me.

In a few minutes he had found someone. A large rough-and-ready woman led us back downstairs to a room near the door we'd come in.

"Wait in here. We'll call you when we're ready."

She turned to leave, then looked back over her shoulder with an afterthought.

"Who's going to go in?"

There was no need to be precise. We all knew why we had come. It seemed though, that the woman had asked the question only out of curiosity or to provoke anxiety, for she offered nothing more, seemed almost not to hear when Jack said, "I'll go," and Mark insisted,
"I'll go with you."

Finally a man came into the room and called them out. The woman was not with him.

"We're ready," was all he said to them.

The man was like some auto mechanic telling them that their car repair was ready for inspection. The waiting room itself was like the place at an old garage where you sit to wait for your car. It was totally without frills or even basic comfort: cement floor, high ceilings, and old suspended light fixture. It was furnished with a broken down sofa—the vinyl dirty, ripped, and taped, the stuffing seeping out of its cushions. Across from where I sat was a very large Coke machine—I recognized it as industrial-sized from having seen similar ones outside my father's various businesses, his cafeterias.

Was this an attempt at hospitality here at the morgue? No, I decided; the Coke machine called to mind instead, whole families seated around, waiting for hours for detectives or medical examiners, or other relatives to come to meet the family after someone they loved had been the victim of a drive-by shooting or a car accident. *Have a Coke*, something to do while you wait with a thirst that cannot be quenched. Or perhaps this was mainly a staff room—a place for employees or medical students, the detectives or policemen, to take breaks, eat their lunches, and relax. But this *Coke* machine, this room, brought *me* no comfort.

Five

COLD WAR (1950s)

The Catholic practice requiring meatless meals on Fridays led to the popularity of eating fish on Fridays, which must have been good for the fishermen of our New England region, and for the little markets that sold their catch. Main South Seafood in our working class neighborhood did a galloping fish and chip take-out business on Fridays. There were so many Catholics in the city, so many fish to fry.

Every Friday evening my mother sent me out for fish. I was often the only child waiting in line among adults I recognized either as the parents of schoolmates or people I had seen so often at church, that their faces were as familiar as family. Standing waiting in the line that stretched out of the storefront and onto the sidewalk, I stared too long at the ancient geranium in the window of the Powder Puff Beauty Shop, shivering from the cold—as I so often did in winter— out without a hat, scarf, or mittens. I was grateful when I finally made it inside the storefront market.

It was very hot inside, especially when I was wearing a winter coat. I felt bad for the women who had to cook the fish, never moving from in front of a row of fryers. These cooking vats seemed to be alive, spitting hot oil. As any child would, I focused on the activity and the strangeness of it. I noticed red blotches on the arms of those women—little burns, I guessed—and their strong Irish faces looked sunburned from the heat of the oil. Sweat beaded up on the ruddy faces of everyone working at Main South Seafood. I watched it roll down the necks of the women who cooked in silence, only nodding to communicate. It wet their brown locks that escaped from the hairnets they had on.

To alleviate my boredom I studied the set–up. I often wondered what it would be like to have a family business like that. I knew that my dad wanted to have a restaurant, but that my mother resisted, believing it was "too risky." Did the family that owned the fish market hate working there? No one seemed to be complaining. No one even looked bothered by the job. Perhaps they didn't care about the heat and the burns and standing so long in one place, because they were making a lot of money. Still, I couldn't understand how they could keep doing the same thing over and over again, the way they did. I used to think I would be bored working like that.

Going to the market and waiting in line so long made me feel like complaining, and I did. I told my father one Saturday morning, how long I'd waited. He didn't know what it was like to go there, how long I'd be gone. He wasn't home on Friday nights. He was always working.

"The line went out the door and down the street as far as the Powder Puff," I said.

My mother interrupted my whining. "They do a terrific business."

My father went right to the telephone, hearing that.

"Who are you calling?" my mother wanted to know.

"I'd like to find out how much that little place makes on a Friday night." It was "a gold mine," he figured.

"Never mind now," my mother said. "What difference does it make?"

But my father didn't hang up. He began dialing some numbers. He got in a few calls in spite of my mother's protests.

This was a scene that I saw played out time and again over the years, when my father was trying to get information about something; whether it was a telephone call spurred on by his entrepreneurial leanings, as that one was, or an attempt to talk to one of our teachers. He'd make calls to comparison price a new kitchen appliance, or he'd call a librarian to research some information he couldn't get from a newspaper. When he made contact and began to talk, my mother always tried to stop him, fearing what, I never understood. Was it his directness, his curiosity, or his pleasure in gaining the knowledge that these telephone calls provided him that my mother disliked?

My father hung up the telephone that day after finding out the cost for this or that. He calculated the numbers in his head and came up with a figure: the fish market's profit margin, he thought. He could do all sorts of calculations in his head at lightning speed, and had little patience for my own lack of interest in mathematics over the years. He was always trying to teach me ways of grouping and efficiently organizing numbers in my head in order to improve my skills. I believe his techniques had some beneficial effect, although I still haven't mastered the art of balancing a checkbook.

"I'd like to have a little place like that myself, one that did that kind of business. They're reeling in the dough," my father said.

"Pipe dreams," my mother said.

Look where you've gotten me so far, she might have been thinking. She was always exclaiming, "We'll be in the poor house yet. I'm robbing Peter to pay Paul." She must have feared poverty. Had her family warned her against marrying my father, knowing he had not finished high school, but not knowing the reason he'd had trouble with his studies— unaware of his intelligence. Maybe even she had come to doubt the wisdom of her decision, and so she'd begun to feel trapped, and that was the reason for her growing bitterness.

Like the children I see at the salon owned by the Vietnamese sisters in North Cambridge where I take my son for haircuts, or the little girl I've noticed helping her mother set tables at the Greek Corner restaurant next door, where we go for lunch after, my father grew up in a neighborhood family business, Testa's market. It was in his blood to want to run a small business himself, having the working class immigrant's dream, one he'd surely inherited.

Besides telling us what we could eat on Fridays and when to go to special masses on Holy Days, the church calendar hanging on our kitchen wall had little lessons above each month about the articles of our faith. I remember particularly, a lesson about God being three persons in one—Father, Son, and Holy Ghost. As a child, this is the way I understood that complicated metaphysical idea. 1) The father created all things, including us; 2) the son died for us; and 3) the Holy Ghost wasn't really a ghost, but rather a spirit represented by a dove, which also meant wisdom and peace. But it was just one God we were talking about, even though there seemed to be three separate creatures. "Like 3-In-One oil," Sister Mary Angelita explained. "It's one kind of oil but it can do different jobs."

Neither the calendar nor Sister Mary Angelita, my third grade teacher, made it any easier for a child to understand these strange ideas. The message was: don't try too hard to understand, just accept what you are told to believe. When we asked too many questions we had to listen time and again to the story from the New Testament of St. Thomas, the doubter, one of Jesus' twelve apostles, who, it was written, received a visitation from Christ after he'd risen from the dead. I supposed that Thomas—or anyone who was in that situation for that matter—would have thought that he was losing his mind, although in all the classroom discussions of visitations and voices heard in the wilderness, there was never any talk of that. The point of this story that earned him the nickname "Doubting Thomas," was that he would not believe that it was Jesus appearing to him, that is not until he had put his hands right into the wounds that were made in Christ's body by the soldiers when they nailed him to the cross. Of course, none of us would want to question Christ the way we would question Sister Mary Angelita, so the point was well made. These illustrations were for me the equivalent of ghost stories, their effect the same: they frightened me into believing what good Catholic children were supposed to believe.

I would suppress any doubt I had—for a while anyway. But I kept asking the questions nevertheless, ignoring Sister's admonitions, the way my father would ignore my mother when she told him not to make telephone calls to get information about something. Sister telling me that we should just believe, have faith, accept the Mysteries, was like my mother saying to my father when she overheard him on the telephone asking questions of a librarian, the clerk at a store, the principal of my school, "What difference does it make to you? Just hang up."

"Everything can change in an instant," Sister told us. "God is all-powerful." "God gives and God takes away." "We have to be prepared at all times for dying, and in that way we will go straight to heaven when we do." These were weighty thoughts for young children, but none of the adults I knew seemed to think so.

When my father wasn't home my mother seemed to be on the phone all the time, and I was drawn to listen in on her conversations. She often caught me eavesdropping. I had an insatiable curiosity about other people's lives—and not just about the people I knew well—but the lives of strangers as well. At my grandmother's house I had been given orders that it was strictly forbidden to listen in on telephone conversations. She had a "party line." This meant that several people shared the same telephone number, and when a call came in you identified if it was intended for your household by listening to the particular sequence—the number and pattern of short and long rings. Of course I knew my grandmother's ring, but eventually I came to know which stranger belonged to each of the other rings as well. Once I had determined that another party's conversation would be well established, waiting a bit before I picked up the receiver quite skillfully—so as not to be heard—I would listen in. I am sure that what I must have heard was ordinary gossip and information exchanged, and although I cannot remember the details now, I delighted in hearing just about anything related to the lives of total strangers.

"M-Y-O-B," my mother's cousin Ann said to me one day, when I asked about something she'd said to my mother about someone I didn't know.

"What does M-Y-O-B spell?"

"M-Y-O-B," she repeated.

"Myob?" I said, sounding the letters out, trying to make a word out of them. "I don't know any word, myob. What does it mean, Ann?"

"Mind your own business," Ann said, emphasizing each word. "And PDQ – pretty damn quick."

"Tunnel vision," I heard my mother saying to someone she was talking to on the telephone one day. I knew she was talking about my father's eyes.

She went quiet. What was the person on the other end of the line saying, I wanted to know. What was this tunnel vision thing? I had never heard of it.

My mother interrupted the person she had called and tried to get across what she was trying to say. "No. No," she said. "He sees everything as though through a tunnel. Yes, a tunnel. It's getting more narrow every day." She paused again and she was shaking her head back and forth, as if saying *No* all the while she listened to whoever it was on the other end of the line. "He's losing his sight, that's why," she said. "It's the peripheral vision—the side vision. It's going."

I could tell that she was frustrated and that was the reason she had so much anger in her voice that day. The person on the other end of the line—whoever it was—just could not grasp the meaning of the words that my father's peripheral vision was slipping.

It was the next step. First he lost his night vision, and then came the gradual shrinking of his visual field. I didn't know it then, but this had been explained to my mother when she and my father went to see a specialist for an evaluation. She was also told that the problem my father had with his eyes was inherited. My mother had called, wanting to let his family know that what was wrong with his eyes, most likely affected others.

Was she talking to my father's mother or father—my grandparents—or perhaps to one of his sisters, my aunt Evelyn or Jean? I am not sure which relative she called first, but I do believe that what I overheard that day was one of the first conversations in my mother's long battle with my father's family over the need to accept the reality of hereditary blindness. I thought that she was talking to someone who had trouble understanding her, someone who didn't have very good English. Maybe it was my grandfather, my father's father. I guessed that from the way she was talking, repeating everything she said over and over.

Because she was telling this person that others in the family might also have the same blindness, I began to worry. If my dad's sisters and brother might become blind, then what about me, or Peg, Kate, and Jack? Could we possibly lose our sight, too? It seemed so, from what I'd heard my mother saying. We were family. For the first time I wondered, how can a person actually live in the world without being able to see? My friends and I sometimes asked each other in the schoolyard at recess, would you rather be deaf or blind? I used to answer, "neither."

My mother became angry that day and all the days thereafter, at what she deemed was "the ignorance of my father's family." This confused me at the time, because I did not know the true meaning of ignorance and therefore could not relate her criticism to their lack of knowledge and the fear that will cause in a person, but rather I thought that she meant I should not love them—and I loved them very much. I have spent time thinking of how fiercely independent the members of my father's family have always been, how proud they are of their family, their accomplishments, and the know-how they possess in spite of some of them lacking a formal or advanced education. I have thought, too, of their fiery Sicilian spirit up against my mother's feisty Irish temper.

Still I must admit some bewilderment when I look at the conflict now. I think I understand my mother's anger better. One *can* ignore all sorts of physical ailments that plague us as human beings—the minor ones as well as those that become more serious and finally catch up with us. The sore throat we have passed off, as "just a cold coming on," sometimes really is more serious, demanding medical treatment. But how, I wonder, does one avoid seeking medical attention when blindness has been rampant for generations? That apparently, is what members of my father's family did. My father was the first to get a diagnosis for his poor—and worsening— vision.

That day in my childhood home, when my mother said what was now wrong with my father's eyes—said it over and over again, each time in different words—I understood her.

She paused from talking and listening, taking the phone away from her ear and staring directly at me in the doorway, realizing I'd been listening—nothing wrong with her peripheral vision. I knew that she would reprimand me later, forbid me once again from listening in on her private conversations. "I saw you out of the corner of my eye," she would say.

"He has to have the cataracts removed," my mother said, going back to her phone call. "We won't know how far the other problem—with the retina—has advanced until he has that operation."

But I had all the confirmation I'd needed. Just as I'd suspected as I'd watched my father and listened to the adults around me talking seriously—and, they thought—privately— there was something more wrong with his eyes, not just night blindness. Still, no one talked to me about it. Why? I wanted the whole story. I wanted my mother to tell me in the same persistent way she'd been trying to talk to the person who was on the telephone. I would listen. I would understand.

I pulled back from the doorway after she'd seen me, retreated behind my bedroom door, out of her view, but still able to hear what she was saying.

"It could take years for him to lose his sight completely. It goes little by little." She was almost yelling. "The doctor doesn't know how long it will be before the tunnel closes completely. We don't know how long it will be before he can't see at all."

I knew that this was very bad news about my dad's eyes. I tried to imagine what it was like to see the world through a tunnel that kept narrowing, the way my mother had said it would for my father. All I could do to understand what I had overheard was to associate it with my child's life. I recalled other not-so-awful tunnel trouble—Alice in Wonderland falling down the tunnel, the rabbit hole. I remembered her changing—shrinking and growing—remembered it happened fast, not slowly, the way my mother said my father's eyes would change. I took some comfort in the fact that by the story's end, Alice was back to normal. Could that possibly happen for my father? I wondered.

Listening in as my mother went on trying to explain the bad news, I needed to know not just what was wrong, but what it would be like for my father to see everything as if he were looking down a tunnel. I got the idea to try looking through a cardboard roll, like the empty one from the waxed paper for wrapping sandwiches. The tube though, was too firm, and I could find no way to shrink my circular view. Then I thought to try using a rolled up piece of notebook paper, which I figured might serve the purpose better, making it possible to change the size of the tube, narrowing the tunnel through which I could see. So I rolled the paper the way I did when Peg and I played pirates and we needed a telescope. This method, too, frustrated me. The paper edges were sharp and gave me little cuts, so I settled on an even simpler solution. I made the "okay" sign with the thumb and index finger of my right hand, holding it up in front of my nose, gradually shrinking the circular view. When the tunnel was almost closed, I squinted, peering through at the smallest crack of light.

My goal was to figure out what my father would be able to see just before he went completely blind. Eventually I got so good at this simulation that I was able to see the world through a tunnel hardly bigger than a pencil eraser. I must have been noticed doing this by the adults all around me, but no one ever asked me about it. I suppose they could not have imagined the seriousness of what I was trying to do and passed off my behavior as some child's game. It must have looked like one. They didn't know what exactly I had overheard, how much I knew, having underestimated my ability to decipher their coded and elliptical talk.

I spent a lot of time with my fingers formed in the "okay" position. In the afternoons I went alone sometimes to my bedroom. I would look out the window, focusing first on the Sadowsky house next door—their front entrance—or the one string of forgotten Christmas lights around the attic window at Roche's house. I moved my view up the street to the McConville yard, or to a tree growing out of the sidewalk, or Mr. Farrell's new car parked in front of his house. With my fingers formed this way, I thought I was able to see what my father's future vision would be like. I gave myself headaches doing this. I would try it, too, whenever I saw something amazing—a circus act, a fireworks display, or the deep cut on my knee. I resorted to looking through the "the tunnel" especially when something affected me as being very beautiful—the maple trees in the park when their leaves changed color, the Christmas tree just after we finished decorating it, a million beautiful things that I had before thought just ordinary. I forgot where I was when I entered these moments of exploration, and I gave no thought to whether or not anyone might notice me doing this.

Focusing on what my father would miss in the days to come led me, I think, to live in his destiny as much as in my own life. I realize, too, that this was indeed a gift, teaching not just empathy for his situation, but feeding as well, a love of detail and the ability to look closely and appreciatively at a great many things. Looking through the tunnel the way my father would in the future, I was able to realize that he would need my help—need everyone's help. How else would he go places and be able to live in the world among people who could see. This was the beginning really, of the course of training that showed me how to be my father's guide. Although I didn't know it then, extreme focus for careful observation was exactly what my father, in the years to come, would ask me to provide for him.

I realized something else as well for the first time, that when my father became blind he was not going to be able to see me or my sisters, my brother, or my mother. When I had been imagining the world, as it would look for him as he lost his sight, I had not considered this at first. But I knew that I would change, as I grew older—that we all would— and that made me suddenly realize that my father would no longer know the faces of those he loved. I worried that when it all went dark for him, he might not love us any more. It crossed my mind, too, that my father wouldn't be pitching fastballs to my brother Jack when he was old enough for that. He probably wouldn't be able to take him to any Red Sox games. I had no idea then how independent he would become, and what a loving, committed father he would continue to be.

At Sunday Mass Monsignor Sullivan gave sermons reminding us to be prepared.

"If we have another war," he warned, "our city might be a target. We have an arms factory over on May Street— Harrington Richardson Arms. Look at the steel, the metal produced here—and the colleges and universities with their big ideas. Why, Worcester would be a prime target," he said.

At school, a man from Civil Defense came to our weekly assembly. He passed out government pamphlets. After school I couldn't concentrate on my arithmetic homework. I studied the plans for fallout shelters in the booklets he'd given us. The man advised that we should all have fallout shelters to go to just in case the Russians dropped the bomb on Worcester.

At home I tried to convince my mother and father that we needed to build a fallout shelter. That was what the man told us to do. My father looked concerned but said nothing. "We would all be a lot safer if everyone had one," I said, parroting the words of the Civil Defense Man and seeing my dad's hesitation. I showed my mother the list of what we needed to store in the shelter and she blew up at me, most likely thinking of other things they had to spend money on—not just the ordinary necessities, but they'd recently learned that all of the water pipes in their Victorian house were made of lead and that the city Board of Health had ordered them removed and replaced with safer materials. The project would be a huge expense, but necessary in order to keep the apartments rented for the income that my mother knew would keep a roof over our heads and pay for basic necessities for the family when my father lost his job. *He can't go on working forever as a machinist with failing eyes,* she knew. She worried he'd lose a hand or an arm if he kept at it. And even with the rental income she knew, too, that it would be a struggle to provide well for four children.

"We don't have money to throw away on this kind of thing," she hollered, tossing the booklet of instructions for building a fallout shelter into the wastebasket.

There were two bedrooms on the west side of the house. When my brother was a toddler and moved out of the crib in my parents' bedroom, being a boy he was given his own room. We girls never minded though, because we enjoyed each other's company. With our three beds side by side— girls' dormitory style, my mother called it—the room I shared with Peg and Kate seemed even smaller than it was. There was not much space for walking around, and no floor space for play. If it rained or if it was too hot to play outside, we stretched out on our beds for a game of "Go Fish" or to color in our coloring books.

There was a large bureau with a gigantic mirror attached to it, placed directly across from the beds. We sometimes danced in front it or we combed each other's hair, braiding or fluffing it, and we admired ourselves. Sometimes we played trampoline and had contests to see who could jump the highest. We shared the bureau, getting one large drawer each, and Peg and I, since we were the oldest and had accumulated more stuff, each got one of the smaller top drawers in which we kept all of our important things—what we thought at the time were diamond and pearl necklaces and bracelets that my grandmother would give us to play with whenever we were bored at her house and she led us on a search through *her* bureau drawers. There were the usual kid things, too—pink rubber balls to slam against the concrete wall of Miller Furniture for games of handball, and jacks and jump ropes, and small boxes of rolls of caps that we exploded by hitting them with pieces of brick that we found in the yard. We kept all sorts of good stuff in the back of those drawers, behind more serious equipment for church—prayer books, rosary beads, lace chapel caps and mantillas, and pairs of white cotton gloves.

Even in summer before the sun had set, my mother put us to bed right after supper. She was tired. "You kids exhaust me," she complained.

It was *so* early that we were not tired enough for sleep. Lying there we made plans for the next day. With Jack out of his crib and in his own room, and with the three of us together, we realized we had the right number for singing rounds. On many nights—for years, I believe—we entertained ourselves this way. We sang, "Row, row, row, your boat /gently down the stream /merrily, merrily, merrily, merrily / life is but a dream." We also sang "Frere Jacques," which we sang first in French and then in English. We sang it in English for our brother Jack, whose name was really John. "Are you sleeping, brother John, brother John?" The door between the rooms was closed, so if our brother heard us singing to him, we did not know it. He was only two and we thought that he was sleeping.

The singing sounded great when the three of us really got going, but Peg would wreck it eventually, by laughing or singing goofy. She couldn't stand to have it perfect, and I got mad. Perfect was the way I wanted things to be. "She's a comedian," Dad said about Peg, but I didn't think Peg was funny when she ruined a song. I got angry with her. I knew that she could sing well in a high-soprano voice—I'd heard her in church—but for some reason she didn't want anyone to know. Sometimes Peg challenged me. "You can't sing opera, like me." Then she imitated the full soprano voice of Auntie Margaret, who sang in the choir at the Cathedral.

There were a lot of good singers in our family. My aunt was often asked to sing at wedding receptions. She sang, "I Love You Truly" at my aunt Jean's wedding. People seated at tables all around her began asking her to sing. "No, oh no," she said. The wedding guests worked hard to persuade her, and then the bandleader went to the microphone and called her to join the band for a song. Everyone clapped and hit their water glasses with spoons; the bride and groom kissed, and finally, my aunt put her own glass down on the linen tablecloth and got up to take the stage.

My mother didn't sing anymore, not even around the house, but my father did. "You'll split a gut," she would say to him when he got started. He stood in front of the bathroom mirror shaving, singing "Pagliacci,"or pretending that he was Mario Lanza or Julius La Rosa. He'd sing "That's Amore," trying to sound like Dean Martin, and he'd sing "Volare," with Italian lyrics, my favorite in his repertoire.

In the room I shared with my sister, the parchment-colored window shades were pulled all the way down. Nevertheless, the room was full of light in the hour before a summer sunset. On a warm evening when the windows were open, if there was a breeze, the shades moved back and forth, slapping against the sills. There were two windows side by side, so those shades became a small movie screen showing the shadows of the swaying branches and the shimmering leaves of the maple tree growing close to the house. I recognized the voices of other children still playing outside, and hearing them we longed to be among them. I was getting too old to be in bed so early—nearly nine. I did not understand why our mother put us to bed so early.

When Peg and Kate fell asleep, I was never tired. I was too curious to be tired, so I took my night watch, climbed out of bed, and crept across the floor to my station behind the bedroom door, left open just enough to allow me to stick my nose in the space where it hung on its hinges, and I could see them—my mother and father and any company they had, sitting in the living room. Like singing rounds earlier in the evening with my sisters, snooping became a ritual for me until I was ten or older, when my mother finally talked directly to me about my father's eyes and the possibility that my sisters and brother and I might also become blind and that we would need to see a doctor for testing.

I could not see the expressions on their faces because the room in which they sat was dark, except for the light from the television. People appeared as shadows, my mother sitting in a rocker by the front door, and my father on the couch beside her chair. I saw them in profile, as if they were full-bodied versions of the framed cut paper cameo silhouettes my sisters and I sat for one afternoon. Their shadows were gigantic, larger than life.

I believed that my mother and father kept some secret that meant something important to me, so each night I sat hoping that it would be revealed. The nuns at St. Peter's School taught the practice of sitting still. "Offer it up for the souls in Purgatory, who long to see the face of God," they said to us in class. I could sit so still sometimes that I thought I had stopped breathing. Having learned to do this proved useful to me as I waited in the dark behind the bedroom door. But I could make out only a word here and there, or some mysterious remark—like the night I heard my mother say, "You can't get blood out of a stone," and my father responded, "I'm doing the best I can. What do you want me to do, Mame?"

That night I'd tried looking through the crack where the door was open, but I couldn't see any stone. It gave off no light. Sitting there I feared that, just like in one of the fairy tales I'd read, when some problem couldn't be solved, when a charm lost its power, that terrible happenings would be set in motion.

I didn't know why they talked about trying to get blood out of a stone. I wondered who gave my father the charm that did not work. In my child's imagination I pictured a witch wearing an old woman's disguise, a talking bird, or a gnome. When my mother sounded convinced that they had no charm, only a stone that she didn't think could work any magic, I sensed that what my parents were keeping from me was something that only special powers would overcome. When my father said, "I'm doing the best I can. I can't do any more," I worried about what it was that was happening to him. Would my father be put to many tests? And how would the spell be broken? In that moment of my childhood, my father seemed like a poor man who'd gone off to market and traded his cow for a few magic beans.

I could never remember going back to bed on those nights I sat waiting to understand. But that is where I woke in the morning, cozy and warm, tucked into my bed in that room with my sisters.

My son Gianni slept—years later—in that old bed of mine salvaged from the family home, his first bed after a crib. It was my father who suggested that I take it for him. When Gianni was younger and in love with fairy tales and adventure stories himself, Mark transformed that bed for him, built a side panel to simulate a pirate ship. I contributed its portholes, giving Gianni a view of an imaginary horizon. I cut out prints of old sailing ships from magazines and glued them inside the cardboard porthole frames. There was a wheel, too—also of cardboard—attached to the bed at the headboard, so that Gianni could pretend to change course on a whim, fending off threats he imagined coming from any direction. And when he climbed in to sleep, he cast over the side a shiny foil anchor. Then he drifted off and I knew that he would sail a peaceful sea all night.

Six

HEIDI (1950s)

Television was new at our house, as it was in houses all over the U.S., my father said. We devoted a lot of our time to it. We ate meals while sitting on the floor in front of our set, watching. Before school there were breakfasts of cereal and milk while Peg and I watched *The Three Stooges* and *The Little Rascals,* and when we came home for lunch we switched on the Boston station to see the *Big Brother Bob Emory Show,* raising our glasses of milk when he told us to do it at the end of the show. Then, the screen went still and serious and we saluted a framed painting resting on an easel, of President Eisenhower. We hummed the song that played, "Hail to the Chief." *"Dah-dah dah-dah-dah-dadadadadadada."* Then before going back to school for the afternoon session, we sang along with the program theme song, about the perils of thinking that the grass is always greener in the other fellow's yard. We were admonished to realize that in our own back yard, the grass was green, too. I sang with all my heart.

We also watched shows about families who lived where there were rows of neat houses, one after another, with little patches of grass out front. Everyone lived in the same kind of house, not like the houses I knew in Worcester, the three-decker apartment houses of many styles, and brick apartment blocks, and large one-family homes, like mansions near Clark University, and on the other—more wealthy— side of the city. And our family wasn't like the families that lived in those television houses. My mother was not a thin, quiet-spoken woman like June Cleaver, the mother on the show *Leave It to Beaver.* She didn't like to cook very much. She didn't make molded desserts of Jell-O with fruit cocktail captive inside, or casseroles that used Campbell's tomato or cream of mushroom soup as the essential ingredient, like those ladies featured in magazine advertisements of her time. My mother wasn't like any of those women, and I didn't know any families either who lived the way the television families did.

We lived in a city where there were many factories. Tanneries and shoe manufacturing companies, steel plants, pressed metal and parts manufacturing suppliers, fabric mills, and a host of other industries were based in the northeastern U.S. cities then, and Worcester was no exception. My father worked in one of those factories. He wore khaki workman's pants and shirt—not a suit like Beaver Cleaver's father wore to work; the television father coming home after a day at the office arrived with his jacket draped over his arm, just in time to eat supper with the family. My father ate the evening meal with us only on weekend days when he wasn't working.

My maternal grandmother didn't have a television. "I don't trust that thing," she'd say. I went to her house almost every afternoon after school. It was a direct walk, about one mile straight down Main Street—all the way downtown really—and I was trusted, even at seven years old—to make the trip leading my younger sisters there, without adult supervision. I thought that at my grandmother's there were other things that more than made up for her lack of a television. She had a piano, and learning to play interested me. And there was a bookcase that held—not just books— but photo albums, too. And for at least some of the afternoon my grandfather—retired from working— was at home and he would help with schoolwork.

Even the closets at my grandmother's house were a child's dream. One was like a small room, unheated and freezing cold in winter, full of long silky dresses and fur coats that we could get lost under. "Come out of there, will ye?" Gram hollered at us when we hid from her. Another closet had shelves chock full of things that could be used for our projects: old greeting cards, jars of pearl beads from broken necklaces, appliques for sewing—all sorts of stuff. When we were seriously bored, my grandmother led us on expeditions through her bureau drawers, bestowing treasure after treasure upon us—rings, necklaces, and bracelets—costume jewelry mostly, pieces like sweetheart pink plastic pop pearls; occasionally though, she'd give us a silver ring, a nice brooch or earrings. And there was also my aunt Margaret's room, with its closet full of the gowns that were, according to my grandmother, worn by my mother and aunt when they went to parties and clubs when they were younger and had boyfriends galore. When I put on those gowns I believed that I was a Hollywood star, just like my mother and aunt had probably felt they were.

There was also Guy Zingarelli, the deliveryman from Cushman's Bakery, who came to the house in the afternoon, selling butterscotch cookies and all-chocolate cakes, blueberry pies, and thick chocolate peppermint patties. "Oh, oh, Mr. Zingarelli's at the door," Gram announced when she heard the doorbell and looked out to see his truck parked in front of her house. She always called him that—Mr. Zingarelli— but I knew his name was *Guy*. I had noticed it under the word *Cushman's* on the left chest pocket of his light grey uniform shirt; both names were embroidered in black thread and written in cursive, the kind of writing I was learning in school. *Guy*. What a funny name. But he was nice and handsome and Gram said that he was Italian, like my father, like me. She called her family the "League of Nations," because, she said, "your mother married an Italian and your aunt Sally married someone who was Polish." She didn't know what kind of a man Auntie Margaret was going to marry; she just wished she'd hurry up about it.

Gram bought a lot from Mr. Zingarelli. She stored some of the baked goods and candies in the sideboard buffet cabinet in the dining room, but not until we had picked out a treat to have right away. She bought so much that Auntie Margaret said that it seemed like she had her own store in the house. I knew that when my sisters and I were leaving she would pack some of it up for us to take home. My dad said that Gram was working on ruining our teeth.

On warm afternoons the Mr. Softee ice cream truck came by, playing its "deedily, deedily, dee" song, which I thought Gram liked almost as much as the ice cream. And in the early evening she always cooked a full supper: meat and potatoes, vegetables, fruit, and dessert—every night of the week, not just at Sunday dinner, the way it was at our house.

A maroon set of books, the *Encyclopedia Britannica*, was a great help in completing my schoolwork. Our set at home, the *Universal Standard Encyclopedia*, came as a bonus for shopping at the A&P Supermarket, and it was generally missing whatever volume I needed most. I wonder now, was it that we didn't buy groceries the week that particular book was issued, or just that there was only enough for necessities? But what I liked more than the expansive knowledge of the encyclopedia at my fingertips, were the books with orange, green, red, or blue spines, the names of writers engraved on them in gold leaf: Tolstoy, Hans Christian Andersen, Lewis Carroll. These were books that gave me a whole world according to the characters who lived in them. "Story books," we called those venerable tomes. There was a copy of *Pinocchio*, and there was *Heidi*, too. I suppose I liked *Pinocchio* for all the Italian names in it, which made me feel more comfortable with my own Italian name—Bonina— in the midst of the Irish Feeherry household. Other Irish relatives, friends, and neighbors regularly visited the Feeherrys. In addition to the O'Briens there were visits from the Bowen, Daniels, Dulligan, and Diggins families.

When I read *Heidi*, the story deeply moved me, because I had by then—I was eight years old in 1958— been called upon to help my father more; his eyesight seemed to be getting worse. As the story goes, Heidi is sent to the mountains to live with her old grandfather. Her presence helps him to be in the world again, after he has been living isolated as a hermit, embittered by life. My father often seemed lost in deep thought when I came upon him sitting alone outside on the stonewall, as I was coming home from the store or a visit to a neighbor's house—or if he wasn't outside he'd be seated on the living room couch when he had time off from work, looking as if his thoughts were deeply troubling him. I didn't want him to turn away from the world as Heidi's grandfather had, when things went wrong for him. I saw the similarities between what Heidi did for her grandfather and the role I played for my father, realized that I wasn't just helping him get from home to church or the A&P, but I was also helping him to take part in the world, to stay with it. The book gave me a new sense of purposefulness. I know now that I benefitted, too, from the experience of helping my father, that while responding to his entreaty, "You be my eyes,"—a request he repeated whenever he needed help—that I was becoming fluent in many valuable aspects of life. But then, I wanted only to be a good girl, a good daughter. I loved my father.

How could a space as small as my grandmother's bookcase hold so many lives, so many different worlds? I was thrilled to have them at my disposal. We had very few books at home. Other than our incomplete supermarket edition encyclopedia, the only books we had in the house other than the library books—which I was continually bringing home— were schoolbooks and my mother's copy of *Gray's Anatomy* from her nursing school days, a volume that would come in handy when I reached adolescence. There were also some of her other texts from her abandoned studies—a book on childhood diseases was one of them—and a shorthand book from her fallback career as a secretary after she quit nursing school. She stopped working at the courthouse as a stenographer soon after she got married. The magic of the many books of poems and stories at my grandparents' house was there for me to discover, not just in words, but in pictures as well. There were in some of them color plates of drawings and paintings and black and white prints—by N.C. Wyeth, Maxfield Parrish, and Rockwell Kent. In my mind I became like one of the sprites at dawn in the Parrish paintings, bathing in a little pool in early morning light, vines overhead dripping with blossoms.

I slid the heaviest books out of the bookcase and lifted them up from the bottom shelf. They were photo albums, the pictures pasted onto blank black pages, the writing saying who was who in white ink. I didn't know these people, didn't even recognize their names.

"Who are they?" I asked.

"Those are your ancestors," my grandfather said.

"Who is Jack anyway?" The only Jack I knew was my little brother.

When I asked her anything, my grandmother always seemed to forget the question. She went on with a story instead. "Oh, I remember Jack at the Worcester Market picnic, having his picture taken wearing only a union suit—long johns—he was a sight for sore eyes—can you see the one? It's in there somewhere. There it is. See. All the other employees fully clothed, even in their butcher's aprons, and there's Jack in his long underwear."

She sighed and then went on.

"Now that one—that's Honey Fitz. Old Orchard was a great place once," she said, referring to the Maine beach town where the family cottage was. "It was a long time ago."

Only the stories associated with the people whose pictures were in the albums mattered to my grandmother. She'd say a name and I'd have no idea who that person was, since she never explained. And so it was left to me many years after I'd first opened those photo albums in the bookcase, to discover the identity of those people and which ones I was related to. And only then did I learn that Jack was Jack McCarthy, my grandmother's brother, known for his kindness and swearing, and that the man my grandmother called Honey Fitz was John F. Kennedy's grandfather, who vacationed in Old Orchard before the family bought property for their compound in Hyannis.

I made a stack of the albums on the couch: the afternoon's provisions. Then I climbed up and arranged my plaid cotton dress all around me. I could feel the burgundy velvet fabric of the couch I was sitting on, smooth and too warm against my legs on a summer day. I would sit so long with those photographs that by the time I was finished looking at them, the skin on my legs would show the imprint of the swirly hearts design carved into the heavy upholstery fabric.

In the oldest of the photo books the people seemed to be from tales like those in the other books that lined the shelves of the bookcase. I had to ask for the stories that went with these characters, for they were not written down. Yes, they were like characters—in costume—women in long, fancy dresses, their faces looking as if they could have been painted in portraits or carved on chunks of ivory for cameos. Who was the woman with the hairdo? "An upsweep," Gram called it. She held a parasol and was walking by a pond.

"Why, that's your aunt Mary McCarthy."

"That is not an umbrella, mind you. It's a parasol," my aunt Margaret O'Brien, Gram's half-sister who was visiting that day, corrected me. "A parasol shades your face from the sun," she said.

"I love to have the sun on my face," I said.

"That's the Mediterranean influence," she said.

She meant, she explained, my "Italian side of the family," only she pronounced it, *Eyetalian.*

"Irish skin is delicate," she went on to explain—even though she herself was, according to Gram, the darker or "black Irish."

Did she mean, I wondered, that I had tougher skin just because I was Italian? My skin, my mother said, was "olive toned," although I didn't understand *her* meaning either, since it seemed not green or black, like the olives I knew.

There were large men with moustaches and beards in some of the photographs. They didn't look like any men I knew, except some I'd seen in old movies on television. These were men with big chests, emphasized by their white shirts, their suit jackets stretched taut over their bellies, the buttons looking as if they were about ready to pop. Men and women together on the beach—all covered up, not the way I knew people to be at the beach when my dad had his vacation from work and we all went to stay in Old Orchard, or when I was at the cottage alone with Auntie Margaret and we became what she called "beach bums." No one on the beach would be dressed this way. I decided that it must have been some performance, these guys dressed in jailbird stripes, looking like they were wearing Charlie Chaplin outfits.

"What kind of a play was it?

But no, I learned from my aunt that it was just a day on Old Orchard Beach, one long ago when that was the way people dressed for swimming.

I recognized the pier in the background and the cupola above the beautiful carousel I loved to ride at the entrance to the promenade. It was all still there. In another photograph there was a long shot of Old Orchard Street, the main thoroughfare, and it was just like one of the postcards I'd seen for sale at a souvenir shop and had been given money to buy it to send to my other grandmother.

"Bathing Beauties," someone wrote in white ink on the black page under another photo of a can-can line at the water's edge. These women were in bathing suits that looked like dresses with flounced hems, and they had scarves tied around their heads. One of them, it said, was Auntie Ceil, Gram's half-sister. I loved her for her spirit and for the fact that she stood so straight and tall. I turned the pages. Glue was dried out on some of the white corners, and the photographs they had held on the page had fallen out of place.

"I have a job for you," my grandfather said, setting me to work restoring the album. "We don't want to lose these. This is part of your history."

He gave me a small glass bottle of LePage's glue and showed me how to do it.

He got nervous watching me as I tried. "Careful now, not too much."

My grandfather liked things to be perfect, and he didn't know that I did, too.

I diligently followed his instructions. I remade the picture frames, careful to put each corner correctly in place, and when the glue dried, I tucked in the missing pictures while he directed me, telling me which one went where.

Seven

CATARACTS (1959)

My mother and father thought that we were all asleep in our beds. Peg, Kate and Jack were, but I was up, sitting on the floor in my usual spot behind the barely open bedroom door, eavesdropping. I was able to hear everything going on in the living room. "This has been the Friday Night Fights, brought to you by Gillette." My father had worked only the early shift, so he was home. All week he had talked about the boxing match. It seemed to be on every man's mind, everywhere we went—the butcher at the A&P when I'd gone with him to shop for the week's groceries the Saturday before—Uncle Tom when he'd called to say *Hello*—and Bill Roche who had been talking about it from his front porch rocking chair.

When Ingmar Johansson delivered the knockout punch to Floyd Patterson, the broadcast went off and my mother and father began a fight of their own. On the rare day when my father was home in the evenings, they always waited to argue at the moment when the lights went off and the house was quiet. It was as if their arguments were on a schedule, like programs on radio or television. For me, when the house was quiet, I was reminded of all that I did not know in life. I felt very small in the world of their arguments and adult mysteries, and as they increased in frequency, I grew more worried.

"You heard what the doctor told you," my mother said that night. Her voice was angry and loud, the way it was when I wouldn't get into the bathtub or go to bed when she wanted. "You don't even know how much you can see, how much damage there is to the retina. You have to have the cataracts removed—then you'll know."

I didn't know what to think, how to understand that things could keep going wrong. I didn't understand then that the world held the potential for all kinds of trouble. I was trying to hold onto a dream that there were all sorts of wonderful things in life.

"What else is there to decide?" my mother said to my father.

"It's just a shot in the dark, Mame," he said.

They yelled back and forth for a while until finally I realized what they were talking about, that my mother was trying to convince my father to have some kind of operation on his eyes. She believed that there was still a chance that my father would be able to see better than he could.

Besides not knowing what cataracts were then, that they blocked light from entering the retina, I didn't know either, that the tunnel vision I had heard about was being caused by the deterioration of the rods and cones in the retina, that these photo receptors are responsible for changing light into the electrical impulses which are then sent to the brain via the optic nerve. I didn't know that this is the process that results in the blessing of sight. Cataracts made it impossible for the several doctors who'd examined my father, to determine just how well the retina was functioning. There was no way to know just how far advanced his blindness was without removing the cataracts.

"You'll never know if you don't try," my mother said, talking to my father in the way that she spoke to me about eating a new vegetable.

My father's answer made clear to me that whatever the operation was supposed to do to improve his sight, the results would not be lasting.

"Why should I?" my father wanted to know. "Why should I have an operation, when I know it's only a matter of time."

My mother stood her ground.

"Because it's the right thing to do. That's why you should do it."

Their arguing stopped and the house became really quiet. The lights went out, and they went to bed.

I wanted my father's eyes fixed, just as my mother did. I knew that was the only thing that could stop the worry I had been feeling and the sadness about my father's situation. I decided also that it was the only way to stop my mother's anger. Lying there in the dark, I thought of her wanting my father to be changed by magic into a man who could see perfectly well, someone who knew immediately what she looked like. She must have known that when he looked at her face he couldn't see it completely, because he was looking through that tunnel and had to turn his head again and again to see a full picture of her, as I had discovered doing my experiments. I already knew that my mother was afraid that my father wouldn't be able to take care of our family financially, but I think she must also have been worried that he would need her to be there for him in an extraordinary way.

I intuitively began to understand that my father's blindness would change us as a family. That my father might feel alone— alienated from others because of his difference, because there was *something wrong with him* in the eyes of others in our parochial world—began to trouble me. I came to realize eventually as well, that this sense of being "different" would extend also to me and to the other members of my family. The possibility of isolation—being considered *an outsider*—is not something a child who is blessed with a loving parent can easily accept. My father was in his early thirties then, and I was almost nine.

If, for some reason, I couldn't go to my grandparent's house when I had a school project that required me to gather information I couldn't find in the encyclopedia at home, I went to the library. I had been working on a big project about UFOs. I had even written to the United States Air Force— with my grandfather's help—and received back a letter from someone named Major Keyhoe. He had the job of reporting on unidentified flying objects for the government, I guess. He'd sent me information, papers printed with charts and numbers that I couldn't figure out, though I tried very hard. There were even pictures to go along with the reports, showing UFOs that had supposedly been sighted. The objects were of all shapes—some as big as and designed almost like airplanes; others were cigar-shaped. No one knew where these vehicles in the sky came from—of if they did, they weren't saying so. I found the mystery enticing.

Researching this subject and doing other kinds of reports for school had taught me that a person could usually discover everything you'd care to know about in books. An encyclopedia was especially helpful. I thought that maybe if I looked there, I could learn why my mother was arguing so fiercely with my father about cataracts. I knew that if I went to my grandmother's house, intending to use the encyclopedia there, my grandfather would likely get involved, trying to help. He enjoyed helping me with homework and I generally appreciated that. "You should have been a teacher," my grandmother would say to him, watching as he explained things I needed to know. But he didn't need to know that I'd been eavesdropping on my mother and father's arguments.

Our neighborhood branch library was not far away. I walked through the university campus to get there, which made my mother worry about me. "I just wish you'd go the other way, that you'd stay away from there," she said. "Haven't I told you that before? Don't talk to anyone over there, coming or going. They're all communists over there."

My mother, like so many people in the nineteen fifties, also thought that the UFOs that had been sighted were either being built by the communists and they were spying on us, or else they thought that our own government had launched them to spy on communists. She favored the latter point of view, probably because it made her feel safe. "Top secret," she said. I didn't believe either theory, nor did I believe that I should be afraid of communists being at Clark University.

In his sermons at Sunday Mass, the Monsignor talked about the Russians and Premier Khrushchev. One week he said that if we prayed really hard, "Khrushchev just might not wake up in the morning." From what he'd said, I understood that we could have a war, so we would be a lot safer if Khrushchev died in his sleep. I was surprised to hear a priest talk of wishing someone dead.

I wasn't worried about the communists being at Clark University, because the Monsignor never mentioned it, and I was convinced that he wouldn't have left out of his sermon such an important piece of information. I decided to ignore my mother's warning about walking through the Clark campus on my way to the library. I felt perfectly safe there. In fact, the only time I worried about it was when I was approaching home. Then I worried that perhaps someone my mother knew had seen me walking through the university gates, and that perhaps that person had called to inform her.

Cutting through campus was a pretty walk in any season. The memory of it will always stay with me. I felt dreamy looking at the colored leaves on the maple trees in fall. In winter, there was refreshing snow piled up high around the iron gates and stuck like frosting to the brick and granite buildings and to the hedges and low bushes. And in the first warm days of spring I was cheered by the sight of the Chinese cherry trees in blossom all along Charlotte Street, and would detour a bit just to look at them and to drink in the sounds of a piano being played at Estabrook Hall on the corner.

I changed my route very little as I grew older, the exception being that as I entered my teenage years, I crossed Woodland Street after Downing, so that I could walk past the lawns where, from the earliest days of the season, students in shorts or bathing suits would stretch out on towels and blankets, and listen to radios blaring rock and roll, some of them playing along on guitars or flutes. The sight enticed me to wish for my own freedom.

On many walks across campus that had begun with my detour in defiance of my mother, something stirred deep inside me, and I felt changed. Besides being a place so unlike any other in the neighborhood, one that made me feel that I was in a different city or town, the university attracted me for another reason, too. I enjoyed being around people I didn't know, people who didn't know me. I was all eyes and ears. I felt tall among the hurrying older students. Perhaps I'd grown, because no one seemed to notice me as different. It was fun being invisible!

Arriving at the public library the day that I was on a mission to learn what cataracts were, I went to the big dictionary always left open on its special stand. I was just tall enough to reach it, to see the words.

"Can I help you with something?" the librarian asked, seeing me there. She was watching me struggling to find what I needed to know.

I had written "C-a-t-e-r-a-c-t-s" on a slip of paper. I didn't think I had the correct spelling of the word so I went to the desk to show her.

"Is this word spelled right?" I felt safe letting her see the word. She didn't know my mother or anyone else in the family, except Peg, who sometimes came with me to the library.

"This isn't an 'e'," she said, changing the second vowel in the word to an 'a,' like the other two, spelling it c-a-t-a-r-a-c-t-s. "Three a's," she emphasized. "Always remember it now. The word is yours for the remembering."

"I will," I promised.

I quickly found the word in the dictionary, listed right after the word catapult, although I found that cataracts had several different meanings. I used the process of elimination to figure out which was the correct one. To start, I knew that my father didn't have "a very large waterfall" in his eyes, and not a "great downpour" either. In fact, I had never seen him cry, not even a little. I considered another possibility— "pathology: opacity of the lens or capsule of the eye, causing partial or total blindness." That must be it, I thought, although I didn't understand what the definition meant.

I copied it out on a piece of paper, which I folded several times so that it was very small and easier to hide. I put it into my coat pocket, deciding to ask my aunt Margaret to explain—I knew I could always count on my aunt Margaret.

When I returned home my mother was talking on the telephone again. I worried that it was Mrs. Malloy or someone else making a report about seeing me near the Clark campus. But no, the phone call was not about me, I determined from the one thing that I was able to hear just before my mother noticed me standing in front of her and ended the call. I learned that my father was going to have the operation that he'd been dead set against.

"There is no cure for it. No nothing can be done. Just pray to God though, that he'll be able to see better for a while at least, when he gets rid of the cataracts," she said, and hung up the phone.

My mother had a stack of prayer cards, worn at the edges and even torn from being shuffled in her hands so much, as she read them over and over again during the day. I got the idea that she thought these cards were magic, that by saying prayers to the saints whose pictures were on the face of each one, she believed she could fix what was wrong in her life. I thought that it would be great to be able to change my father's eyes so that he could see perfectly again. I believed that that was the reason my mother was praying. Since I liked magic, too, I wanted to be able to do some tricks with the cards. The only tricks I knew were with the playing cards and the disappearing ball in the kit my grandfather bought for me at Jack's Joke Shop downtown.

When my mother would forget to put the cards away, I found them left out on the dining room table near my pack of Bicycle Playing Cards. I decided to try them out, but not by using them to pray. Next to my cards, hers looked like a game deck, too. The stack was of the same height, but on the face of each card was a different saint's picture, and instead of an ace, king, queen, jack, or number on the backside, hers had a prayer. There was one for St. Jude, Saint of the Impossible, the hopeless cases. I had heard about him from my grandmother; she mentioned him whenever we watched the *Danny Thomas Show* on television. My grandmother repeated herself. She told me time and again that Danny Thomas had given a lot of money to start a research hospital for children with leukemia and other serious diseases they could die from. "He named the hospital for St. Jude," she'd say, "after the saint of lost causes. That man's a saint himself."

My mother also had a card for St. Lucy, and I noticed that she was the "patron saint of the blind."

One day I asked my mother why these saints were connected to certain things, how that happened. "Is it like a job? Like having something to be in charge of?"

She gave me a crumbling old book then called *Maidens of Hallowed Names*, the stories of women who'd become saints. I read its inscription: "To you, maidens of pure lives, the joy of Christian homes, the hope of sound society, the tender care of Mother Church, this little book is offered. Here you will find a saintly model: try to become her image."

My mother told me a gruesome story about St. Lucy having to serve her eyes to someone on a silver platter. "A lot of them were tortured," she said.

I made the connection then: the prayer card saints were the martyrs, like the stories of the saints in the book she'd given me. The Sisters at school were always telling stories of martyrdom. Being martyred was how these saints got their power. I hoped never to become a saint, even if it did give you power. I was afraid of being chosen, like St. Maria Goretti who was murdered in the movie our class was brought to see downtown at the Loew's Poli Theater. I was afraid too, of having saints talking to me, like the Virgin talked to Bernadette at Lourdes or to the shepherd children at Fatima, or like Jesus did when he rose from the dead and talked to his apostle Thomas. I didn't want to be chosen to relay any messages from God. The idea of it scared me. One of my classmates was a perfect student—a good girl, always kind to everyone. She was chosen. At her funeral Mass of the Angels, the one for a child who dies, the Monsignor said,

"We don't know why God took her away from us when she was just seven years old. God has a reason for everything."

I shuffled my mother's cards into my playing pack. It was a fat deck I made, adding them in. I hoped that I would deal a lucky hand, one thick with saints—the queen next to St. Theresa, the Little Flower. Wouldn't a hand with St. Anthony, who found what was lost, help *me* find the cards I was missing to make a suite in a game? And if I got the big one, St. Jude, *Saint of the Impossible*, I bet that Peg would have to give up all of her aces to me in a game of "War."

I didn't realize then that words are magic, that the cards themselves were useless. The words in the prayers were pleas for help, a rescue, mercy. Reading them over and over, as my mother did, was a way of believing, even when there was little hope.

"Pray for the success of the eye operation that Mary Bonina's father is having," Sister said on Good Friday.

I didn't know that my mother had told my teacher to remember my father in our classroom prayers. I didn't like finding out this way. Hearing my father's name—my last name, too—ring out like that in the tight silence of our stifling classroom, took my breath away.

"Is he going blind?" Larry Murphy wanted to know, hearing Sister's mention of a special intention.

"Did someone hit him in the eye?" Will Hanley asked.

There was laughter then, because Will was always getting into fistfights, wrestling some other kid to the ground. When Sister broke up a fight she said the same thing every time, "If you keep this up, you'll lose an eye!"

"Mary," Sister said. "Do you know why your father is having this operation?"

I was confused. If my mother had told her already, then why was she asking me about it? Was it that it was not my mother who had told her, that she'd heard a rumor started perhaps by old lady Malloy next door, or someone else she talked to? Or maybe my mother had actually asked for prayers, but without giving her all the details, and that was the reason Sister was putting me on the spot while the class listened in. Before that day I hadn't ever thought that Sister Mary Agnes was mean, the way some of the other Sisters were mean to the children. But when she pressed me for answers she seemed like all the rest. "M-Y-O-B," I felt like saying.

Now I wonder, did Sister hope that in describing my father's trouble I might instruct the class, might teach something about God's power, life's uncertainty, and the need to pray for mercy? Maybe she chose me to be the teller of a cautionary tale that day: "Be grateful, children, for what you have in life—for it can all be gone in an instant. Think of Mary's father, of what has happened to him." Is that what the lesson was that day? The nuns were always telling stories to illustrate morals, looking for the lesson in whatever happened in life. I was, I believe, a reminder to everyone, of that tenet of faith, that we must willingly accept whatever God dishes out without questioning.

"Death is like a curtain closing," that same teacher used to say to us, matter-of-factly, our fourth grade hearts heavy, as we tried to understand that irreversible instant. I have often wondered why the good Sisters thought that children ought to be able to carry around the same emotional weight they themselves did? And what about those of us who had enough worry already and did not need constant reminders?

That day, my classmates were quietly watching me struggle, waiting to hear what I would say. My heart beat so fast that I thought surely everyone could hear it. "He has," I began then stopped. I had forgotten the name of what was wrong—forgotten the word *cataracts*. It went rushing from my memory, even after all the effort I'd put into learning it. All I could remember was what my aunt told me the day that I pulled that folded piece of paper out of my pocket for her to have a look at it, and I saw tears in her eyes. "Cataracts," she said, "are something like clouds covering the sun." I knew that I couldn't say that my father had clouds in his eyes.

For years after that day, I sometimes lost my train of thought, especially when speaking in front of a group, or if I were put on the spot unexpectedly, to give an opinion or even to offer knowledge of something that was not personal, something as ordinary as the answer to a math or geography question, an answer I knew as well as my own name. I would begin, and then falter, unable to speak.

Finally the word did come to me, and I blurted it out, my face flushed. "Cataracts," I said, pleased with myself for a moment.

"That's a big word for a little girl," Sister said.

She wrote the word in large letters on the board using the bright yellow chalk left by the music supervisor when she came for our morning lesson. Sister removed the chalk from the pitchfork-like contraption that was used to make bars of music. C-A-T-A-R-A-C-T, she wrote.

I didn't feel like a little girl then. My worry was too big. My embarrassment filled the classroom space. I had told the truth, told what I knew. Now everyone knew.

"This afternoon," Sister said, "let us pray that God in his infinite goodness and mercy will see fit to answer our prayers."

I tried to keep from crying by staring straight ahead. I couldn't though. The word cataract on the chalkboard flashed in front of me each time I blinked away a tear. The yellow chalk was so very wrong for the use Sister had made of it. I dreaded returning from the Good Friday afternoon prayer visit at church, entering the classroom and finding the word still written there in such bright letters, like the title of the latest movie up on the marquee at Loew's Poli.

The lower chapel of the church where we sat in hard wooden pews was dark as cave. It always was, but usually I could stare at the stained-glass windows and that made the place feel less gloomy. But this was a winter day without sun, the church lit only by candles. The cobalt blue windows I loved—no sun behind them—were dark as a starless night sky. In the lower church there were no golden-haloed angels floating, winging their way in a baby blue heaven painted on the ceiling, as there were upstairs. The statues that were placed all around—even my favorite one of St. Francis and the Birds—had been covered up during the last days of the Lenten season, draped with purple cloth. There was a solemn tone to our church visit; on Good Friday of Holy Week, Christ was crucified for us, we were taught.

The only lighted spot was behind the altar rail. There, a many-tiered iron rack of votive candles stood waiting for anyone who wanted to brighten the darkness by striking a long wooden match on the front of the tray and adding another flame to those lights already flickering. Whoever lit a candle decided for what intention it would burn, whatever favor was needed from God, his Blessed Mother, or a saint to whom you were particularly devoted. The whole class knew what I would ask for, but I didn't have money to light a votive candle. I watched Noreen. Her father was on the city council. She stuffed a dollar in the slot, and seconds later had a whole row of candles burning. I wondered what she wanted.

The Stations of the Cross were not covered with purple cloth and I followed "The Way of the Cross" ritual, moving around the chapel with my classmates, stopping at each of the scenes painted in color to look realistic. I wondered how the heavy stone reliefs depicting the scenes of Christ's last hours—could possibly stay up on the wall. I did what I had been told: I meditated on the suffering of Christ, so that I might know how much he loved me.

Eight

SIDEKICK (1959)

Going by car to Boston was only about a one-hour drive from Worcester, but taking a Trailways bus made the trip down Route 9 longer. I was happy to have a window seat. The driver put on the squealing brakes again and again. He stopped near fields where there was not a house in sight: one time to pick up a man, another for an old couple. They looked cold, and I wondered how long they'd been waiting. The driver also stopped at gas stations, where he picked up more riders who had been inside the office. Somehow he knew that they would be there, although you couldn't see inside because the windows were steamed up; that early spring morning the heat must have been on. When the doors opened, sometimes a woman with a tiny baby in her arms or an old man all alone would come out and climb on board. And just before we got into the city, there was a little hut at the side of the road in Chestnut Hill. There, a blind man leaning on a white cane was waiting for the bus with a couple of black women who were dressed in white uniforms.

"Are they his nurses?" I asked my grandmother. I was thinking about my father having to go to the hospital for his operation.

I understood that I was with my grandparents on this bus with my two sisters and my brother so that my mother didn't have to worry about us. She already had enough to worry about. The white uniforms of the women with the blind man reminded me very specifically of my father's situation and I began to worry again, not knowing whether my father would be able to see after the bandages were removed from his eyes. Would the surgery improve his sight or make it worse? The doctor had told him that there was no guarantee. Would he need to have nurses? I had questions, but I didn't ask them.

"No," Gram said. "They aren't nurses. They work as maids in some of the big houses around here."

She seemed sure of it. Still, they didn't look like they were wearing maids' uniforms to me, at least not like the ones worn by actresses who played the parts of maids in the old movies I saw on television. These uniforms didn't include frilly aprons and caps.

"But look, Gram! He knows them. He's talking to them. They must be."

"You don't see colored nurses too often. They're maids. He's talking to them because he can't see them. He doesn't know they're colored."

My grandfather started to tsk-tsk, which was what he did whenever my grandmother said too loudly, something he knew to be wrong. Even when she whispered these kinds of comments, my grandmother could be heard clearly. My aunt Margaret said sometimes that she had a stage whisper. I'd been with her in church when she whispered her opinions about the clothing people were wearing, loud enough for them to hear.

I remember intently watching the blind man that day as he made his way toward the bus. He hesitated at each step getting on. And then when he tried to sit in the first seat he reached, he almost sat on another passenger's lap. He apologized and the person aimed him at the empty seat across the aisle. There, he collapsed in the same way that his cane folded up: so that no one would notice.

I was watching, thinking of my own father, worried that he might be like the blind man on that bus some day, the continued focus of everyone's curiosity.

When we got into the city, at the Trailways Station we ate at the nearby Waldorf Cafeteria, where we could help ourselves.

"Have whatever you want," Gram said.

I was dazed by the sheer number of plates of chocolate cake slices lined up on the shiny aluminum shelf, and there was a row of glass parfait dishes filled with bright red Jell-O and whipped cream topping.

"I'll have that." I pointed to one of the sundae dishes of Jell-O. "Just the cream. I don't want the red stuff."

Gram special-ordered a tall glass dish of whipped cream—a mountain of it—for me.

I liked being able to say what I wanted and to get it.

"Spring is here!" Gram said, and headed in the direction of Filene's Basement where she was going to buy new shoes for me and Peg and Kate.

We found shiny black patent leather Mary Janes in our sizes. She paid the clerk. We wanted to wear them. She said we could put them on after we finished shopping.

We made a couple of stops first—one upstairs in the lingerie department, where my grandmother unbuttoned her silky shirtwaist dress, unbuttoned all the buttons right down to her navel, in order to show the clerk that she wanted to buy *vests*. The sales person, a young woman, didn't understand what she wanted, and that was the reason for her demonstration. *Vests* were the camisoles she wore under her dresses. My grandmother often used different words than the ones other people used to describe things. Besides calling camisoles *vests*, she always called zero *cipher*. The letter z was *zed*. She said *ye* instead of you, and called cancer *catarrh*.

Gram told the elevator operator she wanted the street level. The man pulled the metal trellis on the door closed and delivered us to the first floor. We were just about to enter the revolving door to go out to the sidewalk when Gram said, "Wait," and turned us around. Out of the corner of her eye she'd seen the Barton's candy counter and had remembered that she wanted to buy peanuts to take to the circus.

"Don't they have peanuts at the circus?" I asked.

"They have Spanish peanuts here. They're easier to eat. No shells."

The clerk packaged the peanuts in a miniature hatbox, a very special-looking black box decorated with a colorful design that made me think of confetti or a fireworks display.

It was a box too nice for peanuts. I believed that I would feel rich eating peanuts at the circus from such a beautiful box.

Before we headed to Boston Garden, where the Ringling Brothers Circus was performing, we went first to have our picture taken in front of the wrought iron gate at the entrance to the Public Gardens. If we had time, we would take a ride after on the swan boats in the lagoon.

My brother Jack has the photograph: Peg, Kate, Jack and I standing at the gate with our grandmother and grandfather. The photographer's camera was resting on a tripod and covered by a black cloth. He lined us up in various ways, trying to determine the best places for each of us to stand, and when he was satisfied with his arrangement, he stuck his head under the veil. Some one of us must have moved, because he suddenly jumped out yelling, "Hold it! Perfect! Just like that! Stay still one minute until I shoot." Then he was gone again, under the cloth. When he finished and we'd all resumed breathing, Peg was crying uncontrollably, like she sometimes would when she was afraid. She was afraid of a lot of things: school, the dark, thunderstorms, having her picture taken by this man. I remember I went with Aunt Ceal and Cousin Billy, Peg's godfather, to the Loew's Poli on *her* birthday to see *Snow White*, and she stayed home because she was afraid to go with them if my mother wasn't going, too. That day at the Public Gardens after having her picture taken, Peg could not stop crying because she had been thinking that the man was going to shoot us, like the cowboys in movies on TV shot each other. "One minute until I shoot!" he'd said.

The swan boats seemed to glide over the surface of the water, which was dotted with yellow-green leaves and branchlets the breeze had stolen from willows that ringed the pond. Looking out at the dirty pigeon house as we passed by, I found it just as enchanting as the little islands around the bend, where ducks, as well as real swans, nursed their young.

"Can I buy a program?" I asked my grandfather as we entered Boston Garden. I wanted to show my father pictures of what we saw, so that he would know what it was like.

At intermission I turned the pages of large color photos of the performers in action, and I tried to decide which ones my father would like the most. I thought probably the elephants and the beautiful ladies who wore glittering costumes and rode them bareback. I thought the elephants were the best.

"We don' t even know if he will be able to see them" my grandfather said. "But go ahead. Take your program home with you, as a souvenir."

Going to Boston and the other exciting things we did during school vacation week, helped me forget—or at least not to worry as much—about my father's operation. We ate out in restaurants a lot and we kept busy shopping. We saw a 3-D movie at the Capitol. We didn't see much of it, because it was so scary that we got down on the floor in front of our seats.

"Just keep you eyes closed tight, like I do," I told Peg, who cried throughout the whole show.

When the movie was over I saved the glasses the usher had given out—cardboard frames with cellophane lenses, one red and one blue.

"They don't work as well without the movie," my grandfather said.

I didn't care. I wore them anyway.

When I got home I was still wearing them, expecting my mother to ask what they were, how they worked, where I got them. She didn't ask me any questions, though. She said, "Take off those glasses, will you? Before you ruin your eyes!"

When my father came home from the hospital he was wearing white patches over his eyes, patches that made him look injured, which he was, I thought, seeing the way he was acting. I had expected that that the patches would be black, like the pirate patch Jack wore for his lazy eye. I preferred that people would think of him as a pirate, rather than someone who was injured. I did know that he had been injured. I had heard my mother describing the operation before he went to the hospital, telling someone on the telephone that during the surgery my father was going to be awake, because he had to have his eyes open. She had said the doctors were going to "scrape" the cataracts from his eyes. I didn't know how that could be true, how anyone could stand to have that done to him.

At first my father spoke only when someone asked him a question, and whenever he could, he gave a simple one-word answer. I was beginning to wonder if the operation had done something to his voice. It seemed almost to hurt him to speak. I remembered that once my grandmother told me that the big scar on her neighbor Jay Ramsey's left cheek came from the slip of a surgeon's knife during an operation to remove something that shouldn't have been growing on his left earlobe. Knowing this, I worried that the doctor had made a mistake, had cut some connection to the brain, and perhaps that was the reason my father was having trouble putting his thoughts into words.

During this time I was greatly involved in investigating how the eye works. I had been studying a diagram of the eye in the encyclopedia at my grandparents' house. I knew about the optic nerve going straight to the brain. I knew that nerve was for seeing, but I wondered: was there another one near it that maybe the doctor had mistakenly severed, one that had to do with talking about what is on your mind?

My mother said that there was nothing new that was wrong with my father. "He just needs to get hold of himself."

She never tried to persuade him to go out with her then, to give him the change of scenery that he probably needed. She was not the kind of person who went out walking in the neighborhood anyway. She had even stopped going to church with him. She went to a different Mass or else she didn't go to church at all on Sundays. In school it was drummed into us in religion classes that not going to Mass every Sunday was a mortal sin, so as a child I thought my mother might be going to hell. If I ever mentioned it, she said God would forgive her because she had a good reason for not going.

When I asked him to go for a walk with me, my father answered, "No," giving off a little laugh, like he was both mad and surprised at me for even thinking of such a thing.

"He doesn't know what to do with himself," I overheard my mother telling my grandmother on the telephone that first week he was home.

I had never seen my father in a sitting position for such long stretches. Before, when he wasn't at work he was fixing something about the house or out working in the yard. I was generally with him, so now I missed helping him do things. My mother called me his "sidekick." He said I was "his eyes."

My father had built steps and sidewalks on the property that included two houses with small front and back yards. I helped him measure and nail frames and mix and pour cement. I watched to make sure he was doing things right. He asked me to read the yardstick and to tell him when to stop mixing and where he needed to pour more cement to even out a step so it was level. We cleaned up the yard together, too, raking and then sweeping the sidewalks all around the property. He clipped the hedges out front and fixed basement windows broken by stray balls. In the cellar he drained rusty water from the boiler and had me read the gauge to check the water level as I watched him fill it up to the line, saying "when" so he knew to stop. I helped him change fuses, running up three flights of stairs to see if the lights went on when he replaced a particular one of the many in the box on the cellar wall, and I would holler down the stairs at the top of my lungs to him, when he had found the one that was spent, "That's it. You found it. Okay. Lights on." Or when he didn't, "No, try another one!"

I also helped him pull up weeds that grew up out of the cellar's dirt floor: strange weeds, tall as trees and still green I suppose, because of the many basement windows that let the light in. My father called them "trees of heaven," which I found odd at the time, thinking that a plant with a name like that ought to grow in the attic rather than in the basement.

I was so used to being with my father that, after his operation, when it seemed that he wanted to be left alone, I missed his company as well as all the activity. I sat with him in the living room each day after school, and for most of the day on Saturday and Sunday.

My mother chastised me for not going out to play.

"Go on. Get out. Get some fresh air, will you?" she said, passing through the room time and again on her way to another room—doing what, I could not figure out. She seemed busy all the time, but the clothes that had been washed just piled up on the open ironing board leaning against the wall in a corner of Jack's bedroom. The pile of clothes reached to the ceiling almost. It was a match for the envelopes on her bureau. "Bills, bills, bills, are all that ever comes in the mail."

My father and I continued to sit on the couch side by side for days—how many I don't know—not talking, just staring at the television. He still had the white gauze bandage taped over each eye.

One afternoon a couple of weeks later, I heard my aunt Margaret talking just outside the living room door in the front hallway, saying "Goodbye" to my mother after visiting. I could hear them even though they were on the other side of the closed heavy gum wood door, and the television was blaring in the background. I had good eyes *and* good ears.

"He's not himself," she said. "But who could blame him? Imagine going through all that—and for what?"

"I don't know how I'm supposed to manage, with four kids," my mother said.

If my father heard them, he never did let on. He continued to face straight ahead, just as if he were able to see what was happening on *The Loretta Young Show*.

From what I overheard whenever my mother talked to anyone about us, I gathered that having enough money to take care of us—to feed and clothe us, to keep a roof over our heads—worried her more than how we might feel about the changes in my father. Money was a great worry, especially for my father, who had married my mother knowing that she came from a family of better means—well-to-do professionals –and that meant that he would have to work hard to please her. That fact had not stopped him from pursuing her.

My father was a smart and ambitious man by nature and he was determined to be successful. I can't be sure that anything motivated him to strive with such intensity, other than wanting to take care of his family and wanting to please my mother because he loved her. I do know though, that all the years I watched my father's hard-working ways, it became increasingly clear to me, that to be "comfortable" financially was ultimately what he wanted for his family. He willingly made tremendous personal sacrifices attempting to secure that goal. Was my father's silence after the failed cataract surgery an indication that he was trying hard to understand how his efforts could have fallen so far short of success? Was he wondering, like me, how things in life could go so wrong? He must have been tortured by these questions, but somehow they motivated him, too, because he kept on.

He never wanted any of us to do without. My father loved my mother even as her attitude toward him seemed to change. He could not understand her anger and he told me many times in the years that followed, that it troubled him. He wanted so much to please her.

When he knew that he would be working on a special day— my mother's birthday, Valentine's Day, their wedding anniversary—he would be sure to leave me with money before he left the house for work that day. "Buy your mother some roses," he would say, directing me to stop at Diane's Florists on the way home from school. "Or get a good box of chocolates. Not Whitman's—Schrafft's— or Russell Stover."

I never heard him complain about having to work so hard and having no time to relax with his family. If he complained about anything related to work, it was that he "ought to be making more money." Working as a machinist—a toolmaker with failing eyesight— he kept up double shifts for years; if he worked just one, it was always that one that stretched from mid-afternoon until nearly midnight, and then he walked that mile or so home alone in the dark, struggling with his impending blindness, yet never speaking of the difficulties it presented. My father believed that it was his responsibility alone to provide for my mother—for all of us as a family— and my mother had been brought up the same way, believing it was the man who ought to work. That was the rule of the day. It would be my generation of women who challenged it.

Maybe it was not the stress of our daily lives that brought on such a storm of affliction—poor health for my mother, financial troubles and the like. Some might say that this is just what happens in life. Still, I am convinced that it must have been unrelenting stress that brought on my father's major heart attack when he was only fifty-two. Even my mother was surprised and has said to me, "He was strong, never missed a day of work. I never expected it of him." What's more, when he was brought into the hospital and examined, the doctor, discovering scar tissue on his heart, wanted to know when he'd had his first heart attack. It was only then my father revealed that one Sunday afternoon years before, sitting in the living room and talking to my grandfather, he had felt ill with the very same kind of pain and had never mentioned it to anyone. My father had kept silent that day, and gone to work the next morning.

The days were long. Spring came late. The sky remained a dull gray. It was cold and rainy outside and my father's thoughts seemed dark. I longed for one of his jokes or the stories he told me about what life was like when he was growing up. I knew that my father loved me and I wanted him to know that I understood why he was sad and worried. I didn't know how to let him know this. I didn't think I could in words. Around the time the bandages came off his eyes, the weather turned warmer and we went to church together again. I held tighter to his hand.

As we walked along, my father asked many questions, wanting to know precisely where we were, who was there, and what was going on—so many questions. At first I told him everything I could, even mentioning the people passing by who made faces at us, the ones who had most likely heard about the useless operation, the troubles at work. People sometimes looked at us as if we were doing something wrong, as if we didn't belong in their world. And there were those, too, who walked right by, even though they knew my father.

I turned his attention to whatever might trip him up. I tried to see who was coming toward us before they saw us, and I signaled my father by whispering their names just loud enough for him to hear me before they reached us. Then, my father knew who they were and could call them by name. They stood in the doorway of Finlay's Spa, or they were out puttering around in their yards or on their porches, peering over newspapers, watching us from rocking chairs. Did we leave them wondering, confused, thinking, "Is he really blind?" Or were they asking themselves the question, "If he is blind, then how did he know who I was?" I hoped so. That was my intention. My father's intention though, I think now, was not to fool people but simply to make them include him in their world.

Sometimes, people standing around on the sidewalk in pairs or in small groups whispered, and I heard them. "Would you look at who's coming," they said, when they saw us. I talked louder then, making conversation that would distract my father.

"Don't pay any attention, Ree," my father said, if he overheard them. "Let it go. Some people just don't know."

We would not be cast aside. I would make sure of it. I let my father know who smiled or waved from across the street, who tooted the horn in a car going down the road. I wanted him to know who his friends were, too.

The blue sky was striped with pinkish clouds. I looked at them through the open bell tower of the Protestant church.

In the distance I could see the spire of St. Peter's, our destination on a Sunday morning.

We walked mostly in silence, talking only when people approached us. Past Sellar's Bakery, Gus's Barber Shop, where my father took Jack for a buzz cut. I imagined that the bell tower through which I could see St. Peter's was the keyhole on the front gate to the kingdom of heaven. I told my father what the sky looked like through that giant keyhole tower, so that he would know that we had reached Gardner Street. Then he knew that it was time to cross.

He understood my cues, knew when to step up or down, off a curb, around a signpost, when to avoid stumbling over the tree roots pushing their way through the sidewalk pavement, or when to avoid walking straight into a fruit bin outside the Blue Front Market.

Mr. Callinan is alone today," I said, when I saw him coming. In this way, when the man approached, my father could say, "How are you this fine day, Mr. Callinan?" The man might think then that my father had recognized him. Since I had mentioned that he was alone, my father could also say, "Where's Margaret today?" She was the man's daughter, my classmate, and she was generally with him.

The more people my father greeted, the better he seemed to feel. My father was becoming full of energy again, stepping lively, and with confidence. Getting it right out in the world restored his confidence, made my father think that he was winning at this game of getting around, almost blind.

I watched people staring at us, heard them talking. Someone I didn't know pointed at us, at me. The woman's face was full of fright. Did she fear for us or for herself? As she talked to those in her group, she shook her head. Did she pity us? Was that why she did that—and looked away when I noticed? My father missed a lot, but I saw everything. Auntie Margaret called me "Hawkeye."

Outside St. Peter's church, the crowd from early Mass was getting out, and we went against the current, arm in arm, heading to the front steps of the upper church. It seemed that my father's purpose was above all, to convey that in the eyes of God he belonged with them. He wanted to prove that he was as much a member of the parish as anyone else. By showing up he was directly confronting their fear of difference, the prejudice of those who might have excluded him.

"Good morning, good morning," my father said as he made his way though a sea of neighbors and people he didn't know. Then he went up the stairs and into the vestibule.

Inside the air was thick with incense. We walked right down the center aisle, all the way to a front pew. Sometimes I wished we could sit inconspicuously in the back of the church, but my father wanted to be up front—to be closer to God? I didn't think so. I thought he wanted everyone to see him there.

Once we reached the front, we genuflected in unison and he told me to go into the pew first. We let the cushioned kneeler down gently and dropped to our knees to pray. I looked around at the congregation and saw other fathers with their children. My father was a handsome man. He didn't look like all the rest. For one thing he was an Italian in an Irish parish. On Sundays he was always well dressed. "Dressed to kill," was the way my mother said it. To church he wore a freshly starched shirt. He had stacks of them, cleaned and pressed at the laundry, and folded around cardboard, so that they would stay perfectly crisp. Each time he took a new shirt out of the stack of them packaged in brown paper at White's Cleaners, he gave me the cardboard sheets to write on. He wore nice suits, too, usually dark, some with pin stripes that accentuated his fit build and his dark, Sicilian face. My mother is right: he did have panache. His shoes were always shined, almost so that you could see yourself in them. "You'll wear them out if you polish them any more than that," my mother would say to him, when she came upon him buffing them in the kitchen on a Saturday night before he went to bed.

Mass ended and the priest dismissed us. "Ite, missa est."

"You look like a million bucks," someone said to my father. It was Happy Farrell greeting my father. He lived up the street from us. He was a politician, our neighborhood's State Representative. My father and mother always signed his election papers. I didn't need to whisper Happy Farrell's name to my father. His voice was as unmistakable as the voice of Elmer Fudd or Bugs Bunny. Happy was a match for my father's mood, upbeat, animated, his voice heard over the recessional hymn being played by the pipe organ in the balcony as we filed out.

We passed from shadow to light. I was a camera recording what I saw. I unraveled my word pictures for my father as we moved along a sidewalk or crossed a street. I thought I could go on like that forever, preventing trips and falls, faux pas, and the crash that would finally bring him down. It was not until I had a child of my own that I really understood that none of us is truly able to protect another, though love can make us want to do that. Too soon after this realization, my father was gone, disappeared quite suddenly from the world.

It is true that I was small, but I was sharp and vigilant. Then, we walked side by side, stepping lively.

Memorial Days

FRIDAY AFTERNOON JUNE 4, 1993

In the car on the way back to Cambridge my brother Jack talked a little about the experience at the morgue. Mark and he did not have to view my father's body in person. The identification process took place via closed circuit television. Someone in another room brought my father before a video camera. Jack and Mark sat in a separate room and watched my father's body on a television screen.

"If I didn't know before I went in there, I wouldn't have recognized him at all," Jack said.

"Why? What did he look like?" I wanted to know.

"I don't know," Jack said. "It just didn't look like him."

When he said that, for a split second I thought, maybe it wasn't my father, maybe it was someone else, that there had been some mistake. But I didn't allow myself to run with this false hope.

"Well, it wasn't him really," I said instead. "He's gone. His spirit's gone from his body now. Isn't that what makes people look like themselves, their individual spirit?"

"He didn't have his teeth in and that made a difference. I always saw him with his teeth," Jack said.

Back at the house while we ate take-out food from one of those burger places and planned what to do next, I thought of Emily Dickinson's words for this kind of day, "The bustle in the house/The morning after death/Is solemnest of industries enacted on earth."

Mark would stay with Gianni while I went to Worcester with Jack for the meeting with my mother and Peg to make arrangements with the funeral director. Mark would drive to Worcester later to pick me up, after Gianni returned from day care.

Someone needed to go to the YMCA to talk to a staff person there to let them know of my father's death and to make arrangements for removing his belongings from the room he rented there. There was also the need to go to Massachusetts General Hospital to pick up my father's personal effects. He usually kept money in his pants pocket, preferring that to leaving too much in the cash register drawer, knowing that anyone might reach over the counter to help themselves, and he wouldn't be able to see that. I'd called my friend Joan to ask her to come with me the following morning, when I would take care of these things. Going to the snack bar and newsstand at the John F. Kennedy building at Government Center in Boston—to take inventory and to deal with the perishable food and drink—would have to wait until after the funeral.

At the top of the list was the need to write an obituary as soon as possible, so that it would run in the Saturday morning paper, to alert people who would want to attend the weekend wake and funeral services. We had to hustle to meet the deadline.

"We can do that in the car on the way to Worcester," I suggested to Jack.

We headed west on the Mass Pike, Jack driving into the bright afternoon sun. I had a yellow legal pad on my lap and pen in hand. We talked about our father's work history. I made notes, ordering them according to two chronologies, the two lives he'd led: one before his blindness when he'd worked as a machinist, and the other after when he'd become a businessman.

When we began to list the places where our father had cafeteria and vending stand businesses in Massachusetts for twenty-eight years, we struggled to name them all. We both easily remembered the first, at Worcester Pressed Steel, because we were all so relieved to have him back at work, when he took over the cafeteria there. The company had gone under in 1975.

"He went to Worcester Molded Plastics after the company closed down," Jack remembered.

"Right. Then that one closed and he went where?" I was unable to remember any other Worcester business he had.

"Yes, that was when he left for Boston," Jack said.

Nowhere else to go in the city, I thought. It was the way I'd felt after being laid off from a teaching job in the Worcester Public Schools in the early eighties, and had left Worcester for a government job in Boston—and working in the same city had helped me stay in touch with my father.

In Boston, besides managing a cafeteria he named "Harbor Mist," at the U. S. Coast Guard Building at Northern and Atlantic Avenues, he had previously been the operator of another at the Massachusetts Bay Transportation Authority's administration building at Forest Hills; and throughout the nineteen eighties and nineties, he'd managed—at different times—snack bars at the Federal Transportation Building at Kendall Square in Cambridge, and two in Boston—one at the Veterans Administration Outpatient Medical Building at Court Square and the other— his last location— at the John F. Kennedy Federal Building at Government Center, where he'd collapsed behind the counter.

"That's it. I think we have them all now," Jack said.

I thought we finally had a complete list, too, and we were both amazed at the number and variety of places where my father had operated news and snack concessions and full cafeterias. Neither of us had ever realized how many there had been.

My father kept moving his food service business to new places, always attempting to better his financial situation. His last move came just after my son Gianni was born, when he gave up the large Harbor Mist Cafeteria at the U.S. Coast Guard Building on the waterfront. He traded that for the small financially unrewarding newsstand at the JFK Federal Building. I think that he moved that last time, too, because the cafeteria had become too much for him. He had insisted, of course, that the move was entirely fueled by good business sense: the numbers were better at JFK. He thought that he had reliable sources reporting accurate proceeds to him. He wanted what had turned out to be impossible: to work in a less demanding and stressful place and to make more money than he had been. Someone had given him false information about proceeds, or at the very least had been a good deal less than forthcoming about foot traffic—and what would detrimentally affect his business—the information about major construction plans in the wing of the building that housed the news store concession.

As we drove to Worcester that afternoon, after Jack and I had the content straight, I began, with his help, to write the obituary, arguing with him over sentence structure and style, trying to make a masterful piece of writing out of what was at its core, simply a straight news story. I wanted my father to get his due, and I thought that I could still make that happen.

Nine

INHERITANCE (1960)

It was most likely one of those ordinary grey winter days in New England when I was sick to death of winter, and a serious case of boredom had set in. It was the day my mother told me that I had to be examined to see if I would have my father's blindness. I had been worried ever since I'd overheard her telephone conversation when she was trying to persuade others in my father's family to be tested for the same retina problem my father had. "The doctor is just going to look at your eyes, that's all," she said.

"You can catch it from him?" I asked, figuring that my father might have caught the disease from someone in his own family.

My mother explained that the problem was "in the blood," passed on by a mother or father when a child was born.

I didn't understand.

"Same as eye color, or anything about the way you look," she said.

Her explanation confused me further. I knew that I didn't inherit my mother's eyes. Her eyes were the color of the ocean in winter. "She's got her father's eyes," anyone who knew him would say, when meeting me for the first time.

My mother went on to explain what I'd already overheard but found hard to believe—that it was not just my father who was born with the seed of blindness— that my grandmother, too, had it—that she was blind as well.

How could it be that I hadn't noticed that my grandmother was blind?

"Oh, she's cagey," my mother said. "And if your sister has it, you might, too," she added.

What? What is she talking about? My sister, Peg? I panicked, feeling that my mother meant to include me, too, in her list of victims. I knew my mother had taken Peg to have her eyes examined in Boston, noticing she seemed to have trouble seeing at night. But it was news to me that what was wrong with Peg's eyes was the same thing that was wrong with my father's eyes. I wore glasses, too, because I saw things double when I stared too long at them. I was told that glasses would correct my eyes. I wouldn't need them after a while, the doctor said. I worried: what if the doctor had been wrong, like the one years before, when my father was given glasses and told that they would correct *his* vision?

My sister, Peg?

My mother continued her disclosure. She didn't tell me not to worry, which is what I needed to hear. I could tell that she was concerned—and angry, too. She seemed completely caught up in her anger.

"No one really knows how many people in your grandmother's family were blind before her. Some things we'll never know. She's not telling, even though we know now that there must have been others—or maybe she doesn't know, if they kept secrets as well as she does. Who knows who else has inherited it? It's not only your father."

I was too young to fully understand the implications of what she was saying. Not knowing how this progressive blindness was genetically inherited, my father's Catholic family had had many children, magnifying the numbers of those with the retina problem, so that it profoundly affected the family. In my father's immediate family, four of six children lost sight from retinitis pigmentosa; in addition to my father: his brother and two of his sisters inherited the gene from their mother—my grandmother.

That day I tried hard to get into my head this idea of inheriting blindness. I already knew that people inherited things like money or houses. Hadn't Auntie Margaret inherited the cottage in Maine from her aunt? To inherit a house or money was to get a present. I knew that blindness was no present.

"Can you imagine? Your father is the first one to see a doctor about it! Can you beat that?"

With all the spying I did, the listening in on conversations not meant for me, I'd never learned enough. My curiosity might have made things worse when this revelation did come, for I had been getting mere snippets of truth for so long— bits and pieces gleaned from eavesdropping—inspiration for my imagination. The whispering had let my imagination run wild. As a result I think I'd become pessimistic about our family situation, expecting the worst for myself, seeing how our fate was unfolding. And my mother seemed not to be aware of the kind of crazy connections a child might make based on limited knowledge and magical thinking—and the worry that would result from them.

"What do you mean?"

"Can you imagine," she repeated, "they were trying to hide the fact that they were blind. Not one of them let on. Ever."

How could anyone do that?

When I walked around with my eyes closed, pretending to be blind, to see what it would be like, I had to hold my hands out in front of me or off to the side to avoid bumping into things and knocking them over—and sometimes, I even tripped and fell. I saw my father do those things, too, once in a while. People couldn't help but notice, and wouldn't they ask for explanations? A person having that kind of trouble getting around would have to tell or else be thought of as showing strange behavior.

I mulled these thoughts over that day and in the days to come and always I came to the same conclusion: surely someone in the family in addition to my father must have admitted to having a problem seeing. Even now I have a hard time believing what I was told.

"No," I said to my mother. "Not true. Can't be."

I had never seen her so angry at me for disagreeing with her—and angry with my father's family members.

"Ignorance," she said. "That's what this is all about."

I knew already that my mother viewed some in my father's Sicilian family as unschooled and with ways of "the old country." I don't really know though, what I thought, hearing her say that. But in the years that followed, I gradually became aware of what it meant to the quality of a person's life, not to have a good education, especially when it came to understanding anything related to science or technology. I was eighteen before the point was driven home to me on the day that Neil Armstrong became the first man to walk on the moon. It was summer and I was visiting Grandma Bella in Milford, sitting in her kitchen. The television was on in the den and I ran in to watch. My uncle Pete, my grandmother's brother, whose eyes were also affected, had come upstairs for coffee and conversation. The news excited me and I hurried back into the kitchen to tell my uncle and grandmother. With complete seriousness, my uncle looked at me and said, "That's just a cartoon they're showing. That isn't really happening. The government is just trying to fool us."

I was shocked that day, hearing my uncle's response to a scientific and historical milestone. Was that the way my mother had felt when she first approached the members of my father's family to encourage them to see the research doctors at Massachusetts Eye and Ear Infirmary? They had refused to cooperate—or even to believe at first—what she had learned and was trying to tell them about my father's blindness being inherited.

But on that day when *I* first learned of it directly, when my mother characterized the relatives on my father's side as ignorant for not ever going to see a doctor about their trouble seeing, I was confused. She seemed to be saying that if someone in my father's family—his mother, for instance— had seen a doctor, that maybe something could have been done to stop the blindness from coming on. I had already overheard in many of mother's telephone calls and conversations that there was no cure. I suppose now that she must have been thinking of what the doctors had explained to her, of their need for research subjects and data about patterns of genetic diseases in order to understand them, which was the reason my mother persisted in trying to establish a family tree that indicated who was blind in my father's family. I can't help but wonder now whether my mother—after she had learned all of this—ever considered that it would have been better if she had not had children. The risk would have been explained to her only after she'd been to the hospital with my father, and by then, my sisters had been born and my brother was already on the way.

There was something else confusing me related to my mother's anger at my father's family for being silent about their trouble. It seemed to me that she was blaming them for this disease. As far as I knew then, a problem that you were born with—like deafness or a missing finger or not being very smart or having any kind of illness—came from God. If God gave you suffering weren't you supposed to accept it, learn to live with it? Isn't that what my grandmother and others in her family had done?

As a child attending Catholic school, I reasoned from the same parochial perspective as my grandmother most likely did. Ours was a theology of limitations. Being still a child really, I could not have imagined the bitterness that would overtake my mother in the years that followed—but which, mercifully, dissipated in her very old age. Nor could I anticipate that it would be from then on, enormous work for me to lose myself in anything so completely that I would not be haunted by questions of how I would balance responsibility and commitment to family with my own needs. After this day, even when I would not be helping, I would be considering that perhaps I should be.

Undoubtedly, the events I am describing were a turning point in my mother's relationship with my father and his family. She had experienced what she felt was an overwhelming personal betrayal and rejection. She could only see action or inaction, and seemed incapable of comprehending possible reasons for their silence. There was the religious belief they held to, that God gives out all kinds of trials and suffering—blindness among them—and that the faithful are expected to accept and bear them. That was the way to heaven. Because they were not formally educated people for the most part, they wouldn't have reacted to their problems the way my mother did, having grown up in a family in which her favorite uncle was a prominent medical doctor. She could only focus on the fact that they had intentionally withheld information that had huge ramifications in her life.

On that day when I learned that blindness was profound in my father's family, I tried to view my mother's anger as similar to a bad cold that would pass. Although I wanted her to, I don't think that I ever expected her to calm my fears or otherwise comfort me about what she had revealed. That wasn't in her nature. Things between her and my father had not been peaceful for years, not since the last day he drove his Packard with me in it after the doctors warned him that he should no longer drive. However, I did not anticipate that my mother would never really forgive. "Forgive and forget," my father used to say to her. She would say something spiteful then, and that would touch off another argument. She became dedicated to her arguments. That day she ranted and raved about the relatives, but her anger would grow into active pessimism, extending beyond them and affecting other relationships, activities, and personal goals and accomplishments. "Don't expect anything," she would advise me. "Then if it doesn't work out, you won't be disappointed." And when she knew we were getting tight with anyone, she would warn us, "Your friends will sell you down the river." "Ain't love grand," she'd proclaim sarcastically, when she saw a couple walking down the street holding hands, or witnessed a kiss between Frank Sinatra and one of his leading ladies in a movie she was watching on television. She could not let go of her anger, and so it turned to bitterness.

I was only ten and facing a primal fear head on. I thought that I could see well enough at night—I knew that had been how my father's blindness had begun—but then why was my mother taking me to see the doctor? I worried that the problem maybe just hadn't surfaced yet. Perhaps though, it would be obvious to the doctor when he looked into my eyes with his special light.

I found ways to use my obsession.

I did a science fair project on *The Eye*. The poster I made was large. I drew it in pencil and labeled it in magic marker, using a stencil for perfect block lettering. Because I knew that the eye worked like a camera, I asked my aunt Margaret to lend me her Brownie Automatic, so that I could have something else to put on the display table. I knew that it was always smart to have an experiment if you could, that the judges liked that. I didn't have one and I knew that only students who had experiments won awards at the science fair. I would have had one, too, if I hadn't spent so much time reading about how the eye functions and if it hadn't taken me so long to make my poster. I could have created some optical illusions for the judges. They would have liked that kind of demonstration. I liked illusions—the mirages I saw on the horizon when driving the highway to Maine, the water that seemed to be up ahead on long stretches of straight road on hot summer days.

Because the science fair judges were nuns who taught at our school or priests of the parish, I worried that some one of them who knew my home situation would ask me what it was like for my father to be blind. I thought I ought to be prepared to answer them, so one day I made two black eye patches and wore them for the whole afternoon and right through supper at my grandmother's house. "She does well, not seeing," my aunt said. Gram and Gramps said nothing, and I thought that meant they were thinking what I was thinking: that it was right for me to be getting used to the business of not seeing.

I had to have someone tell me where each kind of vegetable was, and where the slices of chicken were on my dinner plate. "At twelve o'clock," my aunt said, about the mashed potatoes. She knew that this was the way my mother talked to my father at Sunday dinner, so then he could find what he had on his plate to eat. Sometimes when he was eating, the food fell off his fork and back onto the plate and he didn't know it and lifted an empty fork to his mouth. The same thing happened to me.

It was a cold winter day in my memory, but perhaps that is the way I remember it because the place we went to was so gloomy, and I was afraid. I suppose I couldn't help but shiver and get goose bumps. If you asked me then, I would have explained my anxiety this way: "I have a creepy feeling in my stomach."

My heart was beating fast when we entered the clinic at Massachusetts Eye and Ear Infirmary. People were milling around. Even though there was crowd and I was with Peg and Mum—and Grammy had, as she put it, "come along for the ride"—I felt alone nevertheless. No one seemed to know where to go, and when they were told, they just sat waiting, staring off into space, not talking to anyone; this place was, therefore, surprisingly quiet in spite of all the people.

"Where do we go?" my mother said to no one in particular.

How can I get out of here? I thought.

My mother got in line to see a woman who stood behind what looked like a ticket window. But I knew that this was not the box office at the Loew's Poli or the Capital Theater. The woman was not friendly. She had a lot of work to do, I imagined, with all the people who came to the clinic. She needed some information from my mother, who began to rummage in her handbag, trying to find the right card or letter that would give the woman what she wanted. Not finding it, she shook her head and threw up her hands in frustration.

"Oh, I just don't know what happened to that," she told the woman.

My mother was always disorganized about paperwork and bills that had to be paid. Throughout their years together this became an increasing source of frustration for my father, who had to rely on her to produce documents that he could not see to read, but which were required for business or tax purposes, or to qualify for some benefit or loan. Later there came the time after he lost his job, and before he began a new career, when there was some confusion about records of unemployment insurance and Social Security records and payments. I was pressed to help because my mother was unable to sort out information and keep track of files in an orderly way. Problems surfaced. That is why my father asked me to write the letters to government bureaucracies explaining, documenting—in essence justifying—any temporary payments he received as a means of supporting the family.

That day at Massachusetts Eye and Ear Infirmary, the woman finally gave up asking my mother to find the information that had been sent to her in the mail. She handed my mother a card and pointed us to rows and rows of chairs.

"Have a seat over there," the woman said.

The clinic appointments worked like the delicatessen counter at the supermarket. You got your ticket and you waited until you were called.

We were on the far end of a row of chairs at the back. When the people ahead of us moved, we got up to move, too. We advanced one chair at a time. We were like the silent shadows, moving from row to row, waiting in the same way that we would wait when we went to see the priest for confession. We were going to have to sit in each of the chairs that made up our section, and so we sat in the first of many sections of chairs on the journey we were to take through this room. For something to do to occupy the time, I decided to count the number of sections and the chairs in each section, and add them up. There were so many, I kept losing track.

Very slowly, we got closer to the doorway where a nurse appeared every now and then, calling out a name. Then there was usually mumbling and a shuffling of coats and other belongings, until the person who was called joined the nurse and the door was closed again. When a person disappeared, we all moved a little closer.

What went on behind the closed doors down the dark corridor? Whatever it was, it was a well-kept secret. My mother had said nothing to me about what to expect. Perhaps it was a mystery to her, too. I was certain of only one thing while I sat waiting to be called: I wanted to leave. I knew this was no place for children.

"Behave yourself," my mother advised, when I started to whine about wanting to go home. "Act your age," she said. "You're the oldest."

"What time is our appointment anyway?" I asked.

On the way to Boston, as my mother drove down Route 9 she kept saying that we were going to be late. We had a distance to travel to get there from Worcester, a ride of an hour or more. We had gotten a late start, as we usually did whenever we went anywhere with my mother. She was late for everything from church to Thanksgiving dinner with our cousins. She joked about this trait, telling us proudly, it seemed, about working at the courthouse before she was married, how she'd earned the reputation for being "the late Mary Feeherry."

"Never mind. It doesn't matter," she said, about the appointment time. Everyone was given the same time to arrive, she explained. "Nine o'clock. When the clinic opens its doors." She meant, she said, that the appointments were on a "first come, first served" basis.

"Are all of them here to see the same doctor?" I asked, scanning the large crowded room once again, hoping that was not the case.

"Relax," she said. "We'll be here all day. I told you that. Didn't I tell you that?"

She had already been to this place to see the doctor a couple of times with my father, and another time with Peg. Those days they were gone until nightfall.

Peg seemed more afraid than I was. I knew that she was frightened by anything unfamiliar, but she had reason to be scared about her eyes. The doctors had told her she was going to be blind. She already had trouble seeing. Out walking at night, she would cling to my grandmother, my mother, or to me. In thunder and lightning storms she cried like crazy. "Oh, it's only the angels bowling," our mother would say to her, laughing. "What's the big deal?" And then our mother would go over to the fireplace in her room and take the little perfume bottle off the mantel. It was water, not perfume in the bottle—water we were not supposed to drink. It had been blessed, so it was *holy water* brought back from my mother's aunt Mary McCarthy's steamship excursion abroad years earlier. The murky water from the shrine at Lourdes, France, was supposed to be powerful stuff. We had learned that Lourdes was a place where miracles happened. Cripples threw away their crutches. The mute spoke. The blind could see again. Cures had been happening there ever since the Virgin Mary appeared to Bernadette, a young girl as ordinary as one of my sisters or me. When one of us fell or got hurt or when Peg was fearful of thunderstorms, Mum blessed us with the Lourdes water to stop our crying, sprinkled it throughout the house, flicking it from her fingers in every direction. We followed her, looking like altar boys following the priest in a cloud of incense at Mass during the entrance procession. With the holy water ritual, my mother convinced us that we were protected from danger. I wondered why she had never splashed the Lourdes water in my father's eyes—or if she had—why it hadn't worked its magic. I thought, too, that we could use some holy water to douse ourselves while we sat there waiting endlessly, it seemed.

I stared at a teenaged boy whose name had been called. I thought he was cute, even though he had patches over both eyes, and someone—his mother probably—was guiding him, taking his arm, leading him toward the doorway and the nurse who stood there waiting for him.

I didn't know what the doctor could do if he decided that a person had the blindness my father and Peg and Granma and all the others had. No one said anything to me about that. Why else should you go to a doctor, if not for help? All I knew was that you had to keep coming back to this place, like Peg did, like my father did. Every time they'd been to see the doctor, I heard my mother telling someone later, "Oh, the eyes were worse this time." I wanted to believe that the doctor was like the priest who could wipe sins off souls, simply by saying, "In nomine patris, et filii, spiritus sancti, Amen," while waving his hands in the air and making the Sign of the Cross. The priest did this after giving us absolution when we went to confession, and it reminded me of the way a magician twirled his baton in his white-gloved fingers on the way to transforming what was inside the hat, the box, or to bring his sleeping assistant to life after hypnosis. Did doctors, too, perform miracles? Were they like priests or magicians? I hoped so, as I sat waiting to see Dr. Eliot Berson.

I wanted to believe that that was the reason why there was such a crowd waiting. I wanted to believe that the doctor had the power to fix my father's eyes and that he would keep me and Peg and Kate and Jack from ever becoming blind as well. I wanted to believe in miracles and to understand mysteries, but I was told always, "You ask too many questions. Just have faith." I tried not to have a sense of doom, but I couldn't help it. Things had changed about the way we lived. My father was worried about his work situation. "Stop biting your fingernails and do something!" my mother would chastise him when he sat on the living room couch looking deep in thought. She was more impatient than ever, and either sick or tired—or both—most of the time. At school, I felt left out. My aunt Margaret invited me to go places with her more often, and my grandmother was always there, helping out, entertaining all four of us at her house— my sisters and brother as well as me—most evenings, even giving us supper. If I'd interpreted any of these kindnesses before that day at the clinic as ordinary and not meant to make up for difficulties, while I sat waiting for my appointment—for the verdict about my own eyes—I knew for certain that we were a family with big troubles.

My mother said, "Say your prayers that you'll be okay."

I was too afraid to talk or play with Peg and too worried then to ask my mother any other questions. Her answers never seemed to make me feel better anyway. I did pray because I didn't know what else to do. I didn't say the prayers that I had learned in school; I made up my own instead. My prayer was a litany, a list of what I thought were some of the most beautiful things in the world, which I hoped to continue to be able to see. I finished my prayer with promises: to be alert and to notice as much as I could, to find some useful purpose for my sight, to help my father. He needed me he said, "to help navigate."

So I cut a deal with God. I said my prayer over and over again while we waited, hoping that I would never forget those promises. I vowed to try to tell the truth always about what I could see, and I believed that might help me keep my good eyes. I prayed desperately, wanting to be spared.

When it was lunchtime, Gram and Peg went out for sandwiches. In order not to lose our place, Mum and I stayed put. By the time they returned, we'd moved up. The wait was worse once we got close, finally sitting in the last row before the door, some two or three hours after we'd arrived. Then I knew that I couldn't escape, that I would be called soon. Some people didn't answer to their names, and we supposed that they had given up and gone home. But we waited it out, stayed, and finally we did hear our name, barely recognizing it as "Bonina," the way the nurse had called it our. "Bo-nigh-na."

"Are all of you here to see the doctor?" the nurse asked when the four of us arrived at her door. My mother explained that Peg and I both had appointments.

"I'm the mother," she said. "And this is my mother."

We were led then into a small waiting room, like that of a doctor's office, a more comfortable place with upholstered chairs. I felt less nervous being in this room.

"I'll be right back," the nurse said and she left us there alone.

When she returned she was carrying two boxes. From the looks of them, I thought that they held some games to occupy our time while we waited to see the doctor. Because I was bored, I was enthusiastic about the possibility.

"Come sit here," the nurse instructed.

Peg and I went over to the large rectangular coffee table in the center of the room, Peg following my lead but still hesitating a little. We kneeled down in front of the two boxes, which the nurse had placed there. They opened up like other boxes I knew: the pastry carrier I'd seen Guy Zingarelli from the bakery open up at Gram's on so many afternoons, and these boxes opened, too, like our father's toolbox did—with trays like steps. But in this much smaller box there were not jam-filled cookies, cakes, pies, or peppermint patties—nor were there screwdrivers and hammers and nails. Each tray held variously colored tablets. We're going to paint, I thought. But I hesitated—if these were watercolors, as they seemed to be—then where was the water? Maybe the receptionist would get it for us. And some paper and brushes, too, I hoped.

But I was wrong. This was some kind of test. I thought the doctors might be trying to find out how smart we were, although I didn't know what that had to do with anything. When the nurse said, "Put them in order. I'll be back in a few minutes," I was relieved that this seemed to be a test I would be good at.

That was all the direction we were given. No rules. No explanation of what kind of order she wanted. The order was for us to decide, just by looking at these hundred or so colors—all of them different, but many of them very much like another. So many different colors! Take pink, for example. It was as if someone had taken a petal from every pink flower in the world, as if all those different shades of pink were pressed into the little circles in our boxes. And it seemed that the color of every green thing you could imagine had been included, too—colors dark as a forest or our pine green Mercury sedan—or light as the pistachio ice cream that I loved—and every green thing in between. The same thing was true for every color on the color wheel.

I decided to order the tablets from dark to light. I enjoyed this game. I was finished quickly, much sooner than Peg, and the nurse was right there to take it away as soon as I'd completed her assignment. "That's very good, " she said, and I figured I'd passed the first test.

A different person came into the room and asked me to follow her.

"Do you want me, too?" my mother said.

I was feeling brave all of a sudden, after feeling the satisfaction of having ordered the color tablets. When the nurse said, "This isn't to see the doctor yet," and my mother said, "Then I'll stay put," I didn't even mind going in alone.

I sat on a stool. I needed eye drops, the nurse said, so that the doctor would be able to examine my eyes well. "He'll be able to get a better look."

She didn't explain how the eye drops that were put in *my* eyes would make *the doctor* see better, but they certainly didn't improve my vision. The world was suddenly a blurry place.

"Don't worry. It might get even worse, but the blurriness won't last," the nurse said. She told me then that she was going to bring me back out to sit in the waiting room for a few more minutes.

Having blurry eyes—not being able to see well—reminded me quite explicitly of the possibility of blindness for myself. The nurse had me by the arm. She sat me down in a chair and then brought on the worst news I'd heard yet: she was going to put patches over my eyes. "Just for a little while," she said.

I felt dizzy and my stomach was queasy, as I looked around the room just before she did.

The patches were just like those I remembered my father wearing after his surgery, but I hoped that when these were removed from *my* eyes, that I would be able to see again. I thought that must have been the same thing my father had wished for all those afternoons when we sat together in the living room after his eye surgery, waiting for the patches to come off *his* eyes.

Not long after patching me up, the nurse returned, asking me to follow her.

"We're ready for her," she said to my mother.

I waved forlornly to Peg, though I couldn't see her.

Mum said to her, "We'll be right back. You stay with Grammy."

The patches were removed, and for a split second I thought, *I am blind.* I had been brought into a pitch-black room and seated in a straight-backed chair. There were voices coming from beside and behind me, telling me that I had to take some tests in the dark. Soon lights appeared quite suddenly and then went out. A voice told me that I was to *say when* as the lights crept sideways into my field of vision.

When I finally did get to see the doctor he was serious as any priest that I had ever encountered in a dark confessional box on a Saturday afternoon at St. Peter's, when I had lots of sins to tell. He looked at the papers in a folder that had my name on it.

"So, let's have a look," he said then. "Just sit back and relax now."

I couldn't think of anything less relaxing than having such a bright light shining in my eyes, especially knowing why the doctor was looking into them. He looked first at one, then the other eye. I felt his hot breath on my face, and I sat so still that I didn't think that *I* was breathing any more. His face got closer and closer to mine, moving from side to side. He followed this routine for a few minutes, and at last clicked off his light.

When I relaxed and readjusted myself in the chair, I saw my mother who had been standing off to the side while the exam was taking place. She was a big blur to me. The doctor turned to her and she approached us, knowing that it was time to hear the verdict.

"I would say," Dr. Berson said, looking very serious and even pausing for a moment, making me expect the worst, "that there is a ninety-nine and forty-four one hundredths percent chance that you will never have this condition."

"Just like Ivory Soap," my mother said.

It was a funny way for the doctor to state the prognosis, but ingenious too, I think now—that he chose something so familiar and something I associated with being clean. He made clear to me that day that I would probably never be blind from retinitis pigmentosa. Still, I remember thinking of that small chance of having my father's blindness, because the doctor hadn't admitted to being one hundred percent sure.

That day, when I announced my fear to my mother when we were in the car later, she turned to me and said, "He isn't God, you know. He's only a doctor. He doesn't want to fly in the face of God. God is the only one who knows anything one hundred percent."

I think of how differently I approached this same situation with my son Gianni in 1999. By that time, I had read many articles about my father's form of blindness, and when I was pregnant I'd consulted a geneticist at Harvard Community Health in Cambridge, about the likelihood that a child of mine would ever inherit this retina problem. I'd been told that the pattern in the family seemed to indicate that since I didn't have the condition, I wouldn't pass it on to my child. Because the phrase, "seemed to indicate," had been used, I felt that I needed more certainty, so obsessively, I decided to have my son examined. I wanted Gianni to have a thorough examination, using all the latest tests and technology that had been developed since I was a child; then I would believe for sure that there was no mistake, no aberration in the pattern.

Gianni was young—younger than I had been when I went to have my eyes tested—just a month short of his eighth birthday. I wanted him to know exactly what he could expect the doctor and technicians to do. I told him, as I told myself, that I was just "making sure," that I did not expect the doctor to find any problem. I told him he showed no symptoms, explaining to him what that meant.

On the day of our appointment I was pleased to find that what I had remembered as a grueling procedure had been overhauled. We went directly to the office of Dr. Eliot L. Berson, the same doctor my father had seen for his diagnosis and the one who'd examined my sisters and brother and me and many other family members. He had since become renowned worldwide for his research work in diseases of the retina. He was now the William F. Chatlos, Professor of Opthamology and Director of Harvard Medical School's Berman-Gund Laboratory for the Study of Retinal Degenerations at the Massachusetts Eye and Ear Infirmary. When we arrived I was delighted to find that just two or three other patients were scheduled for that morning and we were seen—not in a clinic but in a regular doctor's office. We also learned that Dr. Berson's other duties had taken him away and we would be seeing instead, one of the other doctors in his practice, Dr. Alexander Gaudio.

When it came time for Gianni to have patches put over his eyes, he was told that when he went into the dark room where the first test would take place, that the doctor would have a better idea of how well his eyes worked in the dark because he would wear the patches for a while first. That was all he needed to allay any fear that might have surfaced. As a result he wasn't afraid as I had been, and simply saw the test as a challenge. He made a game of waiting, walking across the reception room while the eye drops and the patches did their work, as if he were playing *Pin the Tail on the Donkey* or the game, *Marco Polo*, which I had seen him play with schoolmates one class trip to Duxbury Beach. He got up out of his chair and headed across the room on his own to the row of chairs lining the opposite wall. The game was to avoid crashing into another waiting patient, or the magazine table. And he asked me to draw eyes on his patches, so I reached into my shoulder bag and took out the makeup pouch I carry, and found—what else but an *eye* pencil—and I drew large dramatic eyes with long curly lashes. Gianni took delight in having me direct him into the little office behind the wall where the receptionist sat, to surprise her with the flirty eyes I'd drawn on his bandages. He brought joy into a situation that could sometimes be grim for the doctors, research assistants, clerks and other patients.

For my son, the technology was state-of-the-art. He sat in front of a small computer and looked at the screen. Each time he clicked a button as light entered his peripheral vision, he must have been reminded of one of his own computer games that challenged his reflexes. When he clicked that button he must have thought it just like the mouse he used when he played computer games at home. In addition to the peripheral vision testing he was also given an electroretinograph. For this test, an electrode was attached to each eye and he sat in front of a computer screen watching while a strobe light was generated. He was told to stare straight on, deeply into the light.

I was surprised to see the next test. Gianni was given a box of color tabs, something like the one than I remembered from my own experience—only smaller, just twenty or so disks—and he was told to put them in order. This had replaced the previous Farnsworth Test, which I had taken. I was told that even though there were a lot fewer color tabs, it was "no less definitive." The purpose of tests like this is to identify difficulties in distinguishing shades and tones of color. This differentiation is the work of the rods and cones in the retina—the photoreceptors.

Gianni took the entire extensive examination in stride and was even able to sit several hours after our arrival, while innumerable photographs were taken of his retina. In the end, as for me, it was determined that his retina functioned well.

In the waiting room that day I had overheard a couple talking. The man had come into the room after being examined by the doctor. He had just been told that he was "going blind." From the way he related his prognosis, it was clear to me that this news was totally unexpected. He thought that he had been referred to the doctor to get a new prescription for eyeglasses. The man in the waiting room hadn't known that eyeglasses were not going to help his vision problem.

Forty years before, my mother and father must have had this same conversation at the doctor's office. I'd seen pictures of my father taken in the early years of their marriage and before, when he wore glasses for something. I wondered: who were the charlatans who had examined my father and this man in the waiting room, and for what reason had their glasses been prescribed?

Mum and Dad at Old Orchard Beach before marriage

Dad (center), brother
and sister: Uncle Tom,
and Aunt Anna

Mum as toddler (left) with
sister Margaret (Auntie)

Mum and Dad in front of
Packard, courting

"Just married"
June 19, 1948

Mum (left) off for honeymoon, showered with confetti by
sisters Margaret and Sally (lower right)

Memorial Days

My father's wake and funeral were being handled by Callahan Brothers at Salem Square in Worcester. When loved ones had passed on, members of my mother's family and many other Irish families in the city had been well cared for by the Callahans, and so new generations remained loyal to the business. As my brother Jack and I drove there, I remembered going as a child with my grandmother when friends of hers had died—to calling hours at the old Callahan Funeral Home on Trumble Street, a small, historic, brick ivy-covered building. Neither the building nor the street have existed since the nineteen sixties, when they disappeared to make way for the Galleria shopping mall. The funeral home was still in the same general area of downtown Worcester, but the new place was modern, bright, open, and with light wood paneling, and it bore absolutely no resemblance to the old place.

Jack and I joined my mother and my sister Peg in a meeting with Phil Callahan. I knew him a little, had met him through a former roommate who ran a halfway house for teenagers called "Come Alive." Ironically, Phil the undertaker was on the Board of Directors. I was glad that he would be the one to handle the arrangements.

Phil was patient and kind with us, his demeanor more that of a grief counselor than a businessman, and I was grateful for that. He took it upon himself to apologize for the condition of the Boston city morgue, because—I guess—as a funeral director he took some responsibility for the failure of his profession to successfully advocate for more dignity and sensitivity, as well a professional staff and a better location. "The legislature doesn't want to appropriate money for death, so the morgue isn't a priority. That's the problem," he said.

"So I apologize. No one should have to go into a place like that, especially under the circumstances."

We worked out the time for calling hours and the funeral. Phil gave my mother a brief talk about protecting her inheritance—my father's hard-earned money—with a trust. I don't know how to say that and make it real, not clichéd—to describe my father's determination related to making money, but I want to make clear the amazing accomplishment of earning it. I think: *hard-earned money*, and that doesn't begin to contain the emotion I feel about his struggle. Like so many colloquial English phrases, it has lost the truth of experience. I think: *money earned with blood, sweat, and tears*. That is dramatic enough, but not my father's style; he was never looking for pity. I will settle on saying that my father earned his money by walking straight into a head wind that never let up his whole life. He kept going—blind, and always against the wind. Yet people who met him and people who knew him, never failed to remark upon his positive attitude and his good nature.

Phil told us that my father's body was already en route from Boston to Worcester. "He should be here soon."

We were standing at the elevator that would take us up to the casket showroom.

Phil hit the "Up" button, but when the elevator arrived at our floor, the door didn't open.

"We'll wait. They're taking it up now," he said, and I understood him to mean that my father's body was on the elevator.

When we got to the casket showroom upstairs Phil left us on our own to choose.

"Take you time," he said. "I'll be in the office if you have any questions."

The experience of choosing a casket for my father's burial was not what I had expected it to be. The idea of a room full of caskets I thought would frighten me. Strangely, it felt no more threatening than a room full of baby cribs. The other thing that surprised me is that although I had always thought that spending money on a casket was a waste, and that everyone who wasn't cremated ought to be buried in the same simple kind of wooden box, I found myself actually *shopping*—looking for the best one of the bunch.

Not metal, I decided. I had always thought that metal caskets looked like cars. The vehicle theme was not lost on me; it made some sense. I knew that in Ghana and perhaps elsewhere, creating elaborate caskets designed as vehicles to transport the soul to the other world, is an art form. I thought though, that these American metal ones reeked of ostentatious opulence. They reminded me, too, of a sleek silvery last-minute "Flight Insurance" desk I'd seen at Logan Airport.

"I think we should get a wooden one. Let's look at those," I said to my mother.

Peg just wanted to get out of the room. Not being able to see much anymore, she was imagining all sorts of macabre; I could tell, just looking at her expression.

"Can you hurry up and just pick one?" she said. "I don't like this place."

I brought my mother over to what I thought was the most beautiful box in the room. It was oak—not highly polished, but with a waxed sheen, like the wood floors in my house that my father thought were beautiful. As I looked at the casket I remembered him coming to our new house for the first time and inspecting the smooth oak flooring. He crouched down to feel the grain of the wood, and said, "Nice wood."

"This one has class," I said. "It's dignified, don't you think."

"Yes, that one's nice," my mother agreed.

"Okay then, get that one. Just hurry," Peg said. "This place gives me the creeps."

I went out into the corridor and found the office where Phil was. "We've made our decision," I said.

He followed me out and down the hall to the showroom.

"This is the one we want," I said.

145

"Well," he said, "that is beautiful craftsmanship—an excellent choice. I can get that one for you."

It was clear from his compliments about our good taste that we had chosen one of the most expensive caskets in the room. The price tags were not visible, or at least I didn't notice them, finding no reason to consider cost, in spite of anything to the contrary I had ever believed before about excess and funerals.

We went into the office to work out the arrangements for the obituary.

"Do you have a picture?" Phil asked.

I showed him the picture I'd taken out of a photo album. Being in a hurry when I'd searched through the books, I didn't think I had chosen the best one I might have, but there was nothing that could be done about it.

"It's in color," I said. "I didn't have a black and white photo. Is that okay?"

"Good. This is fine," Phil said.

He told me that I should give the secretary all the information for the obituary and that she would see to it that it made the morning paper.

"We would like to have it printed in the *Boston Globe* as well as the *Telegram and Gazette* and the *Milford Daily News*," I said.

"It probably won't make it into the *Globe*," Phil said.

"We don't need to put it in the *Globe*," my mother said.

"It should be in the *Globe*. He worked in Boston for years. He knew a lot of people. People will want to know, and people know me, too, from living in Cambridge and working in Boston."

"There's only a slight chance that it would get in. You'd have to pay," Phil said. "And that doesn't guarantee it. If an important person dies they get the space. There's a slight possibility that they'd pick it up if it's a story with human interest."

"If an important person dies?" His words took my breath away. "My father did amazing things in his life."

"I know," Phil said. "I'm sure he did."

I felt—perhaps unfairly—that Phil was trying to humor me though, that he chalked up my reaction to the failure of logic that can accompany grief. But he had not read the obituary yet and I did not think that he knew much of my father's story.

"Do you know?" I challenged him. "How do you know?"

"Cut it out, Ree," Peg said.

Phil tried patiently to avoid any further conflict. He explained again, in slightly different words, the policy of the *Boston Globe* regarding death notices and obituaries. He seemed to want to make it clear that he had no control over this.

"You have to pay a fee," he repeated.

"They usually reserve the space, and then if someone well-known dies, the obituary can get bumped. They *will* print a death notice, though. They're required to do that much."

What does the money matter, I thought, when we have spent how much already?

"I think we should do it," I argued. "It's not that much. I'll pay for it, if you don't want to."

"What are you made of money?" my mother said.

"Forget it," Peg said. "They have a nerve to charge for something like that. I wouldn't be caught dead paying for that."

Peg laughed, realizing that what she said was funny in the context.

Phil smiled at this. It was a kind, smart smile.

My mother seemed not to feel what had happened, and this realization brought to mind something else I remembered. I recalled being with her in the solarium outside intensive care at City Hospital, when my father had had the coronary when he was only fifty-two. I remember thinking then that she felt nothing when she looked me in the eye, a strange look on her face, and said matter-of-factly and cruelly

I thought, "You know, he probably isn't going to make it."
She seemed as matter-of-fact now, and I interpreted her
refusal to try to get the obituary in the *Globe* as an act of
retaliation—conscious or not—against my father for having
lived another life in Boston without her when she'd resisted
moving. And I understood the irony of that, considering that
my father was able to provide well for her when he might not
have otherwise, simply because he'd been willing to work in
Boston.

My mother's lack of expressed emotion was different than
my own. Even though I didn't cry, I was propelled by the
sense that dealing with my father's death was my final
responsibility for him. I already felt that his leaving would
profoundly affect me. He'd had enough. He'd simply had
enough, I thought to myself in moments when there was a
lull in activity.

"It's already written," I said to Phil about the obituary. "I
just have to type it up. Is there a typewriter I can use?"

"Oh, no, you don't have to do that yourself. Our secretary
will do that for you."

"Oh, but she can't. I have to do it. She wouldn't be able to
read it. Jack and I already wrote the whole thing. There are
cross-outs and I was writing it in the car while we were
driving, so it's a mess. No one else could possibly decipher
the handwriting. Look, it's all over the place," I showed him.

The secretary interrupted our exchange.

"Oh, you'd be surprised at what I'm able to read. I'll take
care of it for you."

"No, look at it," I said, going over to her desk, showing
her.

"That's not so bad," she said. "I've seen a lot worse."

But I insisted on typing it myself. I was terrified that my
words would be changed, that something important would be
left out, and that my father's story would not be accurate.

"You shouldn't be doing this," my mother said, when I sat
down at the typewriter. "Let her do it. She knows her job."

"I'm sure she does," I said. "I just want to make sure it's right."

"Oh, for God's sake—you're really something," my mother said.

"Just go. Let me do this. Go on, leave the room," I said. "I can work faster if you're not standing over me."

Ten

OLD ORCHARD (1960)

The family travelled to Old Orchard Beach, our vacation destination for many summers of my childhood, when the pressed metal company where my father worked shut down for two weeks. I also often went to Auntie Margaret's cottage with her alone or sometimes with other members of my mother's family. In Maine, I found that we were in a world that contrasted so sharply with the one of my everyday existence, that I could not help but feel that I was living out some dream. The O'Briens and the McCarthys, my grandmother's family, had built the cottage in the late nineteenth century. Even to this day, when the house is over a hundred years old, it remains with its original Victorian furnishings and without hot water, a bathtub, or a shower. When I was a child there was not even a modern cooking range at the house, but rather a kerosene stove that was portable—like a several burner hot plate on wheels, and there was a regular electric hot plate, too. On rainy days everything turned damp and we would burn pine in the small Franklin stove in a corner of the kitchen, trying to heat up the two-story house that was not insulated from the harsh New England weather.

Every good day we went to the beach. I was dreamy in my new surroundings: dune grass bleached white as the sand from salt and sun, and the sight of gulls ruffling blue sky, landing on grey rooftops of the Brunswick and all the other hotels lining the beachfront. In spite of feeling euphoric, I was as alert as the gulls at their perch seemed to be. I watched everything. Often, I headed down the beach to Googin's Rocks with my sisters Peg and Kate, my little brother Jack sometimes tagging along. We'd explore the tide pools and the roads snails made on the wet strand, and I would search for sand dollars, knowing where to find them. I got good at spotting them stuck in the muddy ridges at the water's edge, even though they blended in, their color when wet only slightly different from the sandy mud. I would bring them back to our blanket where we'd set up camp on the beachfront at the Brunswick, spotting from a distance the old red and white striped heavy canvas umbrella on a tall oak pole, a sunshade that had been used by the family for many decades. Seeing it I would run to put my treasure in my dad's hands so he could "see" what I had found.

Noticing how easily I'd mapped my way, and also assessing my cache of sand dollars, my aunt would say, "good eyes," just the way my grandmother would, when I helped her thread her sewing needle or found something very small she'd dropped on the floor—a tiny button or one of her pearl earrings. Did the adults in my family frequently say things like this to me—complimenting my "good eyes"—or calling me by the nickname "Hawkeye" or "Night Owl"—in order to reassure themselves, because they were worried and watching–not just me, but my sisters and my brother, too--for signs of any problem seeing, knowing more than I did for a time, about the problem with my father's eyes?

Now I know why they worried, given that doctors were only just beginning research on retinitis pigmentosa. So little was known about genetic patterns then. I've learned since that different members of the family have different degrees of difficulty seeing. For some, blindness associated with RP comes on sooner and advances more quickly than for others. My own father and mother had no idea how many of their children—if any of us—would become blind. When RP is autosomal dominant, as it is in my father's family, each child has a fifty-percent chance of having the trait. How many or which children will have it, no one can predict without genetic testing before birth.

My father was newly included in the research, having been referred to the practice at Massachusetts Eye and Ear

Infirmary by his doctor. When he asked the members of his family for their participation in the research and was met with resistance and outright refusal initially, it made it difficult if not impossible to learn just how many and which of his ancestors were blind. One of the reasons so little research had been undertaken was that many people—not just those in my father's family—had been afraid to come forward, afraid to be identified as blind. One in four thousand in the United States are affected by retinitis pigmentosa. Not understanding and afraid to know the purpose or kind of research being done, members of my father's family might have thought that they'd be subject to exploitation for the purpose of experimentation. When people who possess only a basic formal education have afflictions, fear often consumes them, makes them keep private what they believe might embarrass them and leave them open to prejudice or subject them to experimentation, robbing them of their dignity. They are vulnerable and therefore sometimes resort to superstition, believing in curses or old wives tales. The Evil Eye—"Don't look at it!" Religion, too, tells them that there will be miracles for those who are exceptionally good and long suffering. And for any wrong doing, there is the wrath of God.

Only with my father's persistent encouragement did his sister Marguerite and his brother Tom involve themselves and their families in the research with doctors at the Massachusetts Eye and Ear Infirmary. Since Tom had also inherited the retina problem that would lead to blindness, he and his wife, my aunt Louise, took their children to be examined as well. My cousin Steve remembers the sadness of that day, how his mother could not stop crying, that he didn't know why she was crying, or even why they were there at the hospital to see the doctors. My cousin Deborah, one of my aunt Marguerite's twins, remembers her parents trying a game the research doctors at the hospital encouraged, in order to determine if any of them might be experiencing night blindness. It reminds one of a crude version of the game of Frisbee—this played only in the dark using a white paper plate rather than a plastic disc. The doctors explained that they should go out into the back yard at night and have the children stand around in a circle, aiming the paper plate and letting it sail through the air, first to one, then another. They were told that if they watched to see if the children were able to follow the sphere with their eyes as it glided toward or away from them, they might be able to gauge their ability to see in the dark.

I think now of what my uncle Tom remembers about trying to get around in the dark during his childhood. He remembers being out in the woods at night, a Boy Scout with his troop. "They all had flashlights except me. And I was the one who needed a flashlight." But he didn't know then he told me, "that other people could see in the dark." No one had told him. He thought everyone had trouble. "It was dark," he said. "I thought—they all had to have flashlights, didn't they?" In fact, he said, no one at all in the family ever mentioned being blind when he was growing up—not even my grandmother—his mother—who was herself blind. My father's sisters and brother have a story similar to that of the princess in Tchaikovsky's *Iolanta*. In the opera, the king conspires to keep his daughter, born blind, unaware of her blindness, by isolating her from the rest of the world. He keeps her in a garden. Milford was no garden, but surely my father and his sisters and brother were sheltered from the truth there, though people outside the family must have known. When my father went home to tell his sisters and brothers of their real condition, he was doing so out of love—just as the suitor to the princess in the opera is acting out of love, when he reveals the truth that she is blind.

In the evenings after dinner at the Maine cottage, we would make our way down Old Orchard Street—the main drag in town—to the amusement park and the boardwalk on the pier, zigzagging in and out of shops all the way to the beach. There were souvenir and candy shops, but my father was drawn mostly to the electronics shops with their flashing beacons hooked up outside, luring him in. Or maybe he tuned into the sound of several portable televisions and radios all playing at once. He was attracted to these shops also by the possibility of bargaining: he loved to negotiate a deal.

My father was, at heart, a businessman. I didn't know this at the time. Then his boldness in trying to get a reduced price at a shop embarrassed me. I didn't know either, that the men in those shops—like the ones who owned the linen stores with the oriental rugs suspended from the ceiling over every crowded aisle of beach towels and tacky souvenirs—were used to the art of the deal, that they respected it even. On one of these excursions my father got involved with the shop owner, discussing the purchase of a portable television. Bargaining seemed to me, a waste of time—his—the man's—and mine, too, since he was delaying our visit to the boardwalk out on the pier where Omar the Great had a booth. I was anxious also to get to the beachfront vendors who sold pizza, fried clams, and ice cream bars dipped in chocolate and rolled in cashew pieces.

"It's a good deal," I heard my father say to the man about his final offer on the price of a television. "I don't need another TV though. But if I did, I'd buy it for that price."

I thought that the man was going to be angry to learn this after he had spent so much time negotiating with my father. Instead, he seemed to feel complimented. A conversation developed.

I walked over to where my father was standing, stood behind him, and whispered close to his right ear, "Ice Cream. Chocolate. Cashews." I knew how to get his attention.

"Goodbye. See you again," my father said to the storeowner.

We crossed the railroad tracks and headed for the ice cream stand. I spotted an organ grinder and his monkey in front of the entrance to Palace Playland Amusements. They were entertaining the crowd. The man had white hair and wore black-rimmed sunglasses. I got the message that he was blind. Although I made no connection at the time to my father's situation, it was clearly on my mother's mind.

"Oh, would you look at that little monkey!" my grandmother said, seeing it.

The monkey was dancing from person to person, passing a tin cup, moving on when it heard the clink of coins dropped in. I loved the monkey's little box hat and his red suit. I wove my way through the crowd to get closer to it. When I saw the cup, I turned back to my grandmother, who was generous, always digging into her pocketbook and offering us spare change. "Do you have any change, Grammy? To put in the monkey's cup? Okay, Gram?"

My mother suddenly reached her arm—longer than I ever thought it was—into the crowd, and yanked me back to where she was standing.

"There'll be no money for the monkey."

"Why not?" I said. "Grammy says I can give some money to him." I held out the dime she'd dug out of her purse and my mother took it away.

"That dirty old thing," my mother said.

"He isn't dirty. He's cute."

"Oh, Mary, let her," my grandmother said to my mother.

"Here, take this," she said, handing me another dime.

My mother was fuming mad. "There is no need for that man to do that—to be begging on street corners like he is. There are programs. He doesn't have to."

I didn't know then what she was talking about because I didn't think of that man as a beggar. I thought only of watching the *Ed Sullivan Show*, when the trainers with their performing monkeys were on. I thought, too, of the day I'd spent at the circus with my grandmother and grandfather, the day my sisters and brother and I went to Boston with them, the same day my father had had the useless eye operation.

My father reached out to take my hand, so I'd know it was time to move on from the monkey. He wanted to stop to visit The Guesser at his booth in the amusement park, before going to the pier; I led him there. That man would guess almost anything about you. The hand-lettered signs at his booth advertised *How Many Children? —How Long Married Your Age? — The Ages of Your Children?* And he would also guess the weight of anyone willing to submit to verification by sitting on what looked like an extra large produce scale.

The barker hollered out to my father, "Guess the make, year, and model of your car?"

"Oh you can?" my father said, a knowing smile on his face.

"Chevrolet Bel Air!" the guesser yelled, looking confident.

My father shook his head.

"Ford Galaxy!" the guesser tried again.

"I don't own one. I don't have a car," my father said.

The crowd that had gathered around was pleased that my father had stymied the man. People began cheering for my dad. The man tried to give back the money my father had paid him to guess, but he wouldn't take it. He was satisfied I suppose, that he had made his point that not everyone could drive, not everyone owned a car. Or had he simply wanted to test the man to see if he, above all—the man with special powers—could tell that he was no longer able to see well enough to drive a car?

Eleven

HIDE AND SEEK (1960)

There were so many cousins at my paternal grandparents' house in Milford every Sunday that there was one child for every adult. Generally all fifteen grandchildren were present and two sets of grandparents, five aunts and four uncles, at least one grand uncle, and my mother and father. All of us were crowded into the small upstairs apartment in what looked like an old farmhouse. We had a party every week, or so it seemed to me then.

We children played outside in the yard, or sometimes at the playground up the street. We were left alone pretty much, and we liked that. If the weather kept us inside some of those afternoons, the uncle with the loudest voice or most serious demeanor—usually Uncle Ed or Uncle John—would be sent out as messenger from the living room where the adults gathered. That uncle would enter our world, take us by surprise, coming into what was called the TV room, the little den off the kitchen, to alert us to the fact that we were too loud or jumping around too much. "Not in the house," he would say, and we all knew he meant that were expected to follow certain rules of behavior.

"Settle down now," he bellowed from the doorway, his face expressionless. And like toys that had been wound up to run and tumble for a limited time only, our activity ceased. However, being children, we would start up again almost immediately after he left the room. It took little more than a giggle from a silly cousin or an elbow jab from a teasing one.

Except for my uncle visiting once in a while to lay down the law, the adults stayed in the living room. Whenever there was a lull in our activity, we heard what seemed to be, all of them talking at once. I wonder now what they talked about, and whether they were really arguing. It did sound that way,

157

and it still does whenever my Italian relatives get together. I wonder, too, if they ever discussed my father's eyes at those Sunday afternoon gatherings, and whether my mother was sometimes rebuffed for trying to explain that his problem was hereditary, whether she actually did "bite her tongue" instead, as she so often remarked she had to do, being with my father's family.

Of all the wonderful surprises that came of those Sunday afternoons—the food, the sweets, the information we garnered from more worldly cousins—in retrospect, the one thing that stands out for me is the fact that my Irish grandmother and grandfather often "came along for the ride." That is the way my grandmother put it. My Worcester grandparents—"city people" and Victorian in demeanor—seemed to love being in the midst of that small town Sicilian family. I recall that no one in my father's family ever called my Irish grandmother, "Julia"—or by her nickname, "Loulee,"—and no one called my grandfather, "Dave." Gramma Bella would say, "Mrs. Feeherry, would you like a cookie or a piece of cake?" And when my grandmother teased my grandfather for starting to doze off, she said, "Mr. Feeherry, another cup of coffee for you?"

Sometimes my Sicilian grandfather didn't come home until late, so I didn't see him for very long on those afternoons. I knew only a few things about him because he didn't talk much to me, not knowing English very well. On Sundays when he was not at the house, he was usually at the Sons of Italy. "He's a nice man, your grandfather," my mother would say about him. She got a kick out of his accent and appreciated the trouble he went to, to be understood. He was nice, taking me with him sometimes into his big garden to help him pick vegetables, letting me pull up carrots, so that I knew what it felt like to tug at their hairy roots. He led me up and down the garden rows, reaching into his jacket for a saltshaker he kept there to use whenever we wanted to snack on the bright, red, and juicy tomatoes that were hot from the sun. My grandpa was always reaching into his pockets to give us something: coins for our piggy banks, chocolate bars, and every Sunday evening after we piled into our car for the ride home to Worcester, he reached his arm in the back seat window and passed out small bags of Blackstone Valley Potato Chips, to keep us happy during the ride home.

Uncle Touri, who owned the gasoline station up the street where we stopped to fill the gas tank before heading home on Sunday evenings, was my grandmother's brother who lived downstairs with their other brother, Uncle Pete. Uncle Touri's sons Bobby and Tom lived with them. I didn't really know my Uncle Touri, but he had the thickest black eyebrows I had ever seen, and they danced around when he talked.

My uncle Pete had a business delivering chicken feed. A tin sign advertising *Unity Feeds* was nailed to the side of the small chicken house on the property, and it remained all the years I went there as a child. It seems to me now that *Unity Feeds* was the family emblem. When I stayed sometimes at my grandparents' house during summer vacations, Uncle Pete took me with him on his route through small towns with fields and farmhouses—to Mendon and Hopedale, Upton and Bellingham. I didn't know him very well either, and sometimes when he left me sitting alone in the red Ford pickup truck while he took an order or dropped one off and collected what he was owed, I worried that he might not return, and I wondered—*What'll I do if that happens?* But I swallowed my fear and went with him anyway, for the adventure of doing something I had never done before.

When we sat down to eat, the small kitchen was usually steamy from soup cooking in a large pot on the stove: tiny beads of pasta—*pastina*—no bigger than nonpareils really, with bite-sized meatballs floating in a seasoned broth, called Italian wedding soup because it was usually the first course at the celebration dinner. We all loved my grandmother's soup and she knew it, smiling over us, passing around a small bowl of grated Parmesan cheese to sprinkle on top. A few would politely decline, liking the soup without it. "No thanks." I would try almost anything though, especially with my father's encouragement. I watched him freely spoon the cheese over his bowl. "Put some on mine," I'd tell my grandmother. I loved the salty taste of the cheese, and the way the hot soup made it melt in my mouth.

"More?" she would ask always, when we said we had finished eating.

We could always have more.

The children ate first—one family at a time—my grandmother serving and generally one of the aunts helping her. Each family of cousins took a turn at the table. Sometimes we were first and the others had to wait in the den until we finished. We could hear them tickling and teasing each other, rolling off the couch, until they were called to eat. If we ate first, we waited outside for the rest to finish, ready for a game of Red Rover.

My father was the only adult who sat with his children. I expect that the soup was made and served to us the same way it had been offered to him when he was a child—by *his* grandmother. My father became his mother's son again on the afternoons of those weekly visits. One day a week he belonged to Milford. He would hold the spoon level with his mouth, stopping it in midair before taking it in, so that he could inhale the fragrant steam. "Mmmmmm," he'd sing, getting the aroma and anticipating the delicious taste. My father cherished simple things like good soup.

After we ate we knew that there were cookies and cakes. Every Sunday I heard the aunties making plans to bake again during the week. We eyed the trays wrapped up on the side counter in the kitchen, had come to expect them. "Get away from that counter," my aunt Ev would holler, seeing us approaching before dinner. "After you eat!" There were anisette-flavored cookies—chocolate walnut drops frosted in cocoa butter cream icing and vanilla ones with lemon frosting. All the cousins coveted the chocolate ones, so there were dozens of them. There were my father's favorites that

had a thick crust of toasted sesame seeds coating them—
vanilla fingers that had a somewhat dry consistency and even
more anisette flavoring than the others.

"Any seed cookies?" my father would ask, meaning the
sesame ones.

His favorites were always there, and I passed them to him.

I liked the bow ties of light fried dough, which were
sprinkled with powdered sugar and had the slightest taste of
oranges and almonds. There were also miniature cheesecakes
and something called red velvet cake, which was burgundy
red inside, but tasted like chocolate.

"My neighbor knows the pastry chef at a New York
restaurant that's famous for this kind of cake. That's where
the recipe comes from," my aunt Anna said proudly.

All of this food served simply because it was Sunday, and
on Sunday the family visited.

When she wasn't serving us, my grandmother stood next
to the stove, watching the other things that were cooking—
roasted potatoes, macaroni and gravy, and sometimes
bracciole or baccala—salted cod in tomato sauce— roast
chicken, or a leg of lamb in the oven.

In Milford with my father's family, in addition to the band
of cousins to run with after eating all that food, we had my
grandmother's stories. She liked to tell us about what life was
like for her as a young girl. I remember only one of her
stories in any detail.

"When I was little," she began, "we didn't have a library to
go to."

"How could you read any books then?" I asked.

"Many people bought or rented books from peddlers,"
she explained. She settled me on the floor at her feet. She
dramatized all the answers to my questions.

"Let me tell you," she said. She gently, almost inaudibly,
clicked her tongue against the roof of her mouth, the way she
would when she was beginning her story—or whenever there
was a pause in the action and the scene was about to change.

This wasn't a tick, but it was more like punctuation, when she did this I knew that she had a good story to tell. It was a nearly imperceptible sound, but my sisters and brother, my cousins and I, all waited for it after she would begin.

"I'd wait all day, when I knew the peddler was coming," she said.

The room was perfectly silent as we waited to hear her strange story of the way she would get books.

"By and by, I'd hear the wheels of his cart. I'd hear the feet of his horse clomping in the road."

"Didn't he have a car?" one cousin wanted to know, and my grandmother laughed, and said, "No, he didn't have a car."

"I would rather have a horse than a car," another cousin said.

"I waited, listening until I was sure," our grandmother went on. "Until I heard him call, 'Books! Books!' he called. Then I ran down the stairs and out the door."

When she told this story I used to picture her jumping down to the bottom landing of her back hall stairs, a little girl of ten, like me.

"'Hurry before he goes,' my mother called out to me from the upstairs doorway!"

When my grandmother brought the books back from the peddler she read them aloud, first in English, and then she translated them into her mother's Sicilian dialect for her.

"While I read the books, my mother stirred a pot of tomatoes. She strained cheese, kneaded dough for bread, checked the oven temperature. I kept reading."

"Did you read in bed?" I asked. My mother used to catch me with a book and a flashlight under the covers, reading, and she would warn me, saying, *You'll ruin your eyes!*

"By and by," my grandmother said—and she clicked her tongue again, ever so slightly, this time, sounding the bell of disappointment. "The stories had to be put away. The others came home. There were so many children—so many things to do to help—dry their tears, wash their hands and faces.

They were hungry and they teased each other." At this my grandmother turned to Peg and Kate and me, as if she knew the mischief we made at home.

Did my grandmother want to escape the house and her brothers and sisters sometimes, to read or to write a story of her own maybe? Did she hide the books from them in a drawer, where none of the others would look? Did she get up at night when the house was dark and quiet, as I have so often, so that she could peacefully read?

I was in love with the way my grandmother dignified words, and I loved watching her hands, how they moved as she spoke, like small birds in the air around her chair.

My grandmother read for her mother. I would read for my father. From the time I was very young—as young as ten, I believe—I read bills and business letters for him, and sometimes the mixing instructions on the huge bag of Portland cement. When I read the gauge on the boiler I thought, *am I doing it wrong?* I grew afraid of fire or a flood, or some other kind of trouble coming to our house. I learned to read the fuse box whenever the electricity went out, because the wiring in the house was outdated; the fuses would blow because circuits were easily overloaded, with too many appliances running at once in our apartment and the ones above and below us.

I would climb down the cellar stairs into the pitch black with my father—if he were home when this situation arose— the two of us lost in the dark. The leaves on the weed trees growing close to the foundation at the windows, would have blocked out any daylight that might have left. Whether at dusk or later at night, in the darkest reaches of the house, I helped find the source of trouble.

"Over here," my father used to direct me. "This wall," he'd say, feeling for the metal box and finding it, swinging open its door, checking by touch to see if all the glass cylinders were in place.

Then he'd shine a flashlight he had with him—for me.

I could see. I read the darkness, the sign that one of the fuses was burned out.

"They mustn't have light downstairs either," my father said once about the tenants' apartment. "That one that's blown is the main fuse. It feeds the whole house."

I had not realized that night that my father didn't know that there wasn't any light at all in the back hall, not even a little seeping out through the keyhole of the apartment, or underneath the kitchen door as we'd passed by on our way to the cellar. He had kept the flashlight in his pocket until we were at the fuse box. I learned along with him, how to get by in the dark.

My father unscrewed the old fuse and put it into his pocket each time I identified a spent one; then he would replace it with a new one.

The rooms of the house that had been in utter darkness, would light up again.

Cousins were wonderful, I would think, once it got dark and my mother began the forty minute or so drive back home to the city from Milford, cruising along in the Mercury past Lake Ripple. It was the same road my father had driven years before, when he went to the city to take her out dancing.

For the first five miles or so out of Milford, I felt I had no worries. An afternoon of laughing and playing hard had left me carefree. Having cousins was a lot like having friends. Peg and I laughed louder than usual, both of us overtired, recalling silly things that had happened to us during the afternoon. My mother and father put up with our silliness until we got out of control, laughing so hard that the radio playing Frank Sinatra singing "Blue Moon," a song my father liked so much, could hardly be heard above our laughter. My father had been singing along with it and had to stop to reprimand us. Both he and my mother eventually lost patience when we got like this in the car.

The chickens got out of their coop one afternoon, and they went running in my grandfather's garden. It took the effort of all the cousins to herd them out of the rows of tomatoes and down the path back to their little house.

"How did they get out?" my father wanted to know, when we reported the event.

"They walked out," I said.

This set me off—and Peg, too. We laughed even more at the idea of chickens walking rather than scooting as they do.

"I mean," my father said, mad at my wisecrack, "who let them out?"

When we finally stopped laughing about the chickens, and it was quiet except for the static of the lost radio station, I related what I thought was the funniest thing that had happened that afternoon. It was difficult to tell it, I was laughing so hard.

No cousin was ever left out. We played games that didn't require much skill, so that everyone could be included, regardless of our different ages.

"Well, first we played hide and seek. Then we played Red Rover."

"Didn't I tell you not to play that Red Rover game, before someone breaks her neck?" my mother said. She thought the older boys played roughly.

"Yes, you did," I answered. "Anyway, while we were playing Red Rover, someone said, *Where's Jeff?* We didn't see him, so we gave up the game and we all went in different directions, looking for him."

Jeff was one of the younger cousins playing that afternoon.

"Dear Blessed God in heaven!" my mother said.

"We did find him. But he was lost for a while."

"Well, where was he?" my father wanted to know.

"Guess," I said.

"Oh, come on, now. Get on with it," my mother said.

"No, guess, " I said.

"So, tell me," my father said. "Where was Jeff anyway?"

"Stuck on hide and seek," I told him.

Peg started laughing hysterically, yelping really.

"He was sitting in the back yard next door—in the garden on a stone bench near the flowers, just waiting for us to find him. We couldn't see him from where we were."

"Didn't anyone yell *ollie-ollie-umfrie* my father wanted to know.

Peg and I laughed heartily hearing my father say that—*ollie-ollie-umfrie*.

One night, one of our stories had distracted my mother. She almost missed a red light as we entered the center of Grafton. She slammed on the brake, and I hit my head against the window.

"See," she said. "One of these days you kids will cause an accident."

Somehow Kate and Jack slept through all of this; the motion of the car would conk them out by the time we were just a few miles out of Milford.

"Enough," my father said. "Sit back now, before you get hurt."

Sunday was over. He began one his talks. It was always the same things he talked about when we were trapped in the car with him, and he made the most of it, going on and on the rest of the ride home, the twelve or however many miles we had left to go. He was a good talker. I could tell that he meant what he said, that it came straight from his heart.

"You kids don't know how lucky you are," he'd say, starting out.

"We do," Peg and I would say in unison, hoping that if we agreed with him he wouldn't go on with his lecture. But we meant it, too. On Sundays we really did feel lucky.

"Have you ever considered all you have in life?" he'd ask us.

We knew he didn't want us to answer him—that he wanted to list everything for us, to recount all the things we had that he didn't have, when he was growing up. Even if we did say what we were thinking, as we had tried one time when he'd given this talk, even if we went on to list every good thing we could remember, every gift we'd ever been given, he would, we knew, find more that we had not realized. He was trying, he would say, to make an impression on us.

From the speeches he gave us those nights, I was left with the message that everything good could be taken away, and without any warning. I think now, that my father was also lamenting the loss of his former life, of leaving Milford, not having his large family all around him. If he ever thought of moving back though, he never said so. There he wouldn't have had the opportunity to be much more than a blind man from a blind family, and surely he must have known that. Going back each week must have given my father something to push against, our trips were a constant reminder of the life he might have lost, had he stayed. Taking us to Milford each week was a way for him to gauge his progress, to measure just how far he had come from that parochial world. He was showing them as well, that he was proud to be raising his own children to be curious about the wider world, to want to know things. We'd hear an aunt gasp when one of us used what she thought was a fifty-cent word, or if we explained something we'd learned that she didn't know, or when we talked about a museum or concert we'd been to with our other grandfather. We wouldn't understand their surprise or what they meant when they expressed it, "Marone, this one's so smart!" But without those visits, I would have been limited as well, thinking of my reaction to those comments. I would shrug hearing them, not knowing what was meant, thinking: that's not smart—doesn't everyone know that? Yes, by taking us there he showed us, too, the same thing that his speeches were meant to teach us—that we were never to take for granted what we had, that we were not to limit ourselves, and inherent in this advice was the warning that, if we did, the future would be limited for us, just as it might have been for him.

"With all you have," my father said in the car on those rides home from Milford, "you should be the best in everything."

I wondered then if he meant that being the best was a way of keeping what you had from going away.

He repeated those words like a refrain, after each new thing he talked about.

"With all you have, you should be the best in everything."

Memorial Days

SATURDAY JUNE 5, 1993

As it turned out, the June 5, 1993, edition of the *Boston Globe* featured in its limited obituary space, the life of a venture capitalist. My father was given the ordinary space of a death notice.

"A venture capitalist? How do you like that?" I said to Mark, returning from the front steps with the newspaper in hand, open to the obituary page. "He was upstaged by a venture capitalist. Perfect."

To their credit, the *Worcester Telegram & Gazette* printed the obituary verbatim, and the *Milford Daily News* rewrote it, recognizing my father's accomplishments as only a small town newspaper of a tightly knit Italian-American community would, in celebrating the achievements of one of their own. In the Milford headline my father was a "state policy advisor on affairs of the blind." He was that, although never lauded in life in exactly that way for his efforts as a member of various committees and task forces of the Massachusetts Commission for the Blind. He fought ferociously for his own rights as a businessman and for others who were blind. He was wonderful at debating issues. "He just likes to hear the sound of his own voice," my mother used to say about this talent of his. His speaking skills had been cultivated when he'd been in a rehabilitation program and had been encouraged to join Toastmasters, giving extemporaneous speeches to the other members at restaurants after dinner.

When I read the obituary headline in the Milford paper, tears welled up in my eyes. In the details of his life he was again offering a sense of possibility. I was struck first by the irony that he would be honored in this way in his hometown. Then, another realization came: only in death had my father

169

achieved what he set out to do in his family, in his hometown—to make public what no one would talk about.

What I wanted that morning was contact with people who knew my father. I started by visiting the YMCA in Central Square. I wanted to inform the staff of funeral plans. I was prepared to learn that the people at the Y who knew my father might not have been aware of his death unless someone had come upon the notice in the *Globe* by chance. I didn't think that my mother or anyone else had called. I couldn't help wondering though, what the staff and residents had thought when my father didn't return to his room as usual on Thursday night. Maybe they joked lightheartedly that he must have had a date. We often invited my father to join us for dinner, so they could have thought, *He's having dinner with his daughter and her family*—and then maybe they never noticed when he did not return later in the evening. Or they might have worried, like I did, that he hadn't been himself in the days leading up to that night, and so, when he didn't show up they were concerned for his well being. If they stopped to think they would have considered that anything at all could have happened to him, since he travelled back from work using public transportation and walked with a cane and not a dog to guide him.

My friend Joan, who offered to drive, parked her car outside the building. As she did, it dawned on me that the taxi driver who would pick up my father every morning at dawn outside the residence on Massachusetts Avenue in Cambridge, to take him to work in Boston, might not know either that my father was gone. I imagined the cabbie pulling up to the curb on Friday morning, the day after he died, and not seeing my father waiting on the steps, he might have wondered, "Where is John?" How long did the driver wait? Did he leave finally for a call coming in over the radio, a fare too good to pass up? I wanted to think that he parked his taxi and went inside asking at the desk, "Can someone call John and see what's up with him?" I wondered if, as the driver waited, he remembered something my father had said about feeling tired or sick the day before, or if he had suspected on his own when he last saw him the morning he died, that my father didn't look well, was weak, or in some pain when he got into his taxi for the early morning ride over the Longfellow Bridge across the Charles River. Or maybe he was fooled—just as I had been when I talked to my father the night before on the telephone—that everything was hunky dory. I didn't know the man's name—only that he'd been his regular driver for years. I chastised myself for not knowing even the cab company he worked for—Ambassador Brattle? Metro? Yellow? Green? I didn't know, but I *should* have. Two years earlier, when Gianni had been just six months old, my father had arranged for this same cabbie to drive my family to Logan airport; we were traveling to California on a flight that left Logan in the middle of the night. I remembered the man was a little heavy, a regular guy, Italian-American, too, I thought. He had been impressed he told us, by my father's determination and amazed at his ability to get around and to run a business. *You see a guy like that, able to do all that, and it makes you think about all the lazy good-for-nothings feeling sorry for themselves*, he told us, as he breezed through the Callahan tunnel.

I had brought a copy of the *Worcester Telegram* obituary to the Y, expecting that the details of my father's life would surprise everyone on staff who knew him. He kept his other life secret, causing speculation about where he went on weekends—or even during the day perhaps—a mystery, which I believe he cultivated and enjoyed. I imagined the shock, too, of the other residents who knew him as John, the man who sometimes brought them snacks from his cafeteria or leftover chicken salad sandwiches from family parties, a friend who was pleasant and kind to them and liked to talk.

I introduced myself to the man at the desk. He seemed to have known already. Maybe my mother had called after all.

"I've made a copy of the obituary. I thought you might find it interesting. It's got the calling hours and the time of the funeral. It's in Worcester, not Boston, so I don't know if anyone will be able to go. I just thought I'd bring it by."

I was rambling, and the young, good-looking man interrupted me, kindly.

"Some of the guys were asking about it. This is good. Thanks. They wanted to know," he said.

By "the guys," I understood he meant the other residents.

Neither of us knew what else to say for a second, but he fell into his staff role and I was grateful.

"I'll get you the key so you can clean out his room."

"I'd rather wait until next week, after the funeral. We have so many things still to do. That is, if it's okay with you?"

I didn't even consider that someone else might have wanted to rent the room. I didn't know how often he paid rent—was it by the week or the month?—and whether waiting until the following week would mean his things would remain in the room beyond the date for which he'd paid rent. I was concerned only with my own well being at that moment: I would need to have Mark with me when I saw the room at the Y where my father had spent his weeknights for how many years? Being a woman I was never allowed upstairs, and on a few occasions—when my father needed help carrying something—a new window fan in the heat of summer, or a package of whatever he'd bought from a supplier back home at a better price than he could have had it for in Boston—it was Mark who carried it upstairs for him. All he ever said to me about the place was that *It was like you'd expect, like a dorm room kind of,* but I never did believe that.

"It's fine to wait," the desk clerk said kindly.

Joan and I headed then to the sprawling Massachusetts General Hospital to retrieve my father's personal effects. What strange language to use to describe what a person has in his pockets when hauled off in an ambulance. I would like to think of the effects my father left, in terms less material. He lived like a monk in his room at the Y all week, and he gave away everything he earned.

I associated Massachusetts General with a great deal of family history, because the hospital's many buildings surrounded Massachusetts Eye and Ear Infirmary, where my father's retina problem had first been diagnosed, where he faced the prognosis of blindness, where my sister Peg had been diagnosed, and where I had been for eye examinations some thirty years earlier. I suppose it was fitting then, that my father's lifeless body would be brought to this place, I thought.

The clothes my father was wearing when he was brought in were not in the bag of his belongings I was given—his white uniform, his shoes, and the chef's hat that always reminded me of the paper newsprint hats my grandfather used to make for me when I was a young kid. I supposed there wasn't any use having those things.

There was no money either, although I had expected he would have had money in his pockets, collapsing in the early afternoon as he did. Most of his business was transacted during the earlier part of the day. He had collapsed after the morning arrivals, coffee breaks, and lunches—the mainstay of his kind of business. Could it have been that in his last days he was making absolutely no money at the newsstand? Had he just paid out the supplier of a large order? He never carried a wallet: I think he believed that it would make him a victim. A wallet was "a billfold" to him, not a place for carrying identification, credit cards, or pictures of your children and grandchildren. I knew from having worked with him that his method with money was to keep in the drawer only what he needed in order make small change. At the end of the day he transferred that and what he'd weeded out as the day went on, into a crumpled up brown lunch bag—crumpled up, I think, because he used the same one over and over again. Either he was the original recycler or it was one item in his bag of tricks containing clever disguises.

Keeping too many bills—and particularly, large denominations—in plain view in the cash drawer, only invited trouble; my father knew from experience that a junkie had no conscience and would steal from a blind man as well as anyone, so he regularly removed cash from the drawer, organizing it in his pocket according to various folding techniques—his own money origami to indicate fives, tens, twenties—in order not to make a mistake if called upon by a customer who needed change, or to pay a delivery man for an order. I watched him do this, calling on me or holding up a bill before a line of customers, saying, "What's this? And this? This one?" And then he'd do some fast folding and arranging and stuff the newly fattened or dwindling wad of money back into his pocket.

Thinking about this system of his, I could not help but remember the time I'd encountered my father, coming home on the train from work one evening. It was 1990 and at the time I was teaching at New England Medical Center in Boston. At Washington Street Station/Downtown Crossing, I had to change from the Orange to the Red Line, and as it turned out that day I boarded the same car of the same train my father was on, returning to the Cambridge Y from his cafeteria.

I knew the train was coming into the station by the difference I heard in sound as the conductor began to brake. I knew it was time to get off, registering it unconsciously, and I stood up. I was the first in our car on my feet, heading to the door—even though the train was still in the tunnel. Then, I was first off the train, meeting the five o'clock rush-hour crowd head on, pushing my way past the knot of old people, school kids, and suits who edged up to the door to enter the train.

I hustled, weaving in and out and around people to get to the stairway leading to the lower platform, to make my Red Line connection. I flew down the stairs, jumping the last two. I avoided the obstacle course of musicians and their instrument cases full of spare change and recordings for sale. The stairway ended at the open first car of the train. I saw the conductor sticking his head out of his compartment, ready to close the door, and I was in before he did, on my way to Central Square.

When I looked up, I saw my father. He was standing right in front of me, the last person I would have expected to meet by chance. What were the odds of it? He spooked me.

"Well, hello," I said.

Of course he knew my voice.

"Ree." He smiled, as if he'd been expecting me.

He was coming from work that evening on the train headed over the Charles River on Longfellow Bridge from Boston into Cambridge, being at the time, the operator of the *Harbor Mist* cafeteria, which served the U.S. Coast Guard Headquarters building on the Northern Avenue waterfront. Those who worked there and in other waterfront businesses, salesmen making their rounds, mail carriers, occasionally tourists as well, ate breakfast and lunch or had coffee or a snack at my dad's cafeteria. Calling it that name—*Harbor Mist*—was his idea, for the fact of its location and the sometimes damp and foggy coastal weather—and of course, for the fact of his own blindness. When I'd call him on the phone there he would answer, "*Harbor Mist*. Pea soup here."

"There's a seat behind you. Why don't you sit?" I said, when the train gave a jolt.

I suspected I was not the first person to have offered him a seat since he'd boarded one stop before at South Station. Realizing that he was blind, seeing his cane, people were generally willing to give up their seats on a rush hour train, but he politely declined.

"I'm fine. I'll stand. You sit."

"Naw, I don't want to sit. You sit," he said, resisting my offer as well.

"No, that's okay. I'm fine."

I would have loved to sit, but I wanted to talk to him more than I wanted to sit, and if I sat down, it would have separated us. He was happy when we talked, and I enjoyed talking with him as well. I was tired after teaching, but I wasn't on my way home yet. I was going to my night job. I was hungry. I was pregnant. But I knew that my father had awakened at four a.m., and I knew he rarely sat down all day. He was not in the best of health, and was nearly thirty years older than I was. But he looked well—strong, and you'd think—healthy, though a little tired. He wasn't going home to Worcester, to a good dinner, a wife and a comfortable home until the weekend. He was headed to a room at the Cambridge Y, his *home* during the workweek. My mother didn't want to move.

"Where did you get those duds?" I teased him.

I was talking too loudly. A very proper-looking woman gave me the eye. I was insulting a blind man, she thought probably. She knew he was blind because he was carrying his scratched and dented metal cane, which he held like a shepherd's staff.

"What do you mean?" my father asked, his eyes feigning innocence.

"What you're wearing," I said, losing patience.

"What do you mean, what I'm wearing?"

He looked defiant then, rather than perplexed. He knew full well what was wrong with what he was wearing. It was a costume he had on, a disguise.

What people saw of my father on a rush-hour train was the way he survived in the big city. He looked as if he were wearing clothes that came straight out of the laundry bag— un-ironed clothes. His charcoal grey pants were some kind of wool and synthetic blend, and their rough surface gave the impression that the slacks had been washed instead of dry cleaned.

"You have good clothes," I said. "What are you doing dressing like this in public?"

"Do you know what I paid for these pants when I bought them? These pants are from Shacks," he said, referring to a men's clothing store in Worcester. "And this is an Arrow shirt I've got on," he smirked.

"They've seen better days," I said.

The people sitting along the train bench facing us looked uncomfortable. I could tell they were, as they looked up at us hovering above them and talking. Hearing our conversation they resettled themselves in their seats after exchanging glances and raised eyebrows. They didn't know he was my father. What did they think? They saw me as a professional, I suppose. I could have been a lawyer, dressed as I was: nice suit, good shoes, and Coach bag. My brother Jack once told me that I looked like I worked for IBM, when he met me for dinner one day after work. I was a writer then, too, but I had a day job as a corporate trainer, one who taught English to medical and bank employees. I had a night job, too, creating a program to help adults learn to read and write—and I was headed there on that train. I watched the other passengers watching my father and me. I had watched people watch us my whole life. Seeing us on the train together that evening, did they think that I was a lawyer harassing a homeless blind man?

"So what have you got in the bag, anyway?" I asked quieter and more politely.

My father had the brown wrinkled and crumpled shopping bag rolled up and tucked under his arm. I knew what was in the bag, although no one on the train would have guessed. I was provoking him—a low blow, I knew. He was secretly afraid that someone would find out that the bag was stuffed with cash. I hadn't meant to scare him; I just wanted him to stop taking the risk; that is why I confronted him. Still, that he carried money that way, "in this day and age," as my mother would have said, was comical. And he knew it. We shared the joke.

"My snacks," he said, smiling impishly. "Peggy Lawton's."

He was referring to the brownies he sold at his cafeteria. He wanted everyone on the train to think that it was his lunch he had in the bag. He was carting the cash proceeds from his restaurant—his day's earnings—back and forth on the train, and on Fridays he took the whole week's receipts home, stuffed in his suitcase on the Peter Pan bus from Boston to

Worcester. He would have rather been a hero, lose his money being robbed at gunpoint, than have had to pay someone to make bank deposits and still have to worry about whether he was being taken advantage of or not. He didn't have time to go to the bank himself, he said. So he carried "a big lunch" instead.

My father's concern with money wasn't greed. The only fear he seemed to have kept alive, all the years from the time he was certain that he was losing his sight some forty years before, was the worry that he wouldn't be able to provide for the care of his family and his own simple needs. He wanted next to nothing for himself: good comfortable shoes, a Sunday suit with clean shirts, and an occasional meal at a nice restaurant to celebrate a family event or birthday. And if going in disguise, looking destitute was what he had to do to make sure he had those things, so be it. He put his pride in his pocket, he said. It was his little joke on the world of the sighted.

My father and I were the first to move toward the door as the train approached Central Square Station. We had both heard it—the change in sound—registering it unconsciously and automatically, as always. Neither of us needed to see where we were. We simply reached out and grabbed the metal pole, just as we were about to feel the jolt as the train braked. We knew it signaled our arrival. We knew where we were at all times. My father gently took my arm, his left hand on my right elbow, like a key that moved me forward, propelled us both up the stairs and outside to the street.

The woman who worked for the hospital handed me a sandwich-sized plastic bag with my father's name on it. Inside there was a small piece of cardboard, folded in half—the grey cardboard coated with shiny white paper on one side was cracked and peeling from having been folded in many different ways over time. It appeared to be a section of a box top, perhaps one that had held candy or chips. I knew immediately what this piece of cardboard had to do with my father: it was his filing system for money, the one he kept in his pocket instead of a wallet. It was literally his billfold, although I doubt anyone would have recognized it as such, the cardboard meant to fool a pickpocket interested only in cash.

My father would put the cardboard around the highest denominations of bills and those he started out with at the beginning of the day, his petty cash. Also, on a day when he planned to pay off a large supplier—the Coca-Cola salesman, for example—he would fold up a one hundred dollar bill until it was only about the size of a square nickel, then he'd fold the cardboard over it and add a few twenties he had rolled up together pencil thin, folding the cardboard over them, too, and on and on that way, putting a rubber band around the whole thing—so that those bills would be separated from any of the proceeds he would weed out of the cash drawer in the course of a work day.

I was at first saddened by this piece of cardboard I found in the plastic bag given to me by the hospital employee. But then something like pride rose up in me, and I found that I had the irresistible urge to tell the woman, to explain what the cardboard was, to tell her about my father. My reason for doing so was not that she had expressed any interest or curiosity whatsoever. She had assumed the appropriately detached attitude in handing over the little bag of my father's personal effects. She had been trained to do this, yet when I began to talk she was obviously interested—or maybe worried about me.

The woman came out from behind the desk counter into the reception area where Joan and I had been waiting.

"He was blind," I said, suddenly overcome by the fact that my father needed to do things like this, to rig up these kinds of devices in order to remain independent and inconspicuous.

"Oh, I'm so sorry," the woman said.

At that moment I recalled an incident once, when I'd been walking on a quiet street near my aunt's Maine cottage. As I was passing a house near the corner of Ivy Avenue, a woman came running out, down the steps to the road to tell me—a passerby, a stranger— that her father had just died. I was that woman now, telling the office worker that my father was blind. I couldn't stop myself; something like pride made me want to defend my father from pity even in death. I wanted to resist what he resisted. I didn't realize that the woman meant her sympathy for me, that maybe she hadn't been saying that she was sorry he was blind.

"Do you know what he used this for?"

The woman came closer to get a look at the cardboard or probably to make sure that I was all right. It was just a ragged piece of cardboard I had her looking at, not a Cartier watch the EMTs had removed from my father's wrist.

Rest, this woman needs rest, the clerk was probably thinking. She was as stumped as anyone might be in this situation. "It looks like an old piece of cardboard," she said.

"He used it to separate money in his pocket," I said.

The woman titled her head and briefly closed her eyes, when I said this, as if she were trying to imagine how the cardboard might help do that. "Oh wasn't that clever," she said, when I demonstrated.

Clever was a word people frequently used when considering the way my father negotiated the world. It never felt quite right, for I thought it had the connotation of dishonesty. Highly organized, creative, or efficient would have been better words to use to describe his methods. His trick, if he had one, was to try to make people who had anything to do with him, forget that he was blind.

"Was there any money in the safe?" I asked, suddenly aware of what seemed to be missing.

"Maybe I missed something. Let me take another look," she said.

This is what I thought when she returned to say, "I'm sorry. That's all that's in there under that name." I thought: he was robbed—either before he collapsed, and that maybe brought on the stroke or heart attack—or after he collapsed,

by whomever found him or someone who'd administered to
him. I just didn't know.

I thanked the woman and Joan and I left the office.

Twelve

BEAUTIFUL (1961)

I heard my mother calling me, but I resisted leaving my cozy bed. She was going out in what seemed to be the middle of the night, going across town to drive my father home from work. She was afraid to go off and leave us all sleeping, so before she left she made sure that I was wide awake, capable of watching over the house and my sisters and brother. This sentry duty routinely fell to me, since I was the oldest.

"You have to get up. What if there's a fire?"

Once I was awake and out of bed, I didn't really mind.

My father's shift ended at eleven, and I was in charge until he and my mother returned. I understood that it was important to have someone in charge, although I wasn't sure that I would know what to do, if anything like a fire ever did happen. I don't remember my mother ever giving me instructions. Perhaps she didn't want to frighten me, or she figured that there was little chance of any problem occurring in the short time that she would be gone. I never thought to ask what I should do either, not until after she left; then, I worried.

During the day these night watches didn't come to mind. I didn't think of them as being at all strange or troubling. I didn't consider that I was tired at school because of them. I knew that my mother was helping my father, making sure he arrived home safely and didn't have a long walk home when he was tired after working—and I knew that I had to help, too. Besides, I looked forward to seeing my father and being rewarded when they returned. Always hungry after work, my father would bring home a pizza, or he'd have my mother stop at Widoff's Jewish bakery on Water Street for bread fresh out of the oven, still warm.

In the years after my father had given up his Packard and stopped driving forever, and before my mother began to drive and to feel comfortable leaving me on night watch, I used to lie awake in bed, visualizing my father as he walked home alone from work. I thought he must have listened hard, maybe imagining sounds or mistaking some ordinary rustling of papers or fallen leaves in a doorway for some threat, just as he had the night my brother Jack was born, the night I'd found he'd barricaded the back door to the apartment when he came home from work.

Imagining threats is what I did, too, on those nights while I waited for my parents to return home near midnight. The television was on so that I had company, and it was tuned in to the *Jack Paar Show*. I stretched out on the couch, listening beyond the voice of Jack Paar and his guests talking. I heard the innocent slapping of a window shade in the breeze, and it startled me. My brother Jack suddenly began talking in his sleep and I heard him, although he was a couple of rooms away. Katie, asleep in the next room in the bed beside Peg's sometimes let out a six-year-old's cry of "Help!" during a dream she was having. And one night Peg woke up, calling for Mum, and once she found out that she wasn't in the house, it set off her fear. I didn't know what it was like to be in a fire, but it sure was awful being with Peg when she was afraid. She couldn't go back to sleep. She wouldn't believe that our mother was coming back, wouldn't stay in bed. She got up and sat next to me on the couch the whole time she was gone.

"What are you doing up?" our mother asked when she walked in the door and saw her sitting with me.

"I was scared," Peg told her.

"Oh, for heaven's sake! What did you think? That the bogeyman was going to come to get you?"

Peg did not tell her, and neither did I, that she thought that she was gone forever.

One night a June bug caught my attention when I noticed it bumping into the ceiling. I watched it carefully, reminded of *The Outer Limits* television program, of one show in which an ordinary bug—a beetle, a mosquito or some other common insect—became monstrous in size and terrorized a whole town. The June bug though, was only interested in trying to push itself up and out, was used to the sky as its only limit. It didn't like being trapped inside the house. It wouldn't accept it. It went again and again up against the ceiling, clicking its wings as it circled the plaster medallion, where a light fixture had once hung.

"Okay now, get to bed," my mother said just seconds after she and my father came in the door.

I ran to my father and he stooped down to my height and put his cheek out for a kiss.

"Here, let me put this down," he said, sliding the pizza box onto the kitchen table and turning back to pick me up in his arms.

"She's too big for that," my mother said. "She needs to get to bed."

"In a minute, Mame. Let me see her. Let her come have something to eat. Are you hungry?" he asked, turning back to me.

It was not only hunger for food that I had. The biggest reward was seeing my father after work. When I got out of bed in the morning, he was generally sleeping—I knew not to wake him so he could rest up for his shift; then, when I returned from school in the afternoon, he had already left for work. There were times, too, when he was working back-to-back shifts, which meant leaving before I got up in order to be at work for the shift that started at seven a.m. In either case, if I were not awake doing night watch when my mother went out to pick him up at work, I might not have been able to see him until he was home on the weekend. That is the way it was for Peg, Kate, and Jack, who generally missed these midnight snacks with him, although he would always call during his supper break to say "hello" to everyone. Once in a while my mother—probably at her wit's end, alone with the four of us at dinnertime—would drive us to his

workplace, and he would come out into the yard to see us.
We'd stand talking to him through the chain link fence.
Although allowed to leave the machine shop in good weather,
he and the other workers were required to stay on the
property behind the fence, not venture even onto the
sidewalk, where we'd stand and he would talk to us from the
other side, and even kiss us goodbye through an opening.

The scorched cheese of the pizza was delicious I thought,
and the hot bulkie rolls smeared with butter melted in my
mouth. He was in a good mood. He seemed to be happy to
be home and wide-awake, even after working two long shifts.
He asked me about school and whether I had been behaving
for my mother, helping her out when she needed me.

My father tried giving my mother a bite of pizza. She
turned her head away, but he continued to hold it out to her.
"Here, have a piece. Go on." The slice of pizza collapsed in
his hand.

"I don't want any of that spicy stuff. I don't know how
you two sleep after eating like this at this hour."

But I didn't have any trouble sleeping. When I went back
to bed, I was content and slept soundly the rest of the night.

*

"Baby fine," my mother complained, as each silky lock of
my fine hair slipped out of her fingers again and again. She
was trying to make pin curls of it.

"Ow! You're hurting me!" I protested, as she secured a
bobby pin, jabbing at my scalp with it, when she did.

"It wouldn't hurt so much if you would just sit still and
stop wiggling all over the place."

"But I can't sit still when you're hurting me," I pleaded.

"Oh, stop it," she said. "You'd think I was murdering you
or something. Sometimes, you know, you have to suffer to be
beautiful." She laughed.

"I don't care about being beautiful," I lied, running off to
my room, slamming the door behind me.

We went through this argument every Saturday evening, when my mother tried to tame my hair so that it would look nice for church the next morning. The rest of the week it was wild, tempting Sister at school to threaten to take the scissors to it in class—*Get that hair back off your face*—and inspiring some of my classmates to say that I looked like a witch. I did have an abundance of electricity in my hair, and sometimes it stood straight out. I thought it looked more like fluff than hair. My grandmother rummaged through her bureau drawers looking for hair combs and barrettes, to get the curls off my face. *You look like the wild woman of Borneo*, she always said, seeing me standing at her door when she opened it to let me in for a visit. I was no longer the sweet little girl to whom she'd often recited a teasing poem, pretending it was about me. *There was a little girl/ who had a little curl/ right in the middle of her forehead/ And when she was good...*

In the bedroom I shared with my sisters—after one of these bouts— I kneeled on the floor, leaned on the windowsill, and looked out into the Sadowsky's yard next door. Mr. Sadowsky was a hunchback. He talked in a loud, angry-sounding voice all the time because he was deaf. Peg and I were scared of him. He drove like a madman, too, waking us up when he came home late on winter nights, when the neighborhood was in a deep freeze. He drove his un-shiny gray Rambler up our steep hill, turning into his icy driveway; often he had trouble making the incline, and we worried that he would crash over the high New England stone boundary wall and into our house. The wheels of his car spun on the ice and our hearts beat like crazy from the fear he stirred up in us.

I watched him that summer day. With his deformed posture, he looked like an old pigeon as he went around his yard, bending every now and then to pickup stray candy wrappers and other litter. He had no wife and no daughters, only five sons. My mother told me that she thought the boys were ruined for life because their father had put them in an orphanage after their mother died. As hard as I tried I couldn't imagine a girl or a woman living in their family. I didn't know the Sadowsky boys, except Billy, who was just a little older than I was. My sisters and I had been warned to stay away from them. "They all have a wild streak," my mother said.

It was true: from the time they were very young, each of them began to threaten to leave home, whenever their father was angry. Even when he was just talking he sounded like he was yelling. Because he did not hear well, he missed the curses his boys swore against him, and the further misfortunes they wished upon him. He missed, too, their detailed plans for moving to Florida or joining the Navy after they quit school. They all quit as soon as they turned sixteen.

I knew that my father had quit school at sixteen because his trouble seeing presented too many problems. After he did, his brother Tom had tried to quit as well. I had heard the story about that. My father made him go back because he didn't think he had enough reason to leave, his eyes not nearly as bad as my father's were then.

I didn't wonder if any of the Sadowsky boys had reason to quit, as my father had. I imagined they'd left school because they got into so much trouble they were expelled. Billy would be sixteen soon, and I wondered where he was going to go. One of his brothers came home on leave from the Navy, wearing dress whites. That day I'd watched him take his duffle out of the taxi that pulled up in front of the house. I was in awe, thinking how much he must have seen of the world.

The boys next door were always accusing each of other of starting fights, yelling angrily because one or the other of them had taken something that didn't belong to him. It was a common thing when they were all living at home that I would see one brother fighting another out behind the house, and a third flying so fast down the back hallway stairs after the other two, that he almost fell out the door to the yard. Once, I heard one of them yell to his fighting brother, "Give me that knife. You give me that knife."

When these things would happen, my mother would say, "It's a wonder someone isn't killed over there." She'd go out onto the upstairs porch and yell over to their yard. "You cut that out now, before I call someone."

We fought, too. We weren't necessarily any quieter about our arguments; however, we never resorted to knives or weapons. When we were yelling we usually stopped once we remembered the neighbors. *What must they think of the hollering going on at our house?* But not the Sadowsky boys—nothing stopped them, except their father—and he was generally not at home when they decided to act up.

"Those were their formative years they spent in the orphanage after their mother died," my own mother explained. When their father was back on his feet again, he decided to raise the boys himself, but by then, they were too wild to be tamed. It was her belief, she said, that Mr. Sadowsky had done the wrong thing, that he never should have taken them home from Nazareth School for Boys.

I didn't know how any father could give a child away for good, the way my mother thought that Mr. Sadowsky should have done with his boys. I thought of my own father, how happy he was to be with us when he was home from work.

My mother came to the bedroom door, opening it without first knocking. I ignored her and kept looking out the window. I watched Mr. Sadowsky pick up one last piece of litter in his yard. I knew that she had come into the bedroom to reprimand me for running away from her when she was trying to fix my hair. Standing in the room, looking out the window while waiting for an apology from me, she noticed Mr. Sadowsky going inside. It gave her inspiration.

"You think it's so bad living here. You don't know the meaning of bad. We haven't put *you* in any orphanage. No matter how bad things are."

I didn't answer her. I was tired of having to be perfect because we had troubles in our family. I wanted to forget them. I think now, that for my parents—particularly for my mother—if we behaved well and if our outward appearance did not call attention to itself--for example, if my hair were neatly styled for church—people might not notice the problems we had as a family. A bad appearance or behavior was a reflection of one's home life, and my mother was determined to uphold the dignity of her own upbringing, which she believed ought to transfer to the whole family and bring us respect. Her frequent admonition was full of nostalgia for her family's past. *We were refined and don't you forget that*, echoes in my memory. Our responsibility was to put out to the world that our troubles made us no less capable or important than anyone else, nor were they an excuse for failure of any kind. She tried to ingrain in us the idea that we were not to be dismissed and for that, I am grateful.

My father approached this in a more empathetic way, and if I could—if he was not working or otherwise occupied—I went to him when my feelings had been hurt. He knew what it was like to be looked down upon, and would share stories of his own adolescence, of being teased or excluded by other children, or of falling behind and becoming the butt of jokes when at dusk, walking home from school in winter, he could not keep up with the step or run of his classmates.

"Is that what you want? To go live in an orphanage, like the Sadowsky boys did?" my mother chided me that day.

I had watched old movies on television of children living in orphanages and being treated badly. The possibility frightened me, and I believe she knew it. Was this my mother's way of keeping me in line, or did she really imagine that alternative? Was she worrying that some day she and my father might not be able to provide for us?

I didn't want to be the queen, and Sister Margaret Bernard cast me in that role in our classroom play. I was to plead with the king to spare someone's life. Probably it was Joan of Arc, who was going to be burned at the stake or Thomas More who had been ordered beheaded. To tell the truth, I can't really remember how the play fit into history. I am sure it did though, for nothing we ever learned at St. Peter's was free of history—especially religious history.

Participating in class in this way—in a play—required that all my attention be focused on school. I would have no escape. I would be required to give up my daydreams about leaving home, school, Worcester. When I told my aunt that I had dreams of traveling, writing stories, and becoming a singer, she told me that I could do anything anyone else could, if I just put my mind to it. I had become accomplished at not being present in the moment, able to construct an elaborate escape into my thoughts and dreams. "Oh, she's gone again," my mother would say, when I sat in a trance in a busy room, resisting her questions.

If making me the queen in our classroom production was Sister's way of getting me out of my imagination and making me pay more attention in class, I figured, too, that she had another motive in mind, in giving me that part. I thought it was her way of making me fit in, a way of making me part of the group. I didn't think that I could fit in. I had become accustomed to the fact that I was not like all the rest. I knew different things about life than my classmates did. I never expected them to understand what it was like to have a father who was gradually losing his sight and would become blind. It didn't dawn on me that their families, too, might have had other kinds of troubles that were just as serious. We were all supposed to trust in God and pretend that we didn't have a worry in the world, so I never knew what anyone else suffered. But ours was not a wealthy parish, and most of the fathers I knew then, worked in factories just as mine did. The residents of Worcester's Main South neighborhood in the nineteen fifties and sixties still labored primarily contributing to the workforce of the manufacturing industry. Large Irish families predominated—lots of mouths to feed.

I remember feeling awkward up in front of the class, dressed in bright red—a heavy velvet cloak, a costume maybe borrowed from the Monsignor, or from last year's Santa at Denholm & McKay.

At the time I could not have known either, that this was just the first of several theatrical performances in which I would play parts that I suspect now were chosen just for me. At the time of this production I was nearly twelve and I had little or no confidence in the way I looked or in my ability to command attention. The good Sister, my teacher that year, must have thought that the part of the queen was made to order, perfect to help transform me into my opposite. In the roles I played later, the directors cast me in parts that, on the contrary, implicitly paralleled my situation. I was a child playing the part of the nurturing adult, always cast as "The Mother."

Katherine Murphy said, about my debut as Queen, "Sister must have given you the part because you're so beautiful."

She must be teasing me, I thought. I didn't believe that I was beautiful. In the summer my mother frequently remarked to my father, whose skin darkened more and more every day, "You look like an Ethiopian." The historical significance of her comment which I assume now was an oblique reference to the Italian conquest, escaped me then. I knew, nevertheless, that her remarks reflected bias and they hurt me, too, because she seemed to be saying that I looked like I belonged to someone somewhere else. Her comments exacerbated the normal adolescent discomfort about physical characteristics that I was already beginning to feel. My own skin was especially dark when I started a new school year in the fall, after being out in the sun all summer. My hair was fine and very curly—often unmanageable, and more so when the weather was humid, which turned it frizzy and wiry. I was skinny and my clothes were wrinkled. "They may not be ironed," my mother would tell me about my clothes when she ran out of time; permanent press fabrics were not yet popular. I outgrew my school uniform. "The waist is up around your ears," my mother said. I was growing like a weed, she said, and school uniforms were expensive. She called me "a long drink," and I thought of a tall glass of iced tea.

I told my father about Katherine teasing me, saying I was beautiful.

"She's just jealous," he said.

I didn't understand him. Why would *anyone* be jealous of me?

My father must have believed that I was beautiful, and that Katherine would have given anything to have the part I got. But these possibilities never crossed my mind. My father was always trying to build up my self-esteem, whenever he saw it waning.

Thirteen

THE WANDERER (1962)

The nuns were forever passing bones around the classroom, bragging about how special it was to have them because they would bring indulgences. The bones were holy relics—pieces of saints, bones from their bodies.

"Pass it," Sister would say, sending a relic up and down the rows of desks, so that we could benefit from holding the piece of saint in our hands.

"Where is it now?" she asked every once in a while, gauging its progress as it made its way around the classroom.

She didn't like the relic to stay too long with any one of us. She didn't have to worry about me. I had trouble even holding such a thing. The relic rested in the palm of my hand in its minuscule box. I watched it through its glass window. A relic was never more than a speck. A speck of bone—saint's bone, though, I would remind myself. So small I could hardly see it. It did not move. It seemed to have no magic. It gave me the creeps. That was the only power it had over me.

As I understood this practice then, indulgences meant we'd receive special blessings. Holding a relic and saying a prayer to that saint was supposed to bring you favors, like reducing the time it would take before you were allowed into heaven after you died. Only those souls that were in a state of grace would see God right away. The rest of us would have to wait in Purgatory. Purgatory was supposed to be just like heaven, only without God. How long we would have to wait depended upon the kind of life we lived, how good we were.

Indulgences were like money in the bank, Sister said. Of course, if we died with a mortal sin on our soul, then off to hell we went—no second chance—nothing, not even indulgences we might have stored up by praying over saint's bones, was going to help us. I used to think of the state of grace as just another part of the country—tiny, like Rhode Island, reserved only for chosen souls—or big, like Texas, because it was such an important place.

The more I heard about how to get to heaven, the more impossible that goal seemed. Living according to so many rules and regulations seemed impossible. Even thinking of sinning, we were told, was a sin. I couldn't imagine, for example, how I would ever keep on living without questioning what my mother told me to do. If I didn't complain, she would never let me out of her sight. I was sure that I would die of boredom then. If I didn't create excuses about school projects for which I needed to use the library downtown, or of having choir practice, I might not have been able to see my friends as often as I did.

It took us all by surprise the morning Sister brought a television into the classroom, so that we could watch John Glenn blast off. It was amazing—a television in the classroom. We realized the importance of the event.

This was the first of many history lessons taken straight from reality during my elementary and high school education. From my seat at St. Peter's I also watched television news programs and documentaries about the Civil Rights Movement, and the assassinations of President Kennedy, Martin Luther King, and Bobby Kennedy, and there were Vietnam, Watts, and Detroit.

I have something to show you. This is indestructible," Sister said, on that day that John Glenn was launched into space. She sounded the way she did whenever she had a saint's relic to show us.

But it wasn't a relic that she held out for us to see, although she treated it with the same kind reverence she would have attributed to it if it were a speck of saint's bone. What she had in her hand was a small square of shiny, silver grey fabric.

Sister explained that this little bit of fabric had special significance for us.

Absurd as it now seems, I remember thinking: maybe it came from the loincloth Christ had worn at his crucifixion. But I could tell that the color was wrong for it to have been that, which gave me another idea. Had it been snipped off the Virgin Mary's veil or dress? Although I knew that the Blessed Mother's outfit would have been closer in color to the remnant that was passed around that day, it would not have looked so shiny new. But we had been trained to see the religious significance in just about everything put forth by Sister.

"John Glenn's spacesuit is made from this material," she announced.

Everyone ooh-ed and ahhh-ed, and we all started up out of our seats to see it up close.

"Back to your seats. I'll pass it around," Sister instructed.

We wanted to know: *How did you get it, Sister? Did John Glenn send it to you?*

Sister smiled but she wouldn't answer us right away because we were yelling out, not raising our hands. Her smile made us think that she really might know John Glenn. We felt lucky to have her as our teacher.

When she'd finally shushed us, Sister said that we ought to feel honored because we were living in the city where spacesuits were invented and manufactured. "This comes from David Clark Company, a Worcester outfit. We should all be proud."

We were proud.

Mr. Clark, we were told, created the pressured, anti-gravity flight suit worn by pilots during World War II. After the war, when the country entered the space race, Clark changed the suit, adapting it for use in high altitude apace flights, and it was just what NASA needed.

Our excitement as children back then was shared with everyone. The country was beginning to look beyond limits in science and technology, and this is how that played out in our little overheated Catholic school classroom. The atmosphere of possibility was beginning to take hold. Even Sister was inspired by it. Our parochial world could not last.

"Should I pass it around so that you feel what it's like?" she asked that day.

When she did, everyone had a go at the fabric that she had described as indestructible. We scratched our fingernails into it, and someone, perhaps it was Sean—Sister called him a "holy terror" because of his behavior—tore at it with his teeth to prove that it was not forever, that nothing is—except God, we knew. That was, above all, what we had learned at St. Peter's.

Were we hoping that Sister was right, that something to last forever had been discovered? The idea that the fabric might possibly be indestructible was so attractive to us because it was something from present day life and not a preserved religious relic—some static bone fragment encased in glass. I remember taking great pleasure myself in tugging and poking at it, putting it to the test.

John Glenn's spacesuit material traveled up and down all the rows of desks to be handled by each one of us in turn, before finally reaching my friend, Barbara. Because she was the last to examine it, she was the one who had the misfortune of having to get up out of her seat to walk up to Sister's desk to return the swatch of spacesuit material.

"What have you done?" Sister cried when she did, holding the frayed remnant up for even God to see.

An interrogation began then, Sister attempting to determine the identity of the culprit; and when no confession was forthcoming, she doled out a group punishment. "Do you know what this means?" she said.

I remember thinking when Sister asked that question, that John Glenn might be wearing an unsafe spacesuit, but I didn't say it out loud because I knew that that was not the answer she wanted to hear. If there was one thing that I'd learned from my dealings with the nuns at St. Peter's, it was when I ought to keep quiet.

"Silence!" Sister bellowed, when the class began to laugh heartily, all of us pleased with our power to affect the indestructible. "After school today! All of you! I don't care what world event is happening. Detention. Until the one who did this owns up to it."

"Someone always spoils things," Sister generally said to us. But she didn't say it that day. I think she must have realized that we had all had a part in what had happened.

Even if the responsibility for some transgression fell to just one of us, we were always being punished as a group. We instinctively stuck together. There were no snitches. We knew that our collective punishment would be less severe than if Sister doled it out to a single perpetrator. The pointer was always at the ready.

The laughing stopped only when we realized that Sister might refuse to let us watch John Glenn go into orbit. She had grounds for it, we knew. We were all spared that disappointment though—I guess maybe, because Sister did not want to miss it herself.

*

My father wanted me to read the newspaper for him. I read to him about John Glenn going into outer space. "The *Friendship* circled the globe three times in a flight lasting four hours, five minutes, and twenty-three seconds."

Before John Glenn I'd read aloud to my father, an article about how the Russians were beating us in the space race with Sputnik. I'd liked reading about the dog in their spaceship, the little cosmonaut.

"How do you like that?" he said now about John Glenn. "Those Russians aren't beating us anymore."

All this reading made me want to go to the moon. "Would you want to go to the moon," I asked my dad.

He laughed. "I like to have my two feet on the ground," he said.

I stared at it at night from the car window when we were on our way home from a shopping trip to Framingham or Chestnut Hill with my grandmother, or on Sunday evenings when were driving home from Milford, and I kept thinking of what was in the newspapers—that man would reach the moon in less than ten years. I wondered where I would be in ten years, and I wondered what would happen to my father in that span of time.

It was February of 1962. John Glenn was in orbit. I was, too. For months I'd been listening to the Dion and the Belmonts' hit song—"The Wanderer"— played on the radio. I liked the song because I, too, was beginning to roam, and not just in my mind anymore. I had quite literally begun trying to get lost, to extend my boundaries, to see what might happen if I did. I found myself walking on streets that were new to me, in neighborhoods I had previously only been through in a car driven by my mother or my aunt.

I had just turned eleven and was in the sixth grade, free to explore. No one, as far as I knew, was questioning where I was. My mother asked where I was going, and I made something up—the library, Grammy's, to see Auntie at work.

My mother had a terrible fear of what might happen to me if she let me go off on my own. In the fifties and sixties though, children owned the streets, and parents did not think they had to worry as much as they do now about kidnappers, pedophiles, and other predators. "Careful crossing the street," was generally the only admonition for most children.

I saw and tried on the gowns in the back bedroom at my grandmother's house, gowns that had belonged to my mother and my aunt. They were evidence that my mother went places, did different kinds of things in her life once. She surely had adventures if she wore what looked to me like costumes for the movies. I was feeling very big and I reasoned that I was entitled to have adventures, too. Realizing that Mum was once out and about in the world, and thinking over some of the stories I had heard about my father being so independent when he was young, gave me my roaming license. It just wasn't fair to be kept in anymore, I decided.

I was all fired up with curiosity about the city beyond the two neighborhoods I did know—my own and that of my grandparents. I would explore those other places to see for myself how things happened beyond my own neighborhood, beyond my own family. Wasn't this the same hunger my father had had growing up in Milford? I knew that small town. I could see when we visited every Sunday that the lives of its residents varied little from house to house, neighborhood to neighborhood. My father had escaped that town, wanting his own kind of life. Like me, I decided, he must have craved variety. I expected that living in the city as we did, once I set out I would find the variety that was missing in my life.

In fact, Worcester was then and still seems to be, something like a series of small towns contiguous to one another, each neighborhood with its own character. The ethnic configurations have changed from what they were then, but in its essence, even now the city has that small town feeling in many of its neighborhoods. Perhaps geography is the reason—the seven hills—that topography combined with the fact that the population is relatively small, given the size of the city. When I lived there, the West Side was where the wealthier families lived, many of them Jewish. Main Street was like the proverbial railroad tracks—there was the poorer neighborhood of South Worcester on the opposite side from our neighborhood, which bordered the University campus. Green Island at the foot of Vernon Hill was also relatively poor. Both Vernon and Grafton Hills had strong Polish and Lithuanian enclaves, and Shrewsbury Street was Italian. Quinsigamond Village had a Swedish population. On the north side of the city, there were the Salisbury Street mansions built by the most prominent families, those of the industrialists and the founding fathers. And scattered here and there were other less well-defined neighborhoods—some of them almost suburban—solidly middle class.

When I set out to explore the city, no awful thing sent me home frightened or worse. Each time I was able to go off on these journeys—not just hoping—but also expecting that something more interesting than life in my Main South neighborhood awaited me.

I remember feeling very brave on these outings, and I supposed that John Glenn had the same feeling when he left his world and went into orbit. I went farther away each time I began my journey. I had absolutely no destination in mind when I set out. My only goal was to get lost, really lost. All I could think of then was that I wanted to be away from the places and people I knew best, to see what that would be like. Would I become a different person? That possibility pushed me onward.

I kept in mind the memory of my sister Peg being lost once, when we were on vacation in Maine. She had disappeared one afternoon at the beach. I could not forget how scared I was, how worried we all were, when she was gone missing, wandering at the edge of the sea. And I recalled that it felt like an impossible task to find her at the height of the summer tourist season—on that beach that stretched out for miles, blanketed with people—mostly Canadians who spoke only French. *No English. No English*, they would say when I asked them— *Did you see my sister?* My mother said that day, that the search for Peg was like trying to find a needle in a haystack. I can still hear in my mind, the bandleader at the microphone at the patio beach bar of the Brunswick Hotel, calling out over and over, broadcasting for the whole beach. *Lost child! Lost child!* I do not remember who found Peg or how long she was missing, but when I think of it now, it feels like it took forever to find her.

I didn't want to make anyone worry the way everyone in the family had that day. I just wanted to be left alone. My sister had lost track of where she was. I couldn't—even when I tried—and that frustrated me. My visual memory kept automatically mapping the streets I took, making it impossible for me to get really lost in the way I longed to be, far outside the neighborhoods I knew so well. I craved adventure—same as John Glenn—I thought. I wanted something different in my days, and after a while I got it.

When I was out traveling by myself, it began to seem as if an opening in a cloud had let me see the blue sky beyond. I put my curiosity to work. Rather than always having to look ahead at what was right in front of me, the way I had to whenever I was out walking somewhere with my father, I was suddenly free to be going nowhere in particular. If I decided to turn a corner it might have been to see a garden or to take a quick look at a stranger getting into a car, or some kids my own age out in their yard. I may have turned down a side street just because I happened to like the name on a signpost. That's what I did one day when I found that there was an intersection at two streets named for the months of May and June. I felt that when I took that right turn down June Street where I had never walked before, just as if I were walking straight into a new season.

Seeing the world for myself, finding that I was in a place where I was unknown—another neighborhood, an unfamiliar street, I realized that I didn't have to work so hard to be in the world as I did when I was out with my father as his guide. On my own there was no need to pick and choose what I saw, no reason to look quickly, to speak fast—and in only a few words— as I would have to when I was walking somewhere with him. In fact, no one paid any attention to me at all as I walked by.

So I enjoyed what I saw. I could linger and I did. I had the chance to feel color, to see the difference it made in the world, and I realized, too, that I had been missing something, not being in open spaces. In our neighborhood the houses were all right on top of each other my mother used to say.

I didn't know the people who lived in the houses I saw. I didn't care to get to know them even. I wanted to imagine their lives. It would have spoiled things for me to know that they had their own difficult dramas in progress. There were

things happening, people talking, celebrations in progress—
circumstances of all kinds, I suppose, although all I ever
observed seemed without trouble. There were people in those
houses who didn't live as my own family did. In some of the
neighborhoods I saw what looked like the setting for *The
Donna Reed Show* or *Ozzie and Harriet*—small lawns out front,
driveway next to the house. I saw fathers—in the late
afternoon when my own father was still at work at the
factory—entering or leaving those houses, shutting car doors,
playing restfully with their children or dogs out on the lawn.
None of the houses needed paint, like ours—and others in
my neighborhood—did. There was order in those
neighborhoods, the grass green and neatly mown. But above
all there was quiet. I didn't hear a single mother yelling out to
her children.

When I was alone, the streets were not an obstacle course
to be maneuvered. I was not a lookout. With my father, I saw
only so that I could prevent trouble from stopping us as we
tried to get wherever we were going.

I knew how well my father remembered the
neighborhood. Even as his eyesight waned, he could easily
follow the coded language I spoke—short descriptions
designed to make us as inconspicuous as possible. Given my
hints, he always knew what was supposed to be right there on
his left or right. He often surprised me, leaving me asking
myself: did he see that? But the trick of it was that what he
remembered was generally still true because in our
neighborhood, like in the small town of my father's youth,
the place and the people and their activities didn't change
much. Unlike the walks I took alone, when I went off with
my father we walked the same way, to the same destinations,
and ended up being with the same people all the time.

When I was out with my father, the world for me was a
flood of nouns that rushed from my lips. Sidewalk. Man.
Corner. Tree. Signpost. Market. Bus. I noticed only surface,
edge, and matter. I gave him who, what, and where. With my
spoken pictures I created something like the negative of a

photograph. This was how we made our way in the world. Anything extra blurred the picture that my father was trying to hold in his memory of the places familiar to him. And so, I let my father's imagination and his memory fill in my sketch of person, places, and things in space. He wanted it that way. He got mad if I told him too much. Yet I found that sometimes, if by mistake I left out something he remembered, he got impatient and reminded me of what I'd forgotten to mention. He didn't like the idea of something he'd once known, gone missing from the world. It was a delicate balance I had to maintain.

Fourteen

THE TEMPLE (1963)

The year that I was a student in the eighth grade at St. Peter's, Buddhist monks set themselves on fire—self-immolated on the streets of Saigon. The 16th Street Church in Birmingham, Alabama was bombed and children my own age were killed in the explosion. I was listening to Bob Dylan and memorizing lyrics so that I could sing along to "The Times They Are A-Changing." When I went on trips with our church youth group—hayrides in North Brookfield, or to Boston to see the *Ice Capades*—a popular young priest of the parish, a cousin on my mother's side, Father Donald Gonyea, chaperoned us. He was going to help register black voters in the South, and would lead everyone on the bus or the hay wagon in singing, "We Shall Overcome" and "The Cruel War is Raging."

Mr. Ronald Sullivan, my history teacher, was handsome and smart. He challenged me to look at things closely, the way my father did— but in a different way. I had to change focus, move beyond the neighborhood, the parish of St. Peter's, and my own family's situation. He wanted all of his students to take a wider view. In his class we were expected to examine places, people, and events, which we had previously thought had no bearing on our lives. The things he talked about seemed so far removed from what life was like in our Worcester Main South neighborhood. We didn't understand how we were affected by what happened in the outside world, and so our teacher set out to educate us.

"Don't you see what's going on in the world?" he asked us, flapping the newspaper in front of us. He paraded up and down the aisles with it, slapping one story after another, trying to provoke a discussion.

I had a terrible crush on Mr. Sullivan. Many of the girls did. He was young—we'd heard that he had just finished college. He looked like James Franciscus, the actor who played Mr. Novak on a favorite television show about a popular teacher. Mr. Sullivan's teaching methods were similar to Mr. Novak's, so I hung on his every word. He walked around the room—not strutting, as some of the tougher nuns did or priests of the parish, when they visited the classrooms for announcements. He walked, it seemed, because he was trying to meet us on our own territory, rather than holding forth standing or sitting at his desk in front of the class.

He called on us, wanting answers to a barrage of questions, more questions than we'd ever thought anyone could come up with about one subject. We'd answer one, then he'd ask another. We often found that to answer a follow-up question, we sometimes had to contradict what we'd given as our first answer. He got us so mixed up that, after a while we didn't know what we believed about anything. He wanted more than facts learned by rote, which was the method we knew. He wanted us, he said, to evaluate information and to form our own opinions and to learn to support them with facts.

"Mary Bonina," Sister would say, "is your book open to the page we are discussing?" Instead, Mr. Sullivan called me, "Miss Bonina." To Mr. Sullivan, all the girls were "Miss Whoever" and the boys were "Mister Whoever." "And what do you think, Miss Bonina about the Supreme Court decision to ban the Lord's Prayer and reading of the Bible in public schools?" I thought sometimes that if the nuns or the parish priests overheard what was said during our class discussions, Mr. Sullivan would surely be fired. Before he came to teach at St. Peter's, we were not expected to voice our opinions. In his "Current Events" class we learned that sometimes there were no right or wrong answers, that there were only questions and more questions.

We girls wondered about our teacher whenever we got together to listen to music after school. We considered how old he was, whether he had a girlfriend or a wife. Mr. Sullivan was the only man on the faculty, the only teacher at St. Peter's who was not a nun. He wasn't even a priest! He was a welcome change.

We learned the word "charisma" and were asked to enumerate some of the famous people we thought had it. John F. Kennedy, movie stars—like James Franciscus. Like you, I thought, when he said that. Charisma, according to Mr. Sullivan, could help make a politician successful; it was what drew people to someone like Martin Luther King. I understood him to be saying that for anyone who wanted to be popular or any kind of leader—not just a politician—it was important to have this quality. I didn't ask, but I wondered if you were born with it, or if it was something you could develop. "It's your attitude," he said, as if he had read my mind. "It shows in everything about you." I saw charisma in Mr. Sullivan. We all did. It was in his voice, his style of dressing, in the way his hair was cut, and even in the way he held out the newspaper when he got mad at us for not thinking deeply enough. I had never before thought about this, never realized that it was possible to be so completely comfortable with yourself, that your personality would show in everything about you.

He always wore English Leather cologne or the very sweet intoxicating scent of Canoe, which made me woozy as he went up and down the aisles negotiating the narrow way between two rows of nicked oak desks. He was a master at keeping our attention, and I was unnerved by the fact that I never knew when he might yell out, "Miss Bonina!" which would have me blushing and tongue-tied. I longed to be able to convince him of my intelligence. It mattered to me because I saw that he appreciated ideas and opinions in a way that none of our other teachers did. And he was movie star handsome. Only the boldest of us were not sitting up straight in our seats, on edge, and anticipating that we might be called upon next to answer one of Mr. Sullivan's questions. I willingly suffered the anxiety of his method, since he brought something new to life at school. We could see that he loved history, that he loved teaching it to us, and that he truly believed that learning it would change our lives. And he was movie star handsome.

I remember that my after-school routine in those days of early adolescence was to sit alone or with friends for hours in my bedroom—on the floor, crossed legged in the lotus position in front of my portable record player, the same one my father had bought for me years earlier. It seems now as if the turntable was the altar in the shrine my friends and I set up to honor rock and roll. We worshipped the music, imagined ourselves stars, too—traveling the country, appearing on television, loved by the entire world.

I made sure that the door into the living room was always closed, so that my mother passing by would not hear the music and come in to bother me about turning the volume down. Those afternoons I went through my entire stack of 45s. These were records that my father purchased for me, the same way he bought a set of porcelain dinnerware. Each week he bought one record, one plate, or one volume of an encyclopedia, hoping that the purchase of those items offered at a discount to shoppers at the A&P Supermarket as premiums, would amount to a collection. I don't think though, that any one of them was actually ever a complete set.

The records—*the hits*, my father called them—kept me happy for hours. I learned all the songs by heart, singing along until I got them perfect. I learned not just the lyrics, but also every twang, slur, and slide, every wail and whine. When I sang along with my records, I didn't sing the way I'd learned to sing as a member of the St. Peter's Girls Choir, with feigned holiness and heavenly pure round tones. The lyrics were not Latin words that I struggled to pronounce and to translate. What we sang in choir was always about heaven, not earth. I was interested in outer space, but I knew that was not the same as heaven. Heaven was impossible to understand.

I had no trouble knowing how to belt out the lyrics of my records, though. I could easily keep up with the fast pace and sassy words in a song like, "He's a Rebel." It seemed I had the rhythm of it in the pit of my stomach, although my music teachers had taught me that a song originated in the head. It seemed also, when I heard those recordings for the first time that I had always known how to sing songs like them, that they reached my soul in a way that no Latin hymn ever did. I waited for the grinding guitar riff to finish. I knew the timing exactly and liked the song's sentiment. I was beginning to truly like the idea of not doing what other people thought you were supposed to do. I had by then seen *West Side Story* on television. I knew what it meant to be a rebel. I imagined myself as Maria, who fell in love with Tony. When my mother left us alone in the house, Peg and I danced through the three adjoining front rooms, leaping and falling. We moved the dining room table up against the wall to give us more space. Peg did cartwheels, and both of us sang Bernstein's lyrics about being a Jet and smoking cigarettes.

I could also mimic one kind of singer's voice after another, as I went through my stack of records. One day my friend, Kerry, examined the label of one I was particularly good at imitating. She said, "Hey, who is this guy anyway? Gene Pitney is the one who recorded 'Only Love Can Break a Heart.' This isn't Gene Pitney. This is some other guy. This record is a fake." She started going through all my records then. "All Alone Am I" was not sung by Brenda Lee; that was recorded by someone else as well. One by one she discovered, "They're all fakes."

"So what? Who cares?" I said, although I was surprised myself.

My friend meant—but I didn't know it then—that the records were sung by cover artists. All I knew was that I felt lucky to have these records, lucky that my father had bought them for me. I didn't think that he knew that the artists who'd recorded the songs were not the original ones who'd released them a year before and made them into hits. That possibility never crossed my mind either. I couldn't imagine that my father would have wanted even one of them if he knew it wasn't the real thing. It hadn't dawned on me then that he might have knowingly purchased them at the A&P, because it was inexpensive and convenient for him to do so. I believed, and I still do, that he had quite simply wanted to give me a gift of some popular music, knowing how much I liked it. The record shop downtown was located at a distance of about a mile and a half from where we lived. My father wouldn't have had the leisure time or the same ease another man might have had on such an errand, let alone the extra cash it would have taken to buy the genuine article in such a quantity as he had been able to buy those records. I believe that if I mentioned to him what Kerry had said to me though, he'd have given me a few dollars, telling me to take the bus downtown to Arnold's Music Shop to get a record I wanted. I saw that kind of generosity and insistence that I should have—that my sisters and brother and my mother, too— should all have whatever he could possibly provide to make us happy. If it were at all within his power, he wanted us to have what he knew others had. Knowing the sacrifices he made for that, I hated my friend at that moment for deeming my records worthless.

I remember thinking that Kerry had been fooled as much as I had been, that she hadn't known either, until she'd looked at the labels, and then she'd been as surprised as I was. I argued with her also, because I knew that the singers who weren't the Crystals or Brenda Lee or Gene Pitney or any of the other singers who were popular then, *did* sing well, and I thought that they understood the songs, presenting them in the right style. And there was something else, too, that bothered me about my friend's objection to these recordings. By singing along, I was attempting to imitate the singers as perfectly as possible. My friend was criticizing the records because the singers did exactly what I'd been doing.

I didn't know the first thing about originality of style in voice then. All I knew was that my singing was realistic, and theirs was, too. *Realistic,* it said in bold, black script on the inside cover of my suitcase record player. As far as I knew then, from everything I had been taught, realistic was just as good as being true. I had been trained to imitate, parroting everything from John Greenleaf Whittier's "Barbara Fritchie," Joyce Kilmer's "Trees," Longfellow's "Hiawatha," to the Baltimore Catechism—*Q. Who made you? A. God made me. Q. Why did God make you? A. To show forth his goodness and to share with us his everlasting happiness in heaven.* In choir, too, I had imitated, repeating and repeating exercises, bars of music, refrains—trying to get the exact tone, rhythm, and control that our director modeled for us.

My long-time friend didn't understand the value of practice, nor did she enjoy it. How she hated having to repeat exercises or pieces she was assigned to master. The rule at her house was that when she got in from school, her first order of business was to practice piano before getting involved in any other activity. On days when I went to her house after school, I waited patiently for her to finish practicing Beethoven's "Moonlight Sonata." I didn't have to wait long. Practice was a chore for her, so she would breeze right through the sheet music and her book of etudes. For me, practice was a kind of game. I wanted to accomplish things as perfectly as I could.

One day when I was bored I memorized how to spell the name of a body of water in the nearby town of Webster— Lake Chargoggagoggmanchaugagoggchaubunagungamaugg— the popularly accepted meaning of the Indian name being, "You fish on your side, I fish on my side, and no one fishes in the middle." I learned, too, that the Nipmuc Indians and their friends spelled the name in a slightly shorter version, meaning a fishing place at the boundary waters, which was a neutral meeting ground. I also learned the longest poems I could, reciting them by rote for my grandmother. I worked at trying to improve how fast I was able to match the choir director's pitch when she threw a note at me. I learned the slide at the close of a Brenda Lee song. I became pretty good at accents, too, and as I got older, I picked them up unconsciously, whenever I was with a person who spoke with one. This focus on music and language would serve me well later, when I began to take myself seriously as a writer. But at the time, it simply brought criticism—and not just from my friends either. I remember particularly after I began spending more time at Clark University, making friends with students who were native New Yorkers or from New Jersey, I would come home unconsciously talking like them. My sister, Peg, a Main South girl to the core and loyal beyond question to her roots, would yell at me, "Cut it out. Stop talking like that." Peg hated pretense, and I hated it that she saw me in that light.

I have since understood the connection between appreciating and learning from the work of other, more accomplished artists and of discovering one's own voice. That came over time, but then I simply accepted practice as a way to get things right. Practice makes perfect, everyone around me would say—and I watched my father's determination to continue to be engaged in the world as he had been before he began losing his sight, saw how he pursued mastering the ability to complete the simple as well as the more complicated tasks of every day life with his diminishing eyesight, in order to live as fully as he always had.

The argument my mother and father were having was no longer happening in the dark. They had progressed from fighting only when a serious conversation they were having erupted into a full-blown argument. Something had changed. When I heard their voices late at night, I hoped to grasp the tone of their argument, so that I might be prepared for my mother's anger and my father's distance the next day. It was something like getting the weather report on the radio when I was in Maine and the meteorologists reported "scattered thunderstorms," so we were not surprised when we had to run from them if they did blow in suddenly, ruining our day at the beach.

But there was no running from my mother and father's arguments. Insults and screaming accusations filled the apartment every day. The people in my father's family were being "ignorant," because they refused to see the retina specialist, my mother said again and again. My mother acted as if my father's worry about going blind, his fear of losing his job, and his confusion about what he would do next, was uncalled for, that there was something wrong with him for feeling as badly as he did. I didn't understand this because I thought that I would be sad and confused, just as he was, if I were going blind. It sometimes seemed that my mother believed he had intentionally brought blindness upon himself, that his eyes were getting worse, not better, because that was his will.

My sister Peg would become hysterical, trying to get them to stop yelling. Katie was frightened and retreated. She hid under her bed or behind a door. I don't remember where my brother Jack was for all of this. Perhaps he was not old enough—being only five or six then—to realize what was happening, what it meant to him.

Especially when my mother and father weren't getting along, my father would leave the house and go out into the yard. When I came home from school, I sometimes found him there. Being in a higher grade now, I was let out a bit earlier than the dismissal time for my sisters and brother, so I saw him for a few minutes every day around that time, before he left for his three o'clock work shift. I found him sitting alone on the granite wall at the edge of the driveway. He wore a shirt jacket—fine wale corduroy in a rust color, which gave a bronze sheen to his olive skin when the sun was shining. I brought him the cigarettes he asked me to get for him at the Blue Front Market on the way home.

"Did you get matches, too?" he'd ask.

I remember that when I slipped the pack of Chesterfields into his jacket pocket, the corduroy felt warm to the touch from the sun. I hoped that sitting there, he felt warm, that the sunny day took away the coldness of my mother's words and the fear that must surely have chilled him to the bone.

I came home early from school on the day of President Kennedy's assassination.

"Is he dead?"

"Who did it?"

"Why?"

"How could such a thing happen?"

These were my questions and the questions of my classmates, when the announcement had come over the intercom. Sister Superior, our principal, said only, "The President..." then she hesitated. "The President has been shot," she continued. "We must all go home now and pray for him, pray for our country."

Shot? What does she mean, "The President has been shot."

Our questions went unanswered and we filed out solemnly, thinking our prayers as we had been told to do.

There was blood—my blood, too, that day. I hurried home, feeling something new and knowing immediately what it was. I had been expecting it. But on *this* day of all days, for it to happen, that I would be bleeding. He was shot, left bleeding all over Jackie's nice dress. Was there blood my dress, too? I couldn't see it but I could feel that my blood was flowing, too, that day.

When I got to our driveway on Norwood Street, I found my father outside as usual, sitting on the wall in the spot he favored. I thought that maybe there would be no work for him, just as there was no more school for me that day. He looked glum and thoughtful. I learned that my mother had just hollered the news out the window to him. Were there bells ringing from every church in the neighborhood, not just St. Peter's—Christian Science, Greek Orthodox, Presbyterian, Congregationalist? It certainly sounded that way. In fact, I thought that all the church bells in the city of Worcester were suddenly ringing like mad.

My mother heard the bells and opened the living room window above the wall where my father was sitting. She yelled out to him. "He must be dead. He's got to be dead if they're ringing the bells. They're still not saying so on television. What are they hiding it for?"

She suddenly registered that I was there with my father, home early and said, "What are you doing here now?"

"The school let us go early. Because of President Kennedy."

"Where are your sisters and brother then?"

"They'll be coming along. They let the older grades out first."

I remembered Mr. Sullivan saying in history class once, that in the moments right after an assassination—or any time the President of a country was not conscious—even during surgery when he had to be given general anesthesia—it was a dangerous time for our country. I was wondering if that was the reason they'd dismissed us from school. Was our country in danger? Was that why they sent us home early to be with our families?

"Who shot him?" I asked my mother, thinking it might be a plot to overthrow the government.

She didn't hear me and closed the window.

That school year, I was often perplexed about why would the parish priests kept coming into our classrooms, interrupting Mr. Sullivan's interesting class on current events? They didn't come to talk to us about religion, the way they had when we were in the lower grades and would ask during their visit, for a show of hands from those of us who wanted to be priests or nuns when we grew up. They came instead to talk on the topic of *Your Sexuality*. They were scheduling us for lectures to be held in church, going to herd us into groups, take us out of our dreams and away from the world we wanted to live in. *A Day of Spiritual Retreat*, they called it.

"They're all sex maniacs," my sister Peg said.

We girls looked the other way as much as possible when they started talking to us about sex, telling us that we should remember that our bodies were *Temples of the Holy Ghost*. I looked out the classroom window and counted planes or pigeons I could see on the flat roof of the building that housed the lower grades—there were more pigeons than I could keep track of, though I tried. Sometimes I watched the sun go behind a cloud and tried to estimate how many seconds or minutes it would take before it was shining again. On the roof of a house near the school there might have been a man fixing his television antenna and I'd watch him for a while. I would look at anything outside our classroom, just to get away from Father Harrington's eyes. *Don't you dare call on me*, I would think. *Ask me a question and I'll tell you that I have "lost my place."* I didn't care if Father Harrington found out that I had not been paying attention to him as he went over the paper he'd given us about the church lectures. That was the point I wanted to make. I wanted Mr. Sullivan to get back to Current Events. *Doesn't someone have a question about who is next in line to become President, if Johnson gets shot, too?* I thought.

For the next several days I was glued to the television whenever I wasn't in school—everyone in the country was—except people who lived in Washington, D.C. They were in the streets, or at the Capitol Building, where President Kennedy's body lay in state in the Rotunda. I focused, whenever I saw them on television, on Caroline and John, and on their mother. Because I was worried for my own family, I worried for the Kennedys—the children who no longer had a father—and I was worried for their mother, too. For myself, I couldn't imagine life for my family without my father.

Fifteen

HITS (1963)

We had almost no toys in the house. What we did have, we received mainly as Christmas gifts. Most gifts, though, were items of clothing, because necessities came before pleasure. One year, my aunt Cecilia, Grammy Feeherry's half-sister, gave Peg *Mr. Potato Head.* I had a stuffed chicken or rooster, which she'd also made possible—though not at Christmas. One summer night, when I was vacationing at the cottage in Maine with her, she took me to the boardwalk on the Old Orchard pier and allowed me to try a game of skill. I fired a b-b-gun at a wooden target. My aunt was so certain that I would win, that I'd had no other choice. I have a vague recollection that some one of us had a *Betsy Wetsy* doll, but it may be that my memory reflects my longing for one, as I watched television advertisements for it broadcast over and over. The only doll I do remember having is one I still have—not a baby, but a handmade cotton doll of a black woman wearing a bright red dress, an apron, and a kerchief. It was a gift Auntie Margaret gave me, purchased in a marketplace in the Montego Bay port of call on her Caribbean cruise. I have always thought of that doll as a link with the wider world, evidence that there were places and people far different from what I knew of life in Worcester.

I also remember having a game of Chinese checkers, which I received from a Christmas party given for the children of employees at the pressed metal shop where my father worked as a machinist.

We wanted to go to the party.

My father said, "You aren't going and that is that."

The party was an annual event apparently, although I don't think I ever remember hearing it mentioned until December of that year I turned thirteen, just after President

Kennedy's funeral, when my father came home from work telling my mother he needed to give the names and ages of all his children to his foreman, so that gifts could be purchased for them. He asked my mother to write the information down for him.

"What kind of gifts?" I asked, overhearing my father talking to her.

I was not too old for presents. I was also hoping he would take us to the party, and begged him to. I figured that a girl who'd just turned thirteen would probably be given a board game or a kit for making something.

"We don't need their games," my father said.

The ambiguity of this remark was lost on me that day. I didn't know that my father suspected some manipulation. I didn't even know for sure that he was having trouble at work, although I couldn't imagine how he was able to operate the machinery for making tools and parts for cars—detailed, precise work—with failing eyesight. I know he didn't want to worry us, but worry I did. He seemed more tired than usual when he was off from work. Watching him sitting alone in the living room or outside on the wall, deep in thought, I felt, too, that he had some big worry on his mind.

When my father wasn't at home, I worked on my mother about the party.

"Oh, please. Can't we go to the party?" I whined. It would be something different to do. "Pleeeease!"

"You'll get other Christmas presents," she said.

"But all the other kids will be there."

I was hoping to meet a good-looking thirteen-year-old boy.

"What are you talking about? You don't even know them."

"But I can meet them," I said.

"No great loss," my mother said.

Only now, as I try to recall that last Christmas season my father worked at the pressed metal company, do I realize that he and my mother were troubled, worrying about how they would manage. What I didn't know then was that my father's eyesight had become much worse and that he was about to lose his job.

The presents came even though we didn't go to the party. My father brought them home from work. They were wrapped in bright red Christmas paper. Each present was labeled. There was one that had a tag that said, *Girl—Age 13,* and I guessed I was that girl. The other tags said, *Girl—Age 11, Girl—Age 9, and Boy—Age 7,* so there was a package for Peg, Kate, and Jack as well. We broke open the wrapping paper and found Chinese checkers, Colorforms, Play-Doh, and Lincoln Logs. We were very happy. They were the only toys we got that year.

After midnight Mass on Christmas morning we walked fast through deep snow to get in and out of the cold and dark. We hurried too, because we couldn't wait to open the other Christmas gifts under our tree. Peg and I got hats that looked something like Dad's Persian lamb Russian-style hat, the one he wore to church in winter. Our hats were not made of real fur though. You could tell when you touched them, but otherwise they were good fakes. We soon found that the fake fur stuff could be combed into something that looked like a bouffant hairdo, and so we called these hats, *wig hats.*

Peg, Kate, and I unwrapped the biggest boxes, and inside we found leopard-print Dr. Denton pajamas. Mum persuaded us to try them on. When we did we looked like "do-re-mi" wearing them, she said. We pretended to be the Lennon Sisters on the *Lawrence Welk Show* singing "Christmas Island," about how Santa delivered presents there in a canoe. We had the record and had been playing it over and over that Christmas season, dreaming of Hawaii. Mum wore her Hawaiian print muumuu, and we ate cookies called Hawaiian Dreams, made of coconut, chocolate, and caramel.

"What a picture. You three are a sight for sore eyes," she said to us.

But we had no camera in the house.

The only family pictures of that time in my life are the ones my grandfather or my aunt sometimes took of us. They aren't pictures of holidays, birthday parties, or milestones in our family life—or of us as individuals either, like the ones I take of my son. My grandfather took pictures of us standing on his porch, or out in front of his picket fence, or next to the lilacs or sweet-smelling climbing roses. And I have one that he took of me at about this age. I'm sitting on a bench at Lincoln Plaza shopping center, looking bored out of my mind, waiting I guess, for my mother to finish shopping at R. H. White's. You can see that I am uncomfortable with my body and my looks, and although I am thin, the lack of muscle tone in my legs shows that I didn't get much exercise then. We also have some photographs that were taken on the beach in Maine by my aunt Margaret; that's all we have really. It makes sense, I suppose: most kids I knew who had pictures or home movies of themselves, had them taken by their fathers, and that, of course, wouldn't have been possible in our family.

That Christmas Eve though—camera or not—my sisters and I pranced around in our new pj's, feeling like little leopards.

I sang at the top of my voice, the Ronettes' hit song, "I Saw Mommy Kissing Santa Claus," which gave my father the idea of kissing my mother.

"Merry Christmas," he said, looking romantically into her eyes.

"Oh, stop," she said, as if it embarrassed her.

There were other presents, too—a new invention, the electric toothbrush—from Uncle Ed, who was married to my father's sister, Aunt Marge.

"He worked on developing that," my father said proudly, about the gift.

Uncle Ed was an engineer for General Electric.

"He's got a big job," my mother said.

I had wanted most of all a transistor radio and I got it, not realizing at the time, just how happy it would make me. It fit in the palm of my hand and it buzzed with life. There was an earplug with it, so I could fall asleep at night listening. All my friends got radios, too. Hearing new songs as soon as they were released gave us the edge on "cool."

At first we listened mostly to "Dick the Derby" Smith's *Open House* program every afternoon. It was local—radio station WORC—and there was a request line. We dialed the phone number and had songs dedicated to us and whoever was our latest crush. *Open House* was a popular show, so it took us sometimes an hour to get through, but we persisted, dialing the number over and over—maybe one hundred times—before the receptionist answered. *Do you have a request?* When we said we did, she told us to *hold on*, and before we knew it, the show's disc jockey was talking to us. *You're on the air. Who'm I talkin' to?* We spoke fast because we wanted to attach the names of everyone we knew to the song, before he cut us off. *This one goes out to Kerry and Bob, Betty and Mike, Mary and Skip, Sue and Lou...*More often than not, the deejay interrupted us. *Turn your radio down, girls. I'm getting too much feedback.* And everyone listening heard the static that came from one of us putting a hand over the receiver, trying unsuccessfully to muffle the order. *Turn it do*wn, he said.

We should have been doing the homework that waited for us in our green gabardine duffle bags full of schoolbooks, tossed in a corner of the room in which we'd sought the solace of music.

I began saving money my grandmother gave me, whenever I saw her—the change she retrieved from the bottom of her pocketbook, whenever she went looking for packs of sticks of gum and boxes of Chiclets, or the rolls of fruit and peppermint and wintergreen Lifesavers she stocked. My friends and I went downtown after school to spend the money. We drank Cokes and ate hamburgers and fries at Woolworth's. Then we went to Arnold's Music Shop, where they posted a chart listing the top ten Billboard hits every week. One record at a time, I amassed a collection that helped keep me dreaming, and gradually the hits I bought replaced the old stack of 45s my father had bought for me at the A&P.

One night when WORC was playing an entire new album of a favorite group, and I was fighting off sleep to hear it, the telephone rang. It was too late for that I knew. I froze at the thought of my father being awakened by the ring, getting up out of bed to answer the call. Yet I was afraid to run to get it first, afraid to bump into him. It was a Sunday night, so he was home in the evening—no three to eleven work shift— and he'd been able to watch *Ed Sullivan* with us before we went to bed. He turned in early himself to try to catch up on sleep he'd missed during the week. I heard the phone ringing and ringing. Although I was awake, it seemed that it had been hours since I'd heard him go to bed. It certainly was too late for him to be dragged from sleep to answer a call.

"Who's dead?" I heard my mother yell when he finally got up got up to answer and said, "Hello."

No one died in the night though.

"Kerry," I heard my father yell. "What the hell do you think you're celebrating, calling here at this hour?"

That was all. Then he hung up.

I waited for him to come into the room to chew me out. I'd had nothing to do with my friend calling at so late an hour. Her call was not a plan we'd hatched together. I was as surprised as my father that she'd called, and I was angry with her for having been so stupid. Her own father, a big man who worked as a butcher and never smiled, would not have been happy at being awakened from a dead sleep either. I thought perhaps he'd have been even angrier. What was wrong with her that she would do such a thing? What could she have to tell me that couldn't wait until we walked to school together in the morning?

My father didn't come in, but I supposed that I would be in for another one of his lectures, when he was more awake. I invented in my mind what he might say. It would be a lesson, not just a chastisement, I knew. He never missed an opportunity to teach some awareness. *I need my sleep. I work hard for you kids. If I can't get to work, we won't have money for things we need.*

Walking to school with Kerry, I learned that she hadn't been thinking at all. She had been swept away by a dream that had made her forget, I guess, that neither one of us was free to do whatever we wanted, whenever we pleased. She had been playing with the transistor radio dial—that was all. She had found a radio station that played rock and roll—right in our neighborhood at Clark University—and she wanted to tell me right away. "WCUW," she said. "We have to find the studio. The deejays at Clark had the coolest voices she had ever heard. "So cool. And they play great music." She knew we had to meet these boys, find the radio station studio, and go there.

"Go there?" I said. "Meet these boys. They're college students. We're only thirteen. Why would they care about us?"

My father would leave his job soon after Christmas. I'm not sure he knew it that day after Kerry's late night phone call, when he made the remark telling me that if he could not get to work in the morning, we would not have the things we needed. He would leave us for a while and enter a program, the purpose of which was to help people who had been born with sight and had become blind—to help them learn to live in the world without having sight—*rehab*, as it is commonly called. In bed listening to my radio through its earplug, I imagine that the music blocked out the worst of the arguments between my mother and father after he came home from work at midnight. Or else the radio just put me to sleep and that was the reason I never heard a word. Although I cannot recall these later arguments, I believe that the most ferocious of them must have happened just before my father went away. There must have been a great deal of anger expressed by my mother those nights before my father lost his job, just as there had been during the earlier round of changes— my father's diagnosis and his family's initial resistance to cooperating with the doctors at Massachusetts Eye and Ear Infirmary to help determine the family pattern of blindness, the failed cataract operation, Peg's diagnosis, and the ongoing money problems. But I never heard anything, and I thank the little radio for that, and later for continuing to keep me distracted, giving me music to focus on after my father left us to go away to school.

Sixteen

LET GO (1964)

"Charity begins at home," was my mother's line, whenever I returned from school with the message that Sister drummed into us at various times during the school day, that *we all have a duty to contribute*. During Lent especially, we were told to save our money for the *Missions in Africa* and other developing countries in the world. By abstaining from small pleasures such as candy, bowling, or movies, and donating what we would have spent for them, we would be atoning for our sins and saving souls, too.

When I dutifully brought this message home the year that life was changing fast for us, my mother must have been thinking that in no time at all my father would be out of a job.

"What on earth are those nuns thinking anyway?" she would mumble.

I knew that the nuns were not thinking of anything on earth, but rather their sights were set on heaven.

My mother would turn to me then, and say, "And what do you think? That money grows on tress?"

The nuns knew who gave and who didn't. A special time was reserved each day for contributions. Every student with a penny jar or a brown bag or pocketful of change was called up to the front of the room. The money was then counted out and added to the total written in large numbers in the right hand corner of the chalkboard, where it would remain un-erased until the next day when the whole process would begin again. It was a shakedown, a public reckoning, and just as those who gave were praised for taking their obligation seriously, those who did not were noticed and—it seemed to me even then—treated as less important.

"Give up the candy," Sister said every day during Lent. "Offer it up for the souls in Purgatory, and help the Missions instead."

I didn't believe that giving up penny candy—little wax bottles of flavored syrups, Squirrel Nut Zippers, Fireballs or Lik-M-Aid Pixy Stix—would help anyone get to heaven, and so I resisted contributing the spare change my grandmother always gave me and withstood the stares and judgment. I continued to stop by the little Gardner Street storefront that was jam-packed with kids every afternoon at three. Some kids had money to contribute to the Missions and to buy candy, too. Not me. I made a choice. I bought candy.

We pushed and shoved each other to get in front of the glass candy case, instructing the clerks who seemed to know just two words—*What else? What else?* We answered back, pointing to one, then another of the cardboard boxes filled to the brim with treats that sweetened our difficult childhoods—*I'll have two of those and one of those, one of those...*

One day, what I had been worried about for so long finally happened. When I came in from school my father was at home, not dressed in his work clothes. Because no one had given me a reason why he was not at work, why he had been *let go*, and because my mother seemed so angry, I figured that his dismissal must have been his fault, that he must have made some terrible mistake. Maybe he ruined an order for some parts he was making—or a piece of machinery he was using—or he might have fallen and knocked into something or someone on the shop floor.

For many years I believed that my father had to leave his job as the result of some error he made, most probably in public view or with wide-ranging effects—some mistake that resulted in the loss of company profit—something so blatant as to require being let go. It was nearly forty years later when I asked my aunt Margaret what my father had done wrong to bring on the loss of his job. "It was nothing he did," she said to me.

But I did know back then how important it was to keep everything in the house always in the same place—the armchair by the front door, the dining room chairs pushed in so that my father wouldn't knock them over. If my mother decided to rearrange the furniture she had to remember to tell him about it or else there would be a big argument when he returned home. He hated making mistakes. He would gauge where he was by identifying a piece of furniture in the room. There was the time that he headed for what he thought was a doorway. He was disoriented though, because my mother had moved a prized piece of furniture—an inheritance, her aunt Margaret O'Brien's mahogany Governor Winthrop desk— to the other side of the room where it would have a more prominent place. My father walked right into it, and startled, jumping back, hitting his head on the doorframe. Later, I saw that his temple was bruised and swollen.

I have always thought that my father used to keep in his memory a map, including the floor plan of every room he'd ever visited, although in the early days of his blindness he was still learning the art of orienteering. I had worried about his well being from the time I was quite small, especially in the years just before that day when he'd had to leave his job. I feared that the kind of mistake he'd make would result in even worse harm than the toll it might take on his ego or the company's profits. I couldn't help but think this way, for I remembered that day when I was just five and he took me with him for a drive the last time he got behind the wheel of a car, putting us both in danger, depending upon me to help navigate.

When he was out alone in the world and living with the gradual onset of blindness, I felt that my father was always in physical danger. In my worst scenarios he would lose an arm in a machine or receive disfiguring burns from a welder's torch. I realized even then, that the tool shop was a minefield for anyone with poor vision. I can picture him heading to his machine, perking up his ears, whistling the way he would whenever he walked into a situation he knew he needed to approach carefully. He was a terrific whistler, and I believe that he whistled as much as he did as a way of navigating, listening as his sound bounced off objects or people. When he would do this at the machine shop, it would let him know that he was approaching objects of different mass, and the whistling would allow him to project a casual, unworried attitude as well, because he hoped that no one suspected any hesitation. The machine work itself required the concentration of all his faculties, and therefore there was always the chance that he might not hear a warning beep of a driver coming through, as dollies or motorized carts carrying materials and boxes whizzed by him on the shop floor. I thought it would be dangerously distracting for him just to hear those warnings, to be amid all that noise, working at his own machine, and anxious enough already.

Only much later though, did I realize that what I had always thought and most people perceived—as my father's unusual comfort in taking risks—might actually have been evidence of his genius. Perhaps he wasn't ever in quite as much danger as my child's anxiety or anyone's imagination could conceive. Perhaps it was the primal fear of blindness that made me and others think so. For years I did not recognize how careful and precise my father generally was, getting around and doing things in the world. I think of it now whenever I do some simple task without really looking. I reach around the back of the shower curtain, soap in my eyes, unable to see, and I find the faucets to adjust the water temperature, my hands settling on the middle shut off valve, and I use that to orient me and can then find the hot on the left, the cold on the right. When I do this or anything like it without using my sight I think: this is exactly the way my father would have done it.

"You have to have systems for doing things, Ree," he would tell me. And *he* did—whether it was a way to keep in his memory the established arrangement of furniture at home or the floor plan at his work place. It was only when he was in a new situation and not careful, or when things were out of what he understood as the preconceived order, that he faltered: a sidewalk under construction, a dining room chair or the living room desk out of place.

My father had calloused fingertips. In warm weather I could feel their roughness whenever we walked down the street, his left hand gently on my right elbow. Yet he was a perfectionist about everything he did with those hands. How to do things blind was a skill my father must have learned as a child from his mother. She must have been a good mother, even if she was afraid to speak directly to my father or anyone about her own blindness and her fear that he and her other children might also become blind. I know, because she nurtured me—and her other grandchildren, too—and I saw from the way she was with us, that she took her maternal role seriously. I believe that when he was a child, my grandmother must have showed my father her way of doing things with her hands, placing hers over his to teach him what he needed to know. I watched her intently over the years, the way she used those hands, helping one of her grandchildren to learn to tie a shoe, button a coat, or to cut a piece of meat using a knife and fork. Touch was her way of knowing, and even though my father had been born with sight she would have wanted him to learn to use that sense as expertly as she used it, knowing it would be one way to compensate for a diminishing sense of sight if he did eventually become blind. By doing so, she taught him early on how to *pass* later as a sighted man, helped him to develop exquisite manual dexterity, which he relied upon as a skilled machinist, a toolmaker.

I watched my father build frames for new stairs, noticed how he held a nail or used a hammer or hacksaw. I stood by as he refinished wooden door frames, using only a piece of sandpaper to remove the remnants of the last layer of stain, a step he took to make the wood look like new again. He kneaded dough for pizza on the occasional Saturday when he did not have to work, coaxing the simple ingredients into just perfect elasticity, delivering up the best bread crust I have ever eaten. And so it was that I took lessons in perfectionism from him, standing by silently, waiting until he asked me to replenish an ingredient or to go for a utensil or tool, and sometimes just to answer his proud question, "How's that look, Ree?"

I know something else now, too, something that confirms for me that my father didn't have to leave his job because of some mistake he made. It comes from the story I got from my mother just before her eightieth birthday, seven years after my father's death.

Although I was probably still awake after having to get up out of bed to watch over my sisters and brother and the house while my mother went out to pick up my father at work when his shift finished, I didn't overhear this conversation. I was most likely back in bed while they talked, with my new transistor radio turned on, listening through its earplug. I was in a different world—my other world—so I didn't hear my father tell my mother, as she now says he did—that his work station had been relocated next to the furnace.

She was furious, worried about him getting burned, and she could not understand how management would ever do such a thing as to move him to a place where he might be injured. She says they must have known about his eyes. Now, as I consider the situation, I find it amazing that my father had been able to hide his problem for so long.

"They're trying to push you out," my mother said she told him that night, getting angry all over again as she recounted the history. "It's what they do to get rid of a person. Get you to leave on your own, so they don't have to ask you to leave and pay severance. Whatever did they think? He was a man with a family, with four young kids!"

The very next day my mother made the first call to the Commission for the Blind and a man named John Hobin agreed to visit the company officials to find out what was going on.

I heard them arguing as I came up the back hall stairs. I stood outside the door, listening for a while, not wanting to go in until I knew what it was all about.

"I can't get blood out of a stone," I heard my mother say.

I knew then that they were arguing about money again. They were in one of the front rooms and when they heard me drop my duffle bag of schoolbooks on the kitchen chair, it became quiet in the house. I found my father in the living room, sitting on the couch. My mother was in their bedroom, getting dressed. I saw her through the open doorway, admiring herself in the bureau mirror. She was not wearing a muumuu, the cotton shift style dress she wore summer and winter around the house or when were going nowhere special, only out for a ride in the country on a nice day. Instead, she'd put on what my grandmother called "street clothes," a navy blue shirtwaist dress of some silky fabric and a matching cardigan sweater. I wondered where she was going.

My father looked like he was once again thinking too hard about something, his eyes faraway and his brow creased. The television was on, but he didn't seem to be listening, so it just played to no one.

I was quieter than ever, and when he didn't hear me come in, I didn't say "hello." I had tested him in this way many times before. This was a game I played, keeping still as a moon in a painting, so that I could watch him before he knew I was looking. Eventually he would somehow sense that I was in the room. Perhaps he got a glimpse of my outline, or he heard me trying unsuccessfully to stifle the sound of my breathing, or was it that he got the scent of the Ambush perfume that I had started wearing?

"Ree? Is that you, Ree?"

"It's me."

"Perry Mason looks so serious," I said, seeing the television program he had on. "The way he raises those thick eyebrows. I wonder what he would look like if he ever smiled."

It had been our television-watching routine, that my father would generally ask questions about what happening on a show—things he couldn't figure out by listening—like the expressions on actors' faces, things that one would get in the present day, from closed caption television. I had learned by this time, to tell him these things—even without being asked.

I expected my father to raise *his* thick eyebrows when I told him about Perry Mason, in imitation of what he thought the actor looked like. And I expected him to say with a smile, "Like this?" He didn't, though. So I repeated what I'd said, thinking that he just hadn't heard me.

"Shhh," he said, continuing to stare straight ahead.

My father made me want to ask *him* to describe what he was seeing in *his* mind, whatever thought I had interrupted. He acted this way even during the broadcast of *The Millionaire*. Watching this show with him had become a good substitute for watching *Queen for a Day*, a show that had been on the air when I was younger and had watched with my mother. Both shows gave me the idea that money could solve a lot of the problems people had. Watching *Queen for a D*ay used to make me feel that the problems we had weren't so bad compared to what some people experienced. But the fun of watching *The Millionaire* with my father was that the two of us could dream; we would imagine aloud during the commercial breaks, what we would do if we had a million dollars.

My dreams changed from day to day, depending upon the mood I was in or what was going on in my life. My father didn't ever say much about his own wishes, and when I asked him, all he ever said was, "I'd make sure you kids and your mother have everything you need."

I had no idea what it would mean to have a million dollars. I wished for things that I knew would help us get along better—a new car, for instance, so that my mother wouldn't be mad about the Mercury breaking down all the time, sometimes when we were miles away from home and all of us and my grandmother were in the car with her.

Because my father was so quiet that afternoon, I was surprised when the doorbell rang and my father made the joke that was a popular one in our house, whenever anyone rang.

"Maybe it's *The Millionaire*," he said.

It didn't seem funny though, that afternoon. My father delivered the joke flatly, ironically, and instead of smiling as he generally would, he was almost sneering. I saw, too, an unfamiliar expression in his eyes. It wasn't the dreamy but serious look I had often seen before, a look I thought meant that he was thinking, remembering, or the one I saw sometimes that meant he felt lost or sad. When he made the joke this time there was anger in his eyes, and I wasn't used to seeing that from him. He must have been thinking about money, about where it was going to come from since he had been *let go*. It wouldn't have taken an anonymous check for a million dollars to make him feel more secure; a few thousand—or even a few hundred—would have made a difference at the time.

"You stay here," my mother said to me, going to answer the door.

I hung over the hallway railing on our second floor landing, while she went down the stairs to see who was out on the front porch, wanting to come in. She didn't hesitate, so I thought that she must have been expecting a visitor.

"I doubt you'll get much out of him today," I heard her say.

"Well, we'll try anyway," a man said.

They were talking about my father. Although I couldn't see him, I recognized the voice as belonging to the man who'd called on the telephone a few days earlier, asking to speak with my mother. I had been waiting for a friend to call, so I was the one to answer. I was surprised that it wasn't my friend Kerry calling, but I heard instead a man's deep voice. *May I speak to your mother?* I had listened to my mother's telephone call from my vantage point, hidden behind my brother's bedroom door, left open just enough for me to hear her end of the conversation. She looked as if she were listening hard to whatever the man was telling her, and then finally she broke her silence. "What kind of a future do these kids have, if he won't go?" she said, and I had not understood her. I had guessed, of course, that they were talking about my father. There was silence again for a moment while my mother listened to whatever the man had responded. Then she said, "Where down Route 9? Newton? Yes, I know Newton."

I knew it, too. The town was a little less than hour away from Worcester, just before Boston and we knew it well from all the Friday afternoon shopping trips we took with my grandmother.

"What? You mean he's got to go live there? How long?" my mother asked. "Oh my," she said, leaving me thinking the worst.

Even though I associated the town with some of the happier moments I'd spent with my mother, I was shaken nonetheless, by what seemed a forgone conclusion, now that this man had come to visit—my father would be leaving us. That day I didn't know if he would ever return. I had not been given enough information to know. Was it like a prison where he was going, a place where blind people were shut away? Was my father now so different that he would have to live separately from everyone else? The story the nuns told about Father Damien who lived with lepers in a faraway colony came to mind. Would we be prevented from visiting, the way everyone was kept out of a leper colony? I had no way of understanding any of this, except by relying on stories of affliction told by the nuns and priests at St. Peter's. What's more, I knew that leprosy was contagious and that the blindness my father had was hereditary, and I was connecting the two meanings in my mind.

For a long time I had known about people being sent away when there was something wrong with them. Sister Rose, my second grade teacher, was sent away after she made Tommy Russo stand in the closet and then she shut the door on him. I wouldn't go to school for a while after that. I was afraid to say why, afraid that she might do something even worse to humiliate or scare me. Finally, I told my father and he brought me back. Soon after, Sister was gone. "Sent away," we heard.

I knew that not all people who had serious problems were sent away. I noticed some on the street. They were missing arms and legs; some had lost their minds, like Victor, the one we called *The Preacher*. He was harmless, corralling us at the street corner we passed as we came out of the schoolyard on our way home, making us listen to him read the Bible and encouraging us to recite every now and then—which we always did with great enthusiasm—*Praise the Lord!* Others I saw looked like adults, but they were the size of children. I thought, too, of the man who sold the *Boston Herald* newspaper from his post in front of the White Tower Restaurant at Chandler and Main every evening. I saw him dashing against the traffic at the busy intersection to make a sale. I shivered sometimes when I came upon a man, a war veteran who somehow put himself down on the sidewalk in front of Kresge's every day to sell pencils out of his hat. His empty pant legs were folded neatly over where knees should have been, and his crutches were behind him, leaning against the display window. And on the other side of the glass, sitting at the soda fountain, no matter the time of day, there was a woman talking to herself, mumbling and arguing into her coffee cup about the FBI, talking as if there was no one else around.

These people were not sent away, but I could see that they were shut out nevertheless. Even I turned away when I saw them sometimes. I wondered: did they have families or were they alone in the world because of their problems? An even more frightening question surfaced as well: if my father did not go away to Newton, would he leave us anyway, to live a life on the street, outcast the way these people seemed to be, without friends or family? This must be, I realized, what had frightened my mother when we'd encountered the organ grinder and his monkey on Old Orchard Street that family vacation in Maine.

My mother and the man climbed the stairs to our apartment. She seemed happier than she had been in a long time, and that confused me. What was there to be happy about when my father was going to go away? I didn't understand that my mother's change of mood meant that she had found someone she thought was going to help him, help us, too.

"Hello there," the man said to me.

My mother didn't tell me his name, but she said, "He's from the Commission," meaning the Commission for the Blind. "This one's got big ears," she said to him about me.

"Oh, they don't look so big to me," he said kindly. "Look at mine, will you?" and he stretched out his left ear so that it looked enormous.

"I'm John Hobin," the man said to my father.

He was standing up and he went to the door to greet him.

"Find something to do in another room," my mother said to me.

I didn't want to be in another room. I wanted to hear everything they were saying—the plans they were making, without asking me what I thought. I wanted to know what my father thought about having to go away.

In my book of martyrs, many times I had looked for that one saint with the power to help my father to see again. I would search, turning the pages of that very old book with the paper and the glue on the spine so dried out that the binding crackled and crumbled as I did. My grandmother had once talked to me about a visit she'd made to the shrine of St. Anne de Beaupré in Quebec, and about all the crutches that were mounted on the walls of the chapel, probably hundreds of pairs of them, she said. People's prayers were answered and then they could walk away without them. I had thought her story was the proof I needed to believe that miracles were possible.

But with a plan for my father to go away, I felt one thing above all: there would be no miracle. The place he was going was a *school for the blind.*

Sitting quietly in my bedroom eavesdropping, I was hoping to understand something of the conversation that was taking place between my mother and father and John Hobin. I wanted to know what my father thought, to hear—if not his words, at least to decipher his tone of voice. But I heard only two words: "No future. No future." It was my mother's voice.

I thought of one of the first times I had considered the future. There was a song on the *Hit Parade* on television. Doris Day sang "Que Sera, Sera," the lyrics about not ever being able to know what your future held for you. When I'd asked my mother what the words meant she said, "What will happen in your life is out of your hands." As I got older and was disappointed about not getting something or achieving what I'd wished for, she repeated again and again her rule for living. "Don't expect anything, and then if it doesn't happen, you won't be disappointed."

In fact, all over the neighborhood there were women who'd given up. I had a friend who lived alone with her mother. I stopped by her house after school sometimes, so she could change out of her school uniform and into other clothes before going to Vernon Drug for a Coke. I waited at the half-closed front door of her house. I was never invited in. I got a glimpse of her mother moving ever so slowly through the dark apartment. I thought she was sleepwalking. I thought she had no future. She wore a bathrobe in the middle of the afternoon, and her hair looked like it hadn't been combed in days.

John Hobin was speaking. He talked quietly, so I couldn't understand his response to my mother's proclamation about the future. He spoke less forcefully than my mother or father did. Perhaps, I thought, he knew how to help my father.

Perhaps *he* believed in the future. I thought I could hear some hope in his voice.

Because I was shut off in my room, I didn't hear the whole story that day. I learned it from my mother when we talked about it almost forty years later, when it was too late to ask my father about it. That afternoon, when Mr. Hobin reported the results of his visit to the company that had employed him, my mother said he had revealed what he believed was going on. "The work does not require you to be near the furnace," he said. "They want you out," he explained. "There is someone else—perhaps someone you trusted, someone you confided in—who wants your job." He was being "let go," not fired, an arrangement brokered by Mr. Hobin to allow my father to receive unemployment benefits, which along with his earnings from profit sharing, would temporarily take care of us as a family.

Although I didn't hear it that day, I do remember hearing the expression *let go* for weeks after the man's visit. *Let go.* It made me think of a rowboat that had lost its mooring or a balloon escaping from my hand, drifting off who knew where.

I also didn't know until some time after it had been decided that my father would go to the St. Paul's Rehabilitation Center for newly blinded adults in Newton, that he would be away from us for months, but that he would return, having learned to be independent, taught as if he were going to be living entirely on his own. And when he'd completed the program in June of 1964, he would return home knowing how to function as a blind man in the world of the sighted.

But in the meantime, money was tight. I know the stress my father was under financially, having to keep up the property so we had a roof over our heads and so that there was some income from tenants, to pay the mortgage; and he wanted to make sure that our other needs were met. Besides reading for my father— as money troubles intensified while he was trying to establish himself in a new career—he would ask me to write letters for him, too—about bills that hadn't been paid and Social Security checks he was entitled to receive. I typed them on an old Royal typewriter that my maternal grandfather had given me. I didn't really know how to type then, but I could pick out the letters of the alphabet, and I was pretty good at spelling. Not knowing the real technique though, I made mistakes and had to type and retype the letters.

There was one I found in a bureau drawer one day, long after—when I was married and we were going to be moving to our first house. I was packing up, going through drawers and closets, looking at things I'd saved over the years—a news article I'd clipped from the *Globe* about a friend–or a necklace I hadn't worn in a long time—and there it was: my father's letter staring up at me. It had been tucked in behind some small cardboard boxes that held pins and earrings. I don't know why I was drawn that day to find that letter, nor do I know why it had never been mailed. It had my father's signature in ink on it, so it was officially signed. It may have been retyped—there was at least one spelling error; perhaps that is why it was never sent. I didn't remember ever deciding to keep it, and I was saddened by it. I have looked for the letter since, and have not have been able to find it. It may have disturbed me so, that I threw it away.

It was a letter to the Social Security Administration. My father's records, I gathered from reading it, were all mixed up. The letter rebutted a charge that my father owed money to the government, that he'd received payments to which he was not entitled. The record listed all the wrong social security numbers, and my father was trying to set things straight by having me write to them. My mother's number, they thought, was my father's number, and they didn't have the correct birthdates, nor did they know how many children my father had. They were asking him to return the checks he had received. He was worried; I could tell from the tone of the letter. It sounded similar to court testimony. I am sure that the money in question was long gone. It would have been spent, used to pay bills, to buy food, to take care of the family. Although I didn't remember helping my father write that particular letter, I remember all the letters as if they were one, for they had a single purpose. My father was trying to keep his family afloat. He was simply carrying out what he— as the father who supported the family—saw necessary. I remember, too, how he thought deeply, planning what he would write.

While I was typing those letters back then, my friends would have been seated outside on the granite wall, waiting for me to finish to join them for nothing in particular, only to go to Vernon Drug for a Coke or to hang out on the street corner.

Memorial Days

Before the wake I didn't do what I remembered my mother doing when her father and mother and any other relative died. I imagined her at the salon having her hair done and then thought of her with my sisters out at the mall, shopping for something to wear. If I'd opened my clothes closet door and found only jeans— or what my father used to call "knock around clothes"— I might have felt the need. It wasn't that I intended to be disrespectful; I thought I had perfectly fine work clothes that would suffice. I knew my father would want me to look good, so that people would view me as someone who had been brought up well, someone whose family cared about her. But shopping was something I could not fathom at that moment.

Our neighbor Renee rang the doorbell just as we were going to leave for Worcester. She had a fistful of bleeding hearts she had picked in her flower garden. They were freshly cut and the bouquet full enough to bring along to grace the funeral parlor during calling hours, if they survived the hour-long drive.

When we went out to the driveway, we found a white balloon in the yard, its string caught on the fence, so it was trapped—or maybe it was meant for us, tied there—or for Gianni. It reminded me of the mourners I had once witnessed exiting Our Lady of Pity Catholic Church in North Cambridge, across the street from our old apartment. It was a Haitian funeral, and I guess, that of a child. I had heard the clamor of the church bells ringing and looked out to see the crowd of mourners on the church steps that day, wailing as they let loose a large bouquet of white balloons.

At the wake I entered the parlor where my father was laid out, and I saw my mother. She looked like a bouquet of flowers floating around the room, greeting people, and as I got closer I saw that the colorful pattern on her black dress was not flowers—but straw hats with ribbons of many different colors. What did it mean for her to be wearing such a joyous dress? And why one with hats decorating it?

I had chosen for myself a dress I'd had in the closet, matronly by comparison—a maroon and navy blue silk paisley number. It was shirtwaist-styled and a little too big for me, a relic from when I weighed more and had held an administrative position working for the Commonwealth of Massachusetts. It was an expensive dress, which I'd bought thinking it an efficient addition to my wardrobe, appropriate for any situation. The look was certainly subdued. I vowed to give the dress away after the funeral and never to buy another one like it.

So what did it mean that my mother was wearing this cheerful dress? Could it have been the only dress that she could find to fit her, one right in size and cut? I knew the frustration of clothes shopping with her; she was short waisted, petite, and somewhat overweight. But no, I thought, it seemed she'd chosen the dress consciously, as a way of avoiding traditional mourners black. A spirited youthfulness emanated not only from her dress. She was chatty, smiling, and joking with relatives she had not seen in years. Was she regressing maybe, free to become again the young woman she was when she met my father, or a bit later in the early years of their marriage?

"Well, how are you? You're getting fat!" she teased one person. I guess life must be good to you."

You would think that she had just met the man by chance, while doing her grocery shopping or when she was on some other ordinary errand. She offered no remark to indicate that she registered the expression of sympathy the man was offering by coming to the wake. She didn't mention my father until the person paying his respects pressed her, "What happened to John? Had he been ill?" The man was obviously shocked that my father was gone so suddenly. Strangely that shock still did not show in my mother's face.

My mother took the compliments that were showered upon her, how well she looked, how her children had grown, how handsome my father was—and still looked, thanks to the undertaker's skill. "You haven't changed at all," someone said about her forthrightness as she assessed how everyone else had aged.

I knew my father wasn't wearing his teeth. The undertakers had chuckled and said they weren't necessary, even though I'd brought his dentures back from the hospital in Boston. My mother had said, when I asked what to do with them, "Oh, just throw them away, will you?" Somehow my father's mouth didn't sag without his own teeth. My father wore his characteristic knowing, impish half-smile, the corners of his mouth ever so slightly upturned, as if—even in death— life amused him.

The fact that he was missing his own dentures brought back a story my mother told over and over in our family when I was growing up. In the early stages of losing his sight, when he was struggling to adjust to his changing vision, my father had been subject to migraine headaches, which made him violently sick to his stomach. During one such bout, he'd lost his new set of dentures—so ill, he'd flushed them right down the toilet before he'd realized he coughed them out. Panicked and not knowing how he'd be able to pay for another set of teeth, he went immediately to the telephone, calling the Water and Sewer Department, hoping there was some way to get them back. The retelling of this story over the years always brought on vociferous hilarity, as my father considered how very silly he'd been in thinking he'd recover dentures from the sewer.

I saw that my mother had taken my advice and given the undertakers the suit I'd suggested my father be buried in. One Easter Sunday back in the mid-eighties, when he'd taken the family to the Publick House in Sturbridge for dinner, he was wearing this suit. It was new then, and he'd hardly ever worn it after that. "This is the suit I'll be buried in," he said that day while we were sitting at the bar having a drink, waiting for our table to be ready.

And then Roxanne arrived. I had known her since right after college. We'd belonged to the same women's consciousness-raising group. Later we did a stint together as VISTA volunteers. But Roxanne's connection to my family was more complex than all of that. She bore the dubious distinction of being the daughter of the man who'd owned the pressed metal company where my father had worked as a machinist before his blindness forced him to choose another career. Ours was a friendship that I know gave my father some trouble, though he'd never tried to openly discourage it.

Roxanne came to the receiving line, flamboyantly surprised after an encounter with my Uncle Tom, my father's younger brother who bears a striking resemblance to him.

"I thought for a minute that he was your father! I went right over to talk to him. I said, 'You have to be Mary's father's brother. You look just like him.'" She laughed good-naturedly at her own sense of drama. "He was sooooo good-looking," she said, gazing back at the casket.

My father's black hair had turned silver with age. He had dark olive-toned Sicilian skin and despite their ineffectiveness, large, beautiful brown eyes. Peg, Jack, and I all have my father's eyes—and even Kate's eyes that are hazel, have more brown than green in them.

I fixed my eyes on my mother's dress again. Did she maybe mean to wear this dress as an unspoken statement about my father's life? Was she perhaps saying by wearing it, "Hats off to ye!" in the manner of an Irish toast? I would like to believe this.

Seventeen

HOLD MY HAND (1964)

It was five minutes of nine on Sunday night, February 9, 1964, just days before my father would be leaving for the rehabilitation school in Newton. We were all seated around the television in the living room. My maternal grandparents had been invited to dinner and they'd decided to stay to watch *The Ed Sullivan Show*. My grandfather was sitting on the couch next to my father, and my mother and grandmother occupied the two armchairs. Jack, Peg, and Kate were sitting next to me on the rug in front of the television.

A real teenager then, I would have preferred to watch the Beatles' first U.S. television performance with my friends. Like most adolescents I spent hours after school, listening over and over again to each new Beatles release, finding that the music helped me to overcome the usual teenage angst, that the lyrics helped shake off my mother's pessimistic attitude and my own worries about our family situation. The music gave me a renewed interest in life; anything seemed possible, and more so with every new hit record. One day I was in love with Paul, another day it was John or George. I think I got the most solace out of dreaming of Ringo Starr though, because his goofy sense of humor made him seem like someone I might really know. Yet, in a way, they all seemed familiar. What I now believe especially attracted my friends and me to the Beatles was that we knew unconsciously that we shared something much deeper with them than a love of popular music: we knew where they came from. We saw that they were working class kids just as we were, and that they had made it, and they gave us hope that we might, too. But sitting on the rug, watching the Beatles while stuffing popcorn into my mouth, I was thirteen years old and naive about how very far away I was from realizing the fantasies I dreamed up then.

I knew—even before the show started that night—that watching the Beatles with my family and not my friends wasn't going to be all that satisfying. I knew that I could count on my mother to put down any public display of affection or unconscious emotion, so I was going to have to control myself when I heard, "I Want to Hold Your Hand." I wondered how was I ever going to contain my excitement? I'd read news stories of girls fainting and hysterical.

"No talking when it comes on," I announced, making more of a demand than a request.

I knew that my grandmother usually talked all through *every* television program.

"This is history being made," I said, when Ed Sullivan announced that he had "a really big shew" for us.

"That's enough of that," my mother said to me.

Mr. Sullivan, my current events and history teacher had drummed into us that we were living in an important time in history. It was imperative, he believed, that we should be informed, know what was happening in the world beyond our little Worcester Main South neighborhood. "Don't be limited," he'd say to us, following that advice with, "Get out if you have the chance." And I'd think, *Brilliant! I'm all for that.* Mr. Sullivan would quiz us each day before our regular lesson. He's ask us questions about the stories appearing on the front page of the newspaper—about Vietnam, which was a country that I hadn't known about before I was a student in his eighth grade class. While I watched that night in our small living room, I'm sure that I must have been thinking that perhaps the next day in class we'd have an interesting discussion about the Beatles; they'd been front-page news ever since their plane had landed at JFK.

When my grandmother heard Ed Sullivan say, "All the way from Liverpool, England," she lost control and began chastising my mother for allowing me to watch.

"Ye aren't going to let her watch those dirty limeys, are ye?" she said. "I've lost any respect I had for that man," she said about Ed.

When she called him "a renegade from his Irish heritage," I didn't understand.

That night I was not nearly as disappointed when I couldn't hear the Beatles singing above the screams of the fans in the audience, as I was about my grandmother's behavior. She broke the dream for me, the fantasy of being there in that audience, instead of at home with my family on Norwood Street in Worcester, Massachusetts. I was both angry and hurt.

"They aren't dirty limeys," I yelled back. "Don't call them that!"

But my grandmother would not be silenced. "I'm through with Ed Sullivan," she said, like she'd been married to him or something. "That renegade! Walter Brennan and Red Skelton are the only ones I like anymore," she said—meaning, I guessed—*Irish* entertainers. "I'm through with that man!"

She had been to see Walter Brennan on Broadway in *God is My Partner*. When I visited her one day after school, I'd read the *Playbill*. After her trip to New York she had been coming to our house every week to watch Walter Brennan in *The Real McCoys*, since she didn't have a television of her own. Red Skelton always ended his show, putting on a foolish grin and saying, "Good night and may God bless," and so she liked him, too.

"He's a heathen," she proclaimed that night, about Ed Sullivan.

I lost any patience I might have had. "This isn't your house and it isn't your TV, so just shut up!" I yelled at the top of my voice.

I'd thought my grandfather was asleep on the couch, but he began tsk-tsk-ing then. "Tsk-tsk," he would say, whenever anyone said anything he found offensive. And if he really got mad he said, "Dammit to hell!" He probably would have said, "Dammit to Hell!" except that he had been sleeping and he didn't hear exactly what I'd said. The commotion had startled him awake.

"Bold girl! You're a bold girl!" my grandmother said, like it was an unarguable fact.

She was sitting up straight and not relaxing back in her chair, as she had been. She was still wearing her pillbox hat, which was covered in silk feathers that had been dyed salmon pink, so they would look like flowers, and she'd obviously chosen it to match her dress. She never took her hat off when she visited. "So no one asks me to do dishes," she said if I asked her why she left it on.

My adolescent rage was all my grandmother had needed to begin recounting the history of the Irish people, more specifically, their mistreatment at the hands of the English. She was reminding me of my roots and the disloyalty she thought I was displaying toward my ancestors by having affection for the four mop top young lads from Liverpool. Because Ed Sullivan had given the audience the opportunity to swoon over four Englishmen, the history my grandmother had learned by word of mouth—not having had much formal education—came spilling out. And so, she had lectured me from the tapestry-covered wing chair, where she always sat, her throne in our living room.

"The dirty limeys cut off the breasts of Irish women. They did that after they'd had their way with them. Then, they starved them!"

Ringo Starr shook his mop top and smiled kindly. Paul McCartney, who looked like one of the choirboys at St. Peter's, looked romantically into John Lennon's eyes. I read their lips. "I want to hold your hananananananaandd!' Ringo Starr hit the cymbals. The fans were screaming bloody murder. Some of them had tears streaming down their cheeks, and if I didn't know what was really happening and had just seen a photo of the audience, I might have thought they *had* actually witnessed a murder.

"I hate you," I said confidently to my grandmother, wanting her to believe it, yet knowing that I didn't really mean it.

I immediately remembered every nice thing she'd ever done for me. She had been buying my clothes: many years I wouldn't have had a winter coat had she not bought one for me. She had welcomed me into her house whenever I felt like going there after school, even though I arrived, more often than not, without warning. By allowing me to be there she'd kept me from hunger, always feeding me supper of meat and potatoes, vegetables and fruit, the kind of meals we generally didn't get at home except on Sundays; she had fed my sweet tooth, letting me influence her buying of pastries and candies from the Cushman Bakery delivery man. And just as importantly, she'd fed my spirit with her collection of children's books and encyclopedias, her piano and reams of sheet music, the jars of stray pearls for stringing, and the stacks of old magazines and Christmas cards from which I could make collages, what I called "my creations."

It was also my grandmother who, years earlier, had taken charge when my mother could not, when I had been in terrible pain from a toothache. It was something I would never forget. She had walked with me in tow from one dentist's office to another in the tall brick buildings downtown, determined to find someone to pull the aching, abscessed tooth. She wouldn't give up until she finally found a dentist who, without warning, slapped a black ether mask over my face, not giving me time to resist before I was snuffed out. When I awakened with a bloody wad of cotton stuffed where the bad tooth had been, I'd been grateful to her that she'd freed me from such terrible pain.

Even though I realized that my grandmother had been central to my well being, I still wanted to hurt her. How I hated her breaking the dream for me that night. All I was doing was trying to hold onto typical teenage fantasies at a time when reality was bearing down hard on my family and me. What I didn't understand, I guess, was the fact that old history and new history clashed that night. I couldn't have known then, but of course it was only the beginning of all that. There would be many more arguments about history and politics in the next several years as I came to understand about Vietnam and the Civil Rights Movement and the continuing troubles in Ireland and other countries in the world. All I knew then though, was that my grandmother would not let me be.

The Beatles sang "I Saw Her Standing There."

When it was over I went to my room. In the dark tears came and I longed for the kind of peace I often felt while walking home alone across the Clark University campus after being at a friend's house. I wanted nothing as much as to lose myself in my dream of being independent.

Gathered around the television every Thursday evening, our whole family—minus my father—watched *The Donna Reed Show*. My grandmother and grandfather and often even Auntie Margaret were there to see the Stone family work things out quietly at family meetings while they were having dinner. We were different though, struggling all the time— more like the families in plays I would later read in high school and college, the ones I would watch on *American Playhouse* a few years later—more like characters in Eugene O'Neill, Thomas Wolfe, Arthur Miller, or Tennessee Williams. We were dealt a different hand than the Stone family, and although I knew that, even as a teenager I was in love with the kind of life those TV people had. I wanted peace and quiet. No one ever needed to raise her voice on *The Donna Reed Show*. I could imagine the family working out ahead of time, the rules for watching the Beatles on *The Ed Sullivan Show* and everyone pretty much sticking to them.

It wasn't that the Stone kids didn't have any of the problems my brother and sisters and I had. But all they ever faced were the ordinary difficulties of growing up—a first crush, a problem with a teacher, finding a date for a special dance or football game. Beyond the rites of passage and ordinary arguments, what problems did the television Stone family have? None it seemed.

The difficulties evident in our household demanded extremes—either silence or arguments that ended in screaming and crying—nothing in between. Our situation kept changing, becoming more precarious as I grew older. Before my father enrolled in the rehab program and found a new career, going into business for himself, there was never enough money for necessities, even with my father working double shifts for many years. The help of my grandparents, while keeping us out of poverty, must have created tension for my father, especially. We were obligated to them. "Never be obligated to anyone," my mother would advise us, one the few principles of friendship she professed.

Eighteen

RUBY TUESDAY (1964)

My father was in Newton at St. Paul's Rehabilitation Center for Newly Blinded Adults. Because my mother knew that the students at St. Peter's were always brought to church for *The Blessing of the Throats* to observe St. Blaise Day, she said to me, "When you go to church today, pray for your father."

My father's name was Biagio, which in Italian means Blaise. It was therefore, the feast day of his patron saint. What better day then, to ask that blessings be bestowed upon him? I had never heard anyone call him Biagio. Even his mother and father didn't call him that. They called him, "Be" (say "Bay"), and whenever they did, it made me think of the sound a baby lamb or some other little animal would make. To Mr. Roche across the street Mr. Sabuk in the corner house, and Mr. Sadowsky next door, my father was simply, "John." Sometimes though, he had important papers to sign and he asked me to show him where the line was, so that he could sign them properly. When I guided his hand I noticed that he wrote: "B. John Bonina." That was the same way his name was listed in the telephone book. Once in a while, he even wrote his complete name on *legal* papers.

"This is my legal name," he told me, when I asked about it one day.

When my father did write out "Biagio John Bonina," the letters looked fine to start, but eventually they began making their way up hill, just a little at first; then they took off, moving way up diagonally, so that he lost the line entirely. My father's signature ended up looking like the incline of a mountain.

Once, when I wanted to know why he mainly used his middle name, *John*, I asked my mother and she said, "He uses it so that he can be like everyone else." When she said this I thought my mother meant that he was trying to fit in. Surely she knew that my father wasn't like everyone else.

At school, Mr. Sullivan said that the President, Martin Luther King, or anyone with a public life of giving speeches and doing what they did, had people who worked for them called "advance men." Whenever they went anywhere to give a speech those people went on ahead to scout things out, like the Indians guiding the explorers and new settlers, I used to think. That's what I was—a scout, my father's advance girl. It just never made sense to me that my father was not different, and that I was not different because of this fact. I didn't know any other girls my age who had the kind of responsibility I had. Other fathers drove cars, but my father and I were seen walking everywhere. I took *him* places. We *were* different, and people looked at us that way.

Who cared what people thought? But sometimes I considered hiding away in my room to listen to music or to read. I don't need anyone, I'd think. Yet deep down, I knew, too, that my father had always refused to hide; he walked right down Main Street to St. Peter's, like anyone else in the neighborhood might. He found his way to the Communion rail, just as the others did, just as I did on the morning of the feast of St. Blaise.

My father's patron saint, according to the legend I heard, saved a little boy from choking on a fish bone or something that got caught in his throat. The boy would have died if Blaise hadn't come along to help him out.

One by one we filed out of our pews and went to kneel at the altar rail. The priest moved down the line to crisscross a pair of beeswax candles under our chins. He held them there at our throats and quickly recited some prayers to protect us from such a fate, and to ward off any other diseases that might affect our throats. The candles were made in the convent by the parish nuns, the ones who also made the small white circles of unleavened bread, the wafers which the priest would consecrate, transforming them during Mass into *the body and blood of Our Lord Jesus Christ*. I imagined that the nuns operated a little factory over at the convent, producing nothing less than the tools of magic.

The magic didn't work for me. I got colds that made me lose my voice. Dr. Mulvihill had to be called frequently to come to our house, because I would develop tonsillitis and he would have to write a prescription for penicillin, making my mother constantly threaten to send me to the hospital to have my tonsils removed. She never did do it, but only tortured me with the possibility. What was even worse though was that I had become so self-conscious that I was afraid to talk in class even if I knew the answer to a teacher's question. I especially feared speaking if I had an opinion about a topic under discussion, or if I didn't understand and ought to have asked for further explanation of something new we were learning. All these problems with my throat and voice led me to believe that the St. Blaise candle ritual actually worked backwards for some people, *causing* trouble.

All the girls were having their ears pierced. I saved the money my grandmother gave me and added it to any I'd received as birthday and Christmas gifts, until I had enough to buy a pair of gold earrings. I was told that I needed to wear only gold, in order to avoid any infection. After school Kerry, Betty and I went our friend Susan's house.

Susan put ice cubes on our ears. "To numb them," she said. Then she stuck an ordinary sewing needle through each earlobe. When they were pierced through she put the gold earrings in. The radio on the stove counter played the Rolling Stones song, "Goodbye, Ruby Tuesday." I sang some lines passionately—about holding on and not giving up on your dreams or else you'd go crazy.

Susan said, "Don't change the earrings for a long time—until they heal—and sponge them with alcohol as many times as you can every day."

Susan wanted to be a nurse.

While my father was at St. Paul's Rehabilitation Center, my mother drove us there, every Friday after school let out, so that we could visit with him, which helped me not to miss him too much. Our visits replaced the established routine of weekly shopping excursions with my grandmother to Framingham or Chestnut Hill, and dinner out after.

The visiting room as I remember it, was all gray—floors, walls, furniture—and the room was lit by fluorescent or some other type of lighting that wasn't necessarily comforting. It was a large common room—with a feeling of openness, like that of a school cafeteria — a place where, not just my family, but other visitors and even students who didn't have visitors— congregated to talk about what went on at the center during the week. The conversation was often entertaining, students jazzing each other about the mistakes they'd made in cooking class or they laughed about a compliment one of them—a burly guy—had received from the activities of daily living instructor for the "great job" he did on the cloth squares they'd sewn in class to learn basic stitches. They roared about practical jokes they played on each other or their instructors. They were a good-natured group, and they made a point of including me and my sisters and brother in the conversation. I thought some of them might have been lonely, especially those who were without visitors.

All students at St. Paul's Rehabilitation Center—renamed the Carroll Center for the Blind in 1972 after the death of its founder, Father Thomas J. Carroll —were also required to take part in various courses designed to improve their mobility and navigation skills. One Friday night in April, my father said he was taking a course in fencing.

"Fencing? With swords?" I asked. I'd seen my father take all kinds of risks, and couldn't imagine what benefit there would be in a blind person learning the sport of fencing.

"Yes," my father said. He told us he put on protective clothing and a mask and took up a sword. "You have to be quick on your feet and keep your balance," he said, as if he were the instructor. He explained that fencing would help him develop balance as well as coordination and dexterity, which were all important to being able to master getting around while using a cane.

On one of our last visits to see my father at St. Paul's— toward the end of May— the talk in the visiting room was all about the mobility assignments they'd been given. From what was said, it was a difficult course designed to foster in the students the courage and confidence to walk wherever they needed to go—alone, and using only a cane to guide them. My father's mobility instructor, Robert Amendola, was an artist—a sculptor who had worked with engineers to design the Corsair, a top-level Navy plane used during World War II. When the war was over he was assigned to work on a program developed to help veterans who'd been blinded during their service adjust to life again at home. At St. Paul's, Mr. Amendola developed a course on "Videation in Spatial Orientation." He used what he knew about sculpture to help his blind students understand the relationships of various objects within an environment, using sound cues-- while helping his students keep visual images they held in their minds from when they'd had sight—combining the two to achieve what he termed "videating."

A large black man, who was obviously well-liked by the other students, nearly fell off his chair laughing that Friday night of their week of solo flights taking public transportation into Boston from the suburb of Newton. They'd each been assigned a specific place at which they were to meet their instructor.

"I had no idea—no idea at all—where the heck I was." He described taking a wrong turn somewhere in downtown Boston and unknowingly entering a construction site.

"How long were you wandering around?" I asked, fearing my father might end up in a similar situation.

"It was like a wasteland," the man said. "I could hear men yelling in the distance—somewhere way over there," he gestured with his large right hand. "They thought I could hear what they were saying, I guess—above the noise of the heavy equipment," he said. "So, I started walking toward the voices, to find out what they were yelling."

When he said this, all the students—there were generally only about five or six in the room whenever we visited and that was the case that night—roared heartily and we joined in, and that is when the man bent over, laughing heartily as well, until he regained his ability to go on.

"So I just kept on walking. And walking. And the voices and the equipment noise got louder and louder and trucks were beeping all around me."

There were still some chuckles and muttering from the students who were listening, but the expression on the man's face and a more serious tone of voice conveyed that he had realized the trouble he was in at the time and had been frightened. The laughing stopped as the student began to tell the next part of his story.

"Suddenly there was a guy yelling in my face, 'Get out! Get out of here! This is a hardhat area!' he was screaming."

I sighed, relieved that someone had come to the man's rescue, however harshly he had approached.

The mood in the room changed again and the man smiled and said in a polite— and somewhat feminine voice, what he had said to the construction worker. "Well, sir, I'd be happy to leave if you'd just point me in the right direction. I raised up my stick," he said, "so he'd see I was blind." At this, he leaned over and felt on the floor for his white cane and lifted it up, as he had for the man. "What did that fool think, that I was in there walking in circles around ditches on purpose?"

Everyone in the room laughed harder now, at the idea that the construction worker hadn't realized that the blind man was lost and certainly would leave the construction site where he didn't want to be, but that he needed some help finding his way out.

Mr. Amendola's technique of teaching what my father described as "videating," was going to give him a new way of navigating the world— without me—and that would change both of our lives. For a long time after his course in mobility, my father would deflect praise about how well he could get around in the world, always crediting Mr. Amendola for having taught him how.

Besides learning navigational techniques at the Center, my father learned to read and write in the language of Braille, and when he returned home he gave up listening to *Talking Books*, and started reading instead, the braille edition of a weekly, which summarized the important news, published for the blind by the *New York Times*. At the school he'd also taken an extemporaneous speaking course. He joined Toastmasters, giving talks to other members at restaurants after dinner, putting to use the ability he'd demonstrated on the car rides home from Milford on Sunday evenings, and other times when he lectured us about life. He built a large mahogany bookcase, which stood for years in the living room of our family home. He learned efficient ways of doing ordinary household chores and cooking, having been taught all sorts of tricks to compensate for his low vision. He was changed; after all the worry and fear that he would be isolated and unable to live life fully, he was learning that there were other methods a blind man could use to make his way in the world. The Center improved not just my father's skills, but his attitude, too, reviving his sense of humor, which had nearly been squelched all the years he'd been trying to pass, while hoping that his eyes might get better, not worse.

As it turned out, with my father away, my mother was preoccupied. She continued to remind me once in a while, as she had on the feast of St. Blaise, "Remember your father in your prayers." I thought of him on my own whenever I used the record player he'd given me, or if Mum sent me to the cellar to change a fuse that had burned out. Improvements in my mother's spirit weren't tangible. The house was still disorganized, and she didn't suddenly take an interest in cooking or get involved in activities at school or church, or look for a job. I noticed though, that there was a change in her attitude, and I took advantage of that. Whatever occupied her mind, kept her—at least for a while—from watching me like a hawk, so that I was free to strike out on my own a little more.

For all the worrying I did before my father went away, about his leaving us, while he was gone I didn't have much trouble filling up the time I had spent helping him. I still had to make excuses to my mother, for going out with my friends. They were easy to come by. I have research work to do at the library for my term paper, was a favorite. I would say that I was staying after school to work on a project with someone in my class who lives across the city. There were other excuses, too. I have an extra choir rehearsal. Or I would say, I'm working at the hospital today. I had been a candy striper—though City Hospital didn't call them that. We had green-checkered uniforms and were simply called "volunteers." I gave up that job after a while; although I'd needed my mother's signature to join the staff, there was no such requirement to quit. These were lies that kept me out of arguments with my mother and gave me the opportunity to "expand my horizons," what she might have said sarcastically, had she known.

I don't remember how it happened, but I began dating a Clark University student, someone I'd had my eye on. Perhaps he just sat down next to me one day at the soda fountain at Vernon Drug. I don't remember. He didn't talk much, but I did learn that he was from a small town in another part of the state and that he was a little homesick, being just a freshman. He must have been, I realize now, several years older than I was—unless he was a genius and had started college especially early—but I didn't think that was the case. I was so surprised to be with him that I couldn't concentrate enough to even pay attention to what he was saying. And when I talked, I fell into my habit of rambling on about nothing of much importance, what I did when I was with a person I didn't know very well and was nervous. It was the opposite of clamming up, what I did in a group then.

I suppose that I felt somewhat comfortable with him because he seemed something like the kind of people I knew in my life. I was being safe, as usual. He was more like me though, than the Jewish boys at the radio station--the deejays who melted my heart when I listened to their New York voices coming over the airwaves at night. They scared me a bit, because they were undeniably big city boys.

Every afternoon my Clark boyfriend and I walked around the neighborhood. He seemed to like that. We didn't have a particular route or anything; we just walked aimlessly, no destination in mind. I told him all about me and about the neighborhood, who lived in what house, and how much I hated going to St. Peter's. "Everyone is so immature," I said. I told him that I liked to read and that I wrote poems. "Write one for me," he said, and I thought that that meant he was getting serious. I told him that I was the oldest in my family and that I had two sisters and a brother. He had sisters, he said. He told me that he was studying psychology, and I said, "Oh, I'm really interested in psychology."

When I saw anyone I knew from the neighborhood or school, I looked the other way, hoping they wouldn't try to talk to me. My boyfriend put his arm around me when we walked, and when we found some place to sit that was out of the way, a bench at Crystal Park or a stone wall on a quiet street, he kissed me. They were long, aggressive kisses—not like the kisses the boys at St. Peter's gave. That was all we ever did—walk and kiss—no movies or bowling—just long walks and longer kisses.

"She's growing up fast, isn't she?" some nosy person said to my mother. "She looked so much older with his arm around her."

That was the end of my busy after-school schedule, my mother said. She didn't know I had already stopped seeing him.

Although he'd never suggested that we go to his room, his kisses had been getting hotter, and he'd been looking deeper into my eyes. I could tell we were headed there, if I didn't end it when I did.

Memorial Days

SUNDAY JUNE 7 1993 – MONDAY JUNE 8, 1993

During the evening calling hours, Father Frank Scollen arrived to lead us in a recitation of the rosary, the string of prayers I'd said so often as a child, while lying in bed in the dark, pushing the crystal beads through my fingers, moving my intentions down the conveyor belt of prayers, straight up to heaven, I hoped.

My father had a beautiful rosary from Italy, its beads of carved rosewood. I remember him bringing it to Mass on Sundays sometimes. The rosary was not part of the Mass, but often, people—especially old women—sat in their pews dangling their beads, like elongated bracelets on their wrists, using them to pray. I would be fascinated—almost hypnotized watching the different ways people held them and used their fingers to mark their progress as they traced the circle of five decades of Hail Mary beads spaced by single beads indicating the Lord's Prayer—or as we would say, "Our Fathers."

As my father grew older and after all of us had left home, he and my mother slept in separate bedrooms, my father taking over the one that had been Jack's. I saw his rosary hanging on the bedpost there one day, and I imagined him praying on nights when worry kept him awake. I remembered my own sleepless nights when worry had moved me to pray.

My mother had given the rosary to the undertaker and it was entwined in my father's waxy stone fingers; laid out in the casket, he looked as if he had fallen asleep while praying.

Father Frank was an old friend. Like me, he became an activist in the nineteen sixties. The Church didn't seem to know what else to do with him in the decade that followed, so when they created the Urban Ministry Commission of the Diocese of Worcester, they had him head it up. In the seventies he filled as many Board positions as he could with community organizers, myself included, and he took up among other issues affecting poor and working class people, the plight of the United Farm Workers, even bringing Caesar Chavez to Worcester to speak at one of our meetings, and to drum up support for the grape and lettuce boycott. By the time my father died, Frank had become Monsignor, the head priest of St. Peter's Church. Father Frank ministered to the old timers who'd stayed in the parish in spite of the changes in the neighborhood—and to newcomers, too, many of them poor, Spanish-speaking, and Southeast Asian families who'd replaced the hold the Irish once had on the neighborhood. Frank organized basketball leagues and shelters, and whatever else his common sense told him people needed to get along.

He approached me after leading the rosary. "Do you want to speak tomorrow? Say something tomorrow at the funeral?"

He was matter of fact about asking me to eulogize my father, and my response was immediate. I didn't consider it— not even for a moment. "Oh, I couldn't, Frank."

"You really don't want to?"

"It's not that. I just don't think I'd get through it."

"Well, is there anyone else who wants to?"

"I don't think so," I said. "Who is there?"

"You're sure you don't want to?" he asked.

"I know I couldn't. But you'll say something, Frank, won't you? Can you do the sermon or eulogy?"

"Your mother wants to have Father O'Brien," he said. "But we'll say the Mass together. And I'll say something after."

"Father O'Brien? Oh, no. I want you to do it, Frank."

Thomas F. O'Brien, my mother's cousin, was the son of her favorite uncle, "Dr. Tom," the obstetrician who was so worried about my mother's low weight that he'd persuaded her to leave nursing school. I think my mother wanted Father O'Brien to give the eulogy because he was her connection to a vanished affluence. Perhaps that is the reason she has always held him in such high esteem. My mother had seen him only every twenty years or so after she'd married my father—only at wakes, funerals, or weddings. She had always told just one story about him for as long as I could remember—a story about a trip they'd taken as kids during a vacation at the cottage in Maine—to the Passamaquoddy Indian Reservation; her cousin had been disappointed when he did not find the Indians in full dress, but rather, saw them wearing clothes just like his own. The years had passed, and my mother's cousin had had little or nothing to do with most of the relatives. He'd stayed in touch only with a wealthier cousin. This was hard to excuse simply based on a commitment to priestly duties, given the gossip that went around about his many vacations, when as a priest he'd taken the vow of poverty. He'd nevertheless managed a relatively comfortable lifestyle. What's more, I had heard Father O'Brien's sermons before, and to characterize them at best, they could only be described as "ethereal." I'd been present at the wedding of a distant cousin, where many of the attendees had muttered under their breath and raised eyebrows at each other, finding that he was the one going to give the sermon.

But what disturbed me most about designating Father Tom—as my mother called him— the eulogizer, was that he didn't even know my father. I was bewildered, unable to imagine what on earth he thought he could say about my father's life. He had been absent from it. Did he maybe have one all-purpose eulogy he used? I doubted that Father O'Brien kept tabs on my father's struggle or his accomplishments. I was torn—guilty—to let him have the last public word on my father's life. Yet, I knew that even though I wasn't demonstrably grief-stricken, I was too vulnerable to stand up front and speak at the funeral. Besides, I had too much to say. I was angry my mother had asked him to have such an important role in the funeral proceedings, but I was powerless to change her mind.

"She wants him," my brother Jack said. "What are you gonna do?"

"Don't argue with her," Mark, my husband, said. "You won't change her mind. She needs this, I guess."

I do not remember if I chose readings, though I had often been asked to do so for weddings and funerals of other relatives. I did however insist that someone sing "Amazing Grace," a song my father loved. He would sometimes begin a weeknight phone to me by singing that or a Stevie Wonder tune that was popular at the time.

We were staying at the Yankee Drummer Inn in Auburn. My brother's house was in Auburn, too, and although we were invited to spend the night before the funeral there, we declined. After the hundreds of people we saw during the wake, I just wanted to be alone with Mark and Gianni. This was the same motel where twelve years before, Mark and I spent our first night as a married couple. It was Father Frank who had performed the church ceremony that day, too. Because that was the only time we had ever stayed at this motel, I couldn't help but realize that the way I felt contrasted sharply with the mix of elation and exhaustion I'd felt that other night. Tonight our suitcases were not packed for a trip to Quebec City. There would be no knock on the door by room service with a surprise gift of champagne from a dear friend. We had no cause for celebration. We'd checked in here only as a way of keeping it together, trying to preserve our little family bundle in the midst of grief.

In the morning the sun was shining. I had expected rain. I was happy not to have to wear my trench coat or to stand beneath the undertaker's giant black umbrella. It was a beautiful bright June day, and I was happy to be alive. Gianni's blond hair sparkled as we packed the car and left for Norwood Street. My cousin Deborah had enlisted her daughter, Gabriella, to take care of Gianni at the family house during the funeral.

My mother with the reputation for being late—*the late Mary Feeherry*—surprised us by being all dressed and ready to go when the limousine arrived at the house to take us to the funeral home. And once we arrived there was an altogether different feeling as the mourners solemnly and slowly gathered before the coffin was shut and loaded into the hearse for the motor procession from downtown to Main South. People arrived and lined up to kneel in front of my father's body to say goodbye to him, and to offer a last prayer. Mostly, there were whispers or just plain silence; yet every so often, someone who was probably overcome by nervousness, made a silly remark, and a giggle escaped and was stifled. Once in a while I noticed someone reach into the coffin and touch one of my father's hands or his face. The ones who did this were not some of my blind relatives, looking in their own way, but others who had gestured this way for whatever reason. I had seen wives and mothers kiss the faces of the deceased, and some in grief threw themselves on the casket. I'd never known what they meant by doing that.

One by one, people took their turn. A loyal contingent of our Cambridge friends occupied a row among the family. Father Frank led everyone in a final prayer and the crowd gradually thinned out as the undertaker called each name and politely instructed people to get their motors running and line up in the order that allowed etiquette to prevail.

I was sitting next to my mother and saw Phil Callahan, the undertaker, approach her as the room cleared out.

"I have his wedding ring and rosary," he said to her, wanting to give them back before the burial.

"No," she said. "You should leave them."

Phil was obviously surprised and perplexed by her refusal. "You want me to *bury* him with the ring and rosary?"

I didn't understand it either.

"Of course," she said.

Nineteen

WALK ALONE (1964-1968)

While a student at St. Paul's Rehabilitation Center, my father had sessions with a vocational counselor who had identified his interests and abilities and recommended a program in food service management. When he returned home from his months away, full of confidence and with his spirit restored, he enrolled in a training program administered by the Commission for the Blind, working with a blind cafeteria manager in Littleton, Massachusetts, to learn the business.

It was obvious that my mother was also hopeful about my father's work situation, pleased at the prospect of him having his own business in the near future. She willingly drove back and forth from Worcester to Littleton twice a day, to and from the training site; this meant that she was behind the wheel, driving almost six hundred miles during the week. I'm not sure if my father was paid during that time, but there was in our family a sense that he was working again. Even if he hadn't earned a paycheck then, there was the hope that the investment of time he spent learning would lead to a much better situation than he'd had in the past. He would become a small business owner.

When he completed the training program he became the manager of the cafeteria at Worcester Pressed Steel, which had more than two hundred employees in the mid-nineteen sixties. I think now, that it was an interesting move—a kind of synthesis—for my father to take the leap from working as a machinist at a small pressed metal company, to serving food to the workers at this much larger steel processing operation. Perhaps his familiarity with a factory environment helped to insure his success.

My mother worked alongside my father during the lunch hour, and she stayed until the afternoon shift came on at three. I think that they were both happier than at any other time I can remember. My father was making decent money, and my mother was getting out of the house and helping him. She was generally not at home when we got out of school, and that taste of freedom was good for all of us.

In addition to my mother, my father had only one other regular employee, a woman who worked with him in the mornings until my mother arrived—or in case of my mother's absence, stayed on for the rest of the workday. I worked for my father on school holidays and vacations, to give my mother a break and to earn some money. I made sandwiches to order, worked the grill, helped in the kitchen if necessary, and cleared tables. My father sometimes asked me to serve the company officials in their private dining room just off his kitchen. I think that when they came to eat in the cafeteria it made him feel like a real restaurateur. He was like the maître d', as he greeted the officers and trustees. He took pleasure in knowing them all, and loved reciting names like, Mary Louise Higgins Wilding-White, which amused him for the important mergers he understood were reflected in her several names.

I was in awe of the whole cafeteria operation, which featured a restaurant-sized professional, spotless, industrial, stainless steel kitchen, where everything shined and the food was of high quality and delicious. My father was the business owner, manager, chef, cashier, and dishwasher. Every weekday he served a full and continental breakfast, full dinners as well as soup and sandwiches for the noon hour lunch, and continuous coffee breaks during the day, all executed with remarkable organization and precise timing. At any given time during the day, my father worked only with one other person assisting him. His reputation for good service and good food brought a crowd of employees—shop and office workers, and management—to line up for the daily offering of one or two entrees with all the fixings; the daily menu featured real dinners: a large roast of beef, pork, or lamb, baked scrod or chicken, lasagna or spaghetti and meatballs made according to a family recipe. He served a homemade soup every day as well, alternating between chicken, beef stew, vegetable or fish chowder. Whoever assisted him—my mother, his hired staff person, me, one of my sisters—worked the sandwich bar and grill and helped him in the kitchen as needed.

It was often hectic and stressful to be with him in the half hour before lunch was served at noon.

"Ree, take a look at this!" he'd order, having pulled an extra large pan that held twenty pounds of roast beef out of the oven, wanting me to help him check to see if it was ready. He wouldn't be wearing protective mitts on his hands, his fingers so calloused that he did not feel a burn.

I'd sometimes hesitate and he'd get angry.

"What time is it? Out of my way. It's got to be done." Then he'd carry the hot pan in his bare hands over to the counter where the slicing machine was, and I'd close my eyes when he hit the switch, afraid for his safety.

But I never saw him get hurt.

At noon on the dot he took his place at the soup station he set up next to the cash register, and he began listening as customers started to arrive, listening for voices, so that he would recognize the regulars, call them by name, look them in the eye as if he could see them when they slid their trays in front of him or handed him a five dollar bill. He put his hand out to greet visitors, new employees, and occasionally a clueless salesman who would show up at this inopportune time, and he'd be pleasant and hospitable rather than disturbed saying, "Here, have a cup of coffee. I'll be with you shortly. Do you want something to eat? How about BLT?" He'd order one before the salesman had a chance to consider it, "Ree, make him a BLT." Watching him delighted not just me, but I could see how my father's upbeat mood affected the crowd of hungry customers waiting to be served. There was a kind of repartee that went on, with certain more outgoing guys hollering out to him from the rear of the line, impatient or pretending to be.

"What are you doin' up there, knittin' a sweater?" a burly guy once yelled out while I was working the lunch shift.

"Yes sir, this may take some time. You're a big fella," my father shot back, figuring that, I guess, from hearing his booming voice. He regularly addressed the workers as "sir" or "mam," perhaps remembering how rare it is for a factory worker to be treated politely on the job.

My father ladled out soup, never spilling a drop or missing a beat, as quick with a good natured teasing response or joke, as he was at making change at the cash register. He'd flirt with the women, giving them the attention they sometimes enjoyed, often complimenting their looks, imagining them as blonds or redheads, which led to more repartee.

"How do you know what color my hair is? You're blind. Or are you pretending to be blind?" I heard a woman tease him back once.

Stone blind, somehow my father kept all the plates spinning on poles above his head. It was something miraculous to experience and testifies to his genius, especially considering what went on behind the scenes to make it all happen.

He would disappear for a while before the afternoon coffee breaks began. He'd take a break himself, and then head to check his stock in the storeroom, after which he would go to the phone outside the kitchen and call the Coca- Cola distributor or New England Coffee and Tea, or Fairway Beef, to place the next day's orders. He had to keep so much in mind, not having then, the kind of technology available now to assist the blind. There were so many salesmen and suppliers to contact—so much to keep straight—to keep in mind, so that he had the food, paper goods, cleaning supplies, and equipment necessary to properly manage his food service operation. He remembered not just each name and telephone number, but which products he bought from which salesmen. He knew the last time he'd ordered something from each one, and what he paid for it and what his profit margin was; so he knew when pricing changes went into effect. He knew not just where to find every item in the stockroom, but he knew what was left of each. He knew these things as well as he knew the ages of his children.

What it meant to me that my father was working at something he loved and doing well at it, was that I didn't have to spend much time worrying about him, nor did I feel the need to be always at the ready to help out—except as a paid employee when he asked me to work for him. With my father's work situation stable, I was free to concentrate on the ordinary things that teenage girls found important.

My friend Kerry and I somehow found out where the Clark University radio station was, and we devised a plan to meet one of the deejays as he was headed to the studio. From there it was easy to be invited in. WCUW broadcast then from a room at the top of a fire escape at the back of Estabrook Hall, the music building on the corner of Woodland and Charlotte, almost directly across from Clifton Street, where my friend lived. All the time we had been wondering and brainstorming the whereabouts of the radio station, and there it was one day, right under our noses.

We must have had an open invitation to visit, because the way I remember it, we were there a lot and no one ever acted as if we were making pests of ourselves. That first day we went there, we stood outside the door with the WCUW sign posted on it. I turned around once we reached the top landing of the fire escape, and I looked out at our neighborhood from that new perspective up above it all. I thought that it didn't look so bad from way up there. I could see Kerry's porch nearby. I thought of us sitting there on so many afternoons, grooving to the Supremes, the Four Tops, and Aretha Franklin on the record player—or tuned into WCUW, trying to imagine what the student deejays looked like.

More than anything, being invited up to the radio station offered us very specific evidence that our dreams could come true. Sitting behind the console, starting at the *On the Air* sign lit up, we felt important, and not at all like the townies or groupies that I suppose we were then. We were hushed every so often if the deejay named Rockaway, who took his name from the Queens, New York beach that was his home, was about to read a playlist or a public service announcement. We were amazed to find ourselves sitting there among the bodies attached to the voices with New York accents we had heard so many nights, while listening in the dark of our bedrooms to our transistor radios.

The student deejays were our antithesis. They came from out of town, most of them from out of state, a majority from the New York City area, and this meant many things—from minor to more significant differences. When I think of it now, I suppose that some of their families had money and that it would have been obvious to them that ours did not, but the subject never came up. It seemed not to matter. It was rock and roll and Motown that we cared about. The music was everything to us. Above all else, the students were Jewish. We didn't know any Jewish teenagers. I think now we must have amused them, visiting the studio, sometimes showing up still wearing our Catholic school uniforms, and loving not just the Beatles and the Rolling Stones, but the rest of good rock and roll. We often arrived proudly carrying *The Avatar*, the alternative newspaper from Fort Hill Commune, which we bought outside Woolworth's downtown and hid from our families, because the word *fuck* was used as an expletive what seemed like hundreds of times in every issue.

I wrote the usual poems of teenage angst. "I'm lost/Never to be found/Never to find myself," are lines from one that I published in the school literary supplement. More than anything, I wanted to fit in, to be like other teenagers—popular, not an outsider—and I worked really hard at it. I was itching to earn money of my own to buy clothes, records, and earrings. I had what I thought was my own style, but it was really just a reflection of fashion: floral printed cotton "Granny dresses," bell-bottomed jeans, mini skirts, and pea coats. I no longer wanted to wear the kind of clothes my mother or my grandmother would choose for me. So when I turned sixteen, I took a job working on weekends and after school for the Glass family, cashiering at their supermarket in the neighborhood. I gave the job more of my energy than I gave to writing poetry or keeping up with my schoolwork.

In addition to working for my father at the cafeteria and cashiering at the supermarket, I had a regular babysitting job on the north side of city along Indian Lake, a more well to do section of the city, bordering the town of Holden. It felt suburban, and it was near the area where my mother used to take us for car rides on hot summer afternoons when I was younger, all the while talking of her dream of living someday in one of the beautiful houses there. When I worked that job, every afternoon when I got out of school, I caught the #9 Holden bus at Barnard's Department Store downtown, to go to the home of my mother's cousin, Margaret, who had three sons at the time. I was hired to care for the youngest, a toddler. I used to see the family's black maid, who took the same bus I did. She always acted as if she had never seen me before, although we got on and off at the same stop, and walked the same way into the same house. I used to think of Rosa Parks, whenever I saw that woman on the bus, and I wondered if she had been taught not to speak to white people, and that maybe that was why she didn't say "hello" back to me—even though we worked for the same family.

My mother was thrilled when I was invited to go with Margaret's family to Cape Cod as the live-in babysitter for the whole summer one year. I was "at that age," I heard my mother say to her on the telephone, agreeing to let me go away with them. I'd fantasized that being away from home for the summer would be exciting—my first real taste of freedom from my family, I thought. Since my father was independent and successful at his business, I would not worry about him the way I used to when I went to the Maine cottage with my aunt. But it was a lonely and boring time living out that summer on the Cape. I had no freedom to come and go, and spent days with the toddler and sometimes his two older brothers, and was home nearly every evening, babysitting while their parents were at the Country Club.

When I was back home in September my social life resumed. In the fall there were hayrides in the Brookfields, football games out under the lights in small New England towns like Clinton, Leicester, and Spencer and I remember velvet green fields illuminated by floodlights, and the crisp autumn air. I went dancing every weekend at the Comic Strip, Bojangles, and Sir Morgan's Cove, where sometimes rock and roll recording stars played. The weekly dances with a deejay and local bands at the St. Peter's School hall were famous throughout the city, and my friends and I went to those, too. Kids came from all over and sometimes there were fights, but all anyone really wanted those Friday nights, was to be with someone they could hold close by the time the Righteous Brothers' "Unchained Melody" was played—"the last dance" each week.

At school, singing and drama were my main extracurricular activities. In drama I played the part of Mrs. Kirby, the capitalist's wife, in *You Can't Take It With You.* I secretly wished for the part of the anarchist's daughter who falls in love with Mrs. Kirby's son, rather than being cast as a woman I viewed as a "snob," who had the line: "My great solace is spiritualism." In the senior class musical, I played the part of Mrs. McAfee, another mother, and in—of all things—*Bye Bye Birdie*, the celebration of youth and popular music. Instead of swooning over Conrad Birdie, my stage husband Michael Ferguson and I sang, "Kids," the lyrics of parents exasperated with the behavior of their teenagers. I always tried out for other parts—the female leads—but it seemed that whoever was doing the casting could only see me in a supporting role.

Spring of junior year my parents and I went to the "Guidance Appointment," an advising session scheduled to help with career planning—or as it was referred to at St. Peter's—*a meeting to talk about your future.* It was assumed that college prep students would be applying to colleges in the fall.

The guidance counselor at St. Peter's was Jack-of-all-trades—
basketball coach, English, history, and homeroom teacher.
"Journalism," he said, "is no career for a woman." I'd been
writing for the school newspaper, and that was what I was
interested in studying. "She should be a teacher," the
guidance counselor advised.

She should be a teacher. He meant me. I was at that meeting
with my father and mother, although the counselor never
referred to me by name, never even addressed me. There was
no personality test, no consulting with the journalism teacher
or other English teachers, no examination of writing samples.
I wasn't even asked a question or allowed to comment. It was
like being given marching orders. The word came down: "She
should be a teacher."

When we arrived home that night I cried and pleaded with
my mother and father to forget what the guidance counselor
had suggested. "How can he make that judgment?" I asked
them. "He doesn't even know me." The guidance counselor
had been a thorn in my side for three years, bothering me for
whatever reason, whenever he found the opportunity. He'd
singled me out as a shy freshman student, calling on me to
read aloud in his class Elizabeth Barrett Browning's poem,
"How Do I Love Thee?" —while smirking to his coterie, the
athletes who always sat around him. After taking his history
class I'd lost the interest I'd had in the subject in the past.
There wasn't really much teaching going on in his classes.

"You heard what he said. You'll be better off as a
teacher," my mother agreed with him.

"Teachers do have a good situation. They have vacations
during the year, plus they're off all summer," my father said,
perhaps thinking of how difficult it had become for him to
take time off for a vacation, now that he had his own
business. "I wouldn't mind that."

At least someone realized finally that I could sing. The
same year that college planning began, I was given a solo for
the Glee Club's spring concert, assigned to sing "You'll
Never Walk Alone" from the Rodgers and Hammerstein

musical, *Carousel.* Sister Mary Albert, the new director of the all-school chorus, the glee club, believed that I could carry it off. Everyone in the family came to hear me perform—my mother, father, Peg, Kate, Jack, aunts and uncles and grandparents from both sides of the family sat up front.

I stepped down from the riser very carefully, and I walked to the microphone. Each foot felt leaden. I saw the audience watching every move I made. They were listening intently to my voice. I figured that they were all wondering if I was going to get through it all right. When I began, I could hardly hear myself singing. People were smiling though. They were smiling at me and I had never expected that. I thought only that I'd be scrutinized, the way I had always been when I was out in public walking with my father. I expected to see people with furrowed brows or squinting eyes in the audience. That was what I was used to seeing, when people looked at me. But they smiled, enthusiastically, it seemed—not just out of politeness—and they were clapping energetically when I finished.

Later, I listened to compliments from my family. Aunt Jean, my father's youngest sister, said how proud she was of me. "I don't know," she said, "how you ever stood there so bravely. I could never do that." "Very good, Ree," my father said. My mother withheld her response until I asked for it. "Not bad," she said.

I wondered if she were thinking that I could have done better. "I messed up on that high note, I think," I said to her.

She said nothing back. I think now that as she sat there in the audience watching me on stage, my mother was probably thinking of her own singing days, of hitting the high notes.

Our concert was such a success that we took it on the road. We went to nursing homes to sing selections for the residents, and at the Worcester State Hospital for the mentally ill we performed the entire concert program, including my solo.

The nineteenth century hospital loomed over Route 9, identified by its huge clock tower. We entered and began our walk down the long hall.

"Stay close. Single file," Sister said.

We walked in a line that was reminiscent of the safety patrols we'd formed for walking home from grade school. Down, down, a long corridor to what I think now was a locked ward. In my memory, the door had no window. It was like the heavy metal door of a storage room. It opened without making a sound and the patients crowded around us as we came in. We were something to look at in this grey room without any pictures on the walls, only signs like *No Exit* or *Private* on some of the doors. Every girl was wearing an ivory or white pleated skirt with a white lace blouse tucked into it, held in place by a purple satin cummerbund. The boys had on dark pants and they wore purple satin bow ties with white shirts and purple cummerbunds, too. The school song played in my head whenever we were dressed for a concert. "Saint Peter's, Saint Peter's, purple and white…" The door had opened for us, but this was no gate of heaven we were entering.

We were singing "Paper Moon," about a scene cut out of paper and cardboard, like the paper dolls I made as a little girl. I counted three men and one woman whose mouths were open all the time, so that they were drooling. Their jaws slackened, I know now, because they must have been heavily medicated.

"You can stay there," Sister said, when it was time for my solo. She meant that I didn't have to leave the group and move out front.

We had no microphone. We didn't need one here. It was a small, stuffy, crowded room. With all eyes on me, with my heart beating strong and my legs so weak that I thought they might give out, I started to sing. I don't know how I did it. I was singing, "You'll Never Walk Alone," a song with lyrics full of irony within this context, about walking through storms yet holding your head high. A young woman was staring at me, her face expressionless. She didn't look much older than I was—five years maybe. I could see in her eyes, the emotional storms she had weathered—in fact, all the faces in the audience showed the scars of trauma. Some were white and puffy, some red as if sunburned; some foreheads— of what must have been middle-aged men and women—were as lined as those of old people. I tried to look above the sea of sad faces. I knew even then, only sixteen, that the words were ridiculous in their message of hope. Yet the song expressed what I saw in my father's eyes, and I concentrated on that idea to get me through it. The song that I was singing was one of inspiration and dignity. I was singing and they were listening. I was telling them a story. I was giving them a talk, like one of my father's talks. I was singing them a lullaby on a dark night in a dark place, and I was going on with it to the end.

The lyrics of the song were like one of the speeches, the little lectures that my father used to give to me and to my sisters and brother when he had us in his power, when we needed a good talking to, especially if we complained to him of life's unfairness or worry. Just as those talks always were, this was a song about going on and about the endless possibilities of love. I didn't know what it meant to the people I sang for, to hear this song. I didn't even know if they could hear me, if they could grasp any meaning at all in the words, or if they heard something familiar in the music. But I went on with the song, unwavering, singing it better than I ever had, telling the audience at the hospital not to be afraid of the darkness or storms that might come up, but to just keep walking.

I was singing. I was singing a song so ridiculous in its hope, so clichéd. But I knew about the dark. I knew how to get around in the darkness of the world. I'd watched my father learn to do it and not to be afraid, and I had learned from him. Singing this song was about that as much as anything. It was a song out of love. I knew about love from being my father's eyes.

Memorial Days:

MONDAY JUNE 7, 1993

In addition to his clothes, these are the things my father left behind. He had a black thorn walking stick from Ireland, a souvenir given to him by Eleanor Reardon, the woman my maternal grandfather married when he was seventy-nine and Grammy Feeherry had been dead for several years. Although it was not of much use as a navigational tool, my father had nevertheless used the walking stick for dressy occasions, instead of his beat up metal cane—the blind stick. He had two of the latter—one of them a collapsible fold-up variety that he used because it was unobtrusive when he was safely seated somewhere—and the other, like a shepherd's staff. The only other blind-person gadgets he had were a manual braillewriter and a braille watch, but I don't remember seeing them after he died.

In winter he wore a black Persian lamb Russian-style hat with a Stetson label, a relic of the panache he'd had as a younger man. I once showed my friend Pierce an early fifties photograph of my mother and father standing in front of his black Packard, and Pierce remarked, "Wow, he looks like one of the Beats." He wore chinos and a knit V-neck sweater. His dark hair was combed in the style of the day, and he held his arms down close to his sides, a cigarette between two fingers of his right hand. My mother stood beside him, wearing a very traditional dark dress with large flowers on it.

I asked my mother, if I could have my father's hat as a memento. I keep it wrapped up in tissue paper in my closet, and once in a while, I take it out to look at it, and it reminds me of my father's spirit.

On the morning of my father's funeral, our procession moved down Main Street from downtown, the route to Main

South sharply revealing the changes that had taken place since I was a child. We passed through the Piedmont neighborhood, where I'd spent so many afternoons of my childhood visiting my grandparents in the house in which my mother lived while growing up. Before I left Worcester, when I was working as a community organizer and a VISTA (Volunteers in Service to America) volunteer, I lived on Piedmont Street, too—just two doors down from that house, in one that had belonged to the Mahoneys when my mother lived there. Mr. Mahoney had been Mayor of Worcester, but when I lived in that house, it was owned by a large New England company, which manufactured and marketed plumbing supplies. With expansion in mind, the company had bought up many of the houses on the street for pipe yards and storage facilities. When I lived there the house was rundown as most of them owned by the company were, and the central heat was set on high all winter, forcing the tenants to open windows in order to breathe freely. When I lived in that house, the neighborhood had been designated a poverty zone and houses were going up in flames at night. In the late seventies, I rented a place on Castle Street, the next block over. I used to call that apartment the penthouse, because it was on the top floor in a Victorian brick building next to a row house, and on an incline—so it loomed over the others, the last building on the street directly across from an overgrown wood called Castle Hill, an abandoned city park.

Seeing the neighborhood as the funeral cortege went by, I saw that it had further deteriorated in the years since I'd left. Beacon Pharmacy, which was just around the corner from my old Castle Street apartment, was still in business, as was the busy phone booth island, where prostitutes and drug dealers and those looking to buy, congregated.

Our limousine followed the hearse and the driver headed to the house on Norwood Street that had been our family home. He would pause there briefly, as was the tradition in Worcester—and many other cities— before taking us to the church for the funeral Mass.

Riding through the old neighborhood, I felt, nevertheless, like a stranger. I remember that once, I could not get lost walking its streets, although I sometimes tried, craving, as I did from a very young age, experiences that veered from the usual. I looked out the window, trying to remember what used to be where in the neighborhood. Was anything unchanged?

Large houses that had been funeral homes during my childhood had been turned into offices, nursing homes, and rooming houses. St. Peter's School had stopped offering an elementary through high school education. Faced with the financial problems that came with dwindling numbers of churchgoers, the Catholic diocese had designated it as a Central Catholic elementary school, and the high school had merged with another one, Marian High School, an all-girls school situated in the more affluent northwest section of the city where I used to babysit for my cousin's toddler. The auditorium that was in the newest of the two St. Peter's school buildings was now a shelter for the homeless, my brother said. It was the place where I'd gone with friends as a teenager on Friday nights to dance to rock and roll.

Except for St. Peter's, all the churches that had been located near our family home on Norwood Street—there used to be four other denominations within a stone's throw of each other—were gone, either defunct or relocated to other parts of the city or the suburbs where their congregations had moved. Others had been turned into Pentecostal churches ministering to Spanish-speaking congregations. The one at the corner of Oberlin had been the Christian Science Church, where I would stop on my way to school to look into the glass case at the edge of the sidewalk, where the newspaper, *The Christian Science Monitor*, displayed what someone who was a Christian Scientist was thinking about John Glenn, the Cuban Missile Crisis, or any one of the political assassinations. At one end of Norwood Street was the Armenian Apostolic Church with its round basilica architecture unique to the neighborhood, and at the top of the hill on the corner of Woodland was the Congregational

Church. Across Main Street at the foot of Norwood was the Presbyterian Church, for which I had the greatest affinity, because I loved walking south on Main and staring as I did, through its keyhole bell tower, watching the clouds pass through, and the sky as it turned pink at sunset.

There was a discount clothing store and restaurant now where the five and ten cent store and Alexander's Ice Cream Creations used to be, and a temporary work agency, where the Cat's Paw Shoe Repair was. Lester's Pharmacy became a check-cashing place, and the site of Vernon Drug was the studio for Clark University's radio station, WCUW—I loved it that one of my youthful haunts had replaced another. Only Main South Seafood and St. Peter's church remained as they were.

The neighborhood also presented a depressing scene of vacant lots and empty buildings and storefronts. Some of the old time residents who had stayed through it all had kept up their property, but most of it was dilapidated or looked so in its new context.

The procession took a slight detour off Main and up Norwood to pass our old house. I had no private place in the house, nowhere to be alone unless I happened to be lucky enough to be at home when Peg and Kate, who shared a bedroom with me, were not. I was crowded out, too by the television characters constantly talking in the background. I think that if my childhood had a soundtrack, it was that of the television yakking from morning until night. I never watched much—not the way Peg did. Was she hungry for the image—for pictures of life that over time would disappear for her, as they had for my father? Was watching television her way of filling up her memory with the sights of places she might not visit, experiences she might not have before she lost her vision, so that she, like my father, would be able to *videate*?

When we got to the driveway in front of the house, I saw in my mind the ghost of my father outside, sitting where he used to—on the granite wall under the small oak that graced the corner entrance of the driveway. Squirrels scooted around in the grass behind him. He was outside for no other reason than the fact that the sun was shining and that it was spring. He liked to feel the warmth of the sun and to listen to the birds. His Packard was parked nearby, glistening in the sun, waxed and buffed to a perfect sheen, the way he always kept it. Sitting where he did, at the edge of the property on the corner near the front sidewalk, gave him the opportunity to greet any of the neighbors walking by. They came up the hill after getting off the bus at the corner of Main, or they headed back with a dozen doughnuts or hot cross buns from Sellar's Bakery, a new buzz cut from Gus the barber, or a pound of apples and a pound of plums bought at Blue Front Market. Hearing and recognizing their footfalls, he waited for them to reach the driveway, waited to greet them. He waited for me to come home from school. He waited for my mother to call out the window—"John! Telephone!" about work or about rehab, about retraining or about a possible business opportunity. He waited to find out what he would do, where he would go next. He waited for my mother to get ready to leave for whatever appointment they had. He didn't wait anxiously as I would. He was seated there in a moment of his life—and whatever moment it was—he savored it. His whole body tuned into the place where he sat. He could hear the cars braking on Main Street when the drivers stopped fast behind someone making a turn. He could hear the church bells. He could feel the light breeze on his face and the firmness of the granite stone where he sat. He could hear the sneakered feet of a teenaged girl—his daughter—running up the street toward him, to greet him.

ACKNOWLEDGMENTS

I would not have finished this book—or even begun it—
without the support of many friends whose interest in my
story helped me to realize that my father's life was remarkable
by anyone's standards. Two people were particularly vital in
the last stages of the work and I thank them both for their
help and their enduring friendship. John Dufresne didn't let
me give up on this book when I thought I had, and his
comments on the manuscript greatly helped me in one of the
final edits, while Edward P. Jones gave the final draft his
meticulous attention, inspiring me to polish it. Thanks to
them and to Ellen Cooney as well for also commenting on
the finished memoir so generously and enthusiastically.

Those who reached out in friendship very early on gave
me the confidence to grow as a person and a writer: Larry
Fask, Jacqueline Lawn, Edward, Nancy Sawyer, Paul
Groesbeck, my women's group, Mike True, and the rest of
my large Worcester community. Thanks to David Huddle
and Mary Elsie Robertson. I'm grateful for evenings spent at
Harvard Square's James and Devon Gray Booksellers, in the
company of the memoir group led by Richard Hoffman, who
inspired me with his own family story; the technique,
criticism and good advice gleaned from the writing group put
me on the right road to start. I wish, too, to thank the
Massachusetts Cultural Council for providing necessary
professional development grants to study memoir.

So many others—the faithful—listened to me talk about
the work and its pleasures and frustrations, read parts or all of
the book in manuscript, offered referrals, attended readings
from it, published chapters in journals, offered residencies
and retreats for the writing and editing—all so necessary to
keeping on with it. Dick Lourie, Constance Emmett, Joan
Eisenberg, John Corccoran, Paul Horan, Sue Hand, Kathryn
Jackson, Abbi Sauro, Irene Rohe, Larry Aarsonson, Jodi
Rothe, John Skoyles, Leslie Wheeler, Angelika Festa, Jesse
Rabban, Kerry Costello Mayotte, and Liz Adamski. Thanks

to the Bedford and Quincy Massachusetts Public Libraries for inviting me to read from the manuscript and to lecture and offer workshops on writing memoir; thanks to the Vermont Studio Center and especially the Virginia Center for the Creative Arts for residency fellowships for the writing; and to Louie Cronin, Maureen Rogers, Rosemary Booth, and my other colleagues at the Writers' Room of Boston, Inc.

Gloria Mindock has been my saving grace for championing this book when others passed on it—she is the kind of cheerleader every writer needs in a publisher. She and her partner Bill Kelle have been terrific.

I'm grateful to members of my family for their cooperation and encouragement, especially to those who shared anecdotes about my dad, verified facts and dates when possible—my aunts Evelyn, Jean, and Marguerite and my Uncle Tom. Thanks, too, to cousins Deborah, Steve, and Jeff, and my sister Kate for sharing their experiences.

Thank you Rachel Walker for so generously honoring my father as you did.

The Worcester Historical Society and the Carroll Center for the Blind in Newton, Massachusetts helped me with my research.

And finally, thank you to my Cambridge family: Andrai Whitted who donated his considerable technical and artistic talent, contributing so brilliantly to the cover design; to my son Gianni for always believing in his mom's book; and to Mark, for enduring readings from the manuscript-in-progress, night after night, for years—but especially for his love and kindness—even in the toughest moments.

Mary Bonina has published two collections of poetry, *Clear Eye Tea* and *Living Proof*. She is also the author of *Lunch in Chinatown*, a chapbook of poems inspired by the experience of teaching the English language to recent immigrants in their work places. Her poetry and prose has been featured in *Gulf Stream, Salamander, English Journal, Hanging Loose,* and in many other journals and several anthologies, most recently in *Entering the Real World: VCCA Poets on Mt. San Angelo*, celebrating forty years of the Virginia Center for the Creative Arts. Commissioned by composer Paul Sayed, she wrote a suite of three poems, *Grace in the Wind*, and Sayed's composition for piano, cello, and soprano voice had its world premiere at the Longy School of Music of Bard College, Cambridge, Massachusetts in November of 2012. Bonina is a graduate of the M.F.A. Program for Writers at Warren Wilson College. In addition to being a Virginia Center for the Creative Arts Fellow since 2001 when she was named the finalist for the Goldfarb Fellowship in non-fiction, she is also a member of the Writers' Room of Boston, Inc. where she is working on a novel and a new collection of poetry. She lives in Cambridge, Massachusetts with her husband, poet Mark Pawlak and their son, Gianni Bonina-Pawlak.